THE AMERICAN LEFT

In this Bill Sandeson cartoon of 1965, Lyndon B. Johnson gazes from the White House as Congress tries to tease out a socialist result by calling it something else. The president added the artist's original to his personal collection.

THE AMERICAN LEFT

Its Impact on Politics and Society since 1900

Rhodri Jeffreys-Jones

EDINBURGH
University Press

For Effie, George and Sadie

© Rhodri Jeffreys-Jones, 2013

Edinburgh University Press Ltd
22 George Square, Edinburgh EH8 9LF
www.euppublishing.com

Typeset in 11/13 JaghbUni by
Servis Filmsetting Ltd, Stockport, Cheshire,
and printed and bound in Great Britain by
CPI Group (UK) Ltd, Croydon CR0 4YY

A CIP record for this book is available from the British Library

ISBN 978 0 7486 6887 8 (hardback)
ISBN 978 0 7486 6889 2 (webready PDF)
ISBN 978 0 7486 6891 5 (epub)

CONTENTS

PREFACE AND ACKNOWLEDGMENTS

When I returned to the UK in 1966 after two years studying at the Universities of Michigan and Harvard, a Welsh-language novelist and feminist greeted me with the words, "Ah, so you are back from the land of the free." It was a familiar bit of sarcasm. Before my visit to the object of her derision, I had held a similar view. My stay there peeled the scales from my eyes. Yet today, when I explain to friends my project for a book on the liberating impact of the American left, they still remark, "Well, that will be a short book, then."

Until recent years, many Americans would have agreed with that skeptical take on the achievements of their nation's left. The pages that follow are an attempt to show why there is reason to take issue with such a view. At one hundred thousand words it is still a short book, but I hope it says enough to dispel some doubts.

I would like to acknowledge gratefully the funding support that made the project possible. Early assistance came in the shape of a Twenty-Seven Foundation Award from the Institute of Historical Research, and of a Charles Warren postdoctoral fellowship at Harvard University. Two further grants enabled me to take the research to its conclusion, from the British Academy and from the Carnegie Trust for the Universities of Scotland.

The frontispiece cartoon of 1965 by William S. Sandeson appears by courtesy of the LBJ Presidential Library, Austin, Texas and is reproduced with permission from the Fort Wayne, Indiana *News-Sentinel*, for which I am thankful.

Over the years, I benefited substantially from the generosity of individuals who advised me in person or through correspondence, and/or commented on drafts of my work. I give them my profound thanks. It has been a long running project and some of my helpers have now moved on to the great university in the sky. I nevertheless record my gratitude to them all: Jonathan Bell, John Berg, Paul Buhle, Bob Cherny, Martin Chick, Jim Compton, Robert Crowcroft, Colin Currie, Donna Davey, Phillip Deery, Mel Dubofsky, Owen Dudley Edwards, Sidney Fine, Todd Gitlin, David Greasley, Nigel Griffiths, Huck Gutman, Oscar Handlin, Hywel Harris, Michael J. Heale, Lyn Jones, Michael Kazin, Kevin Kenny, Robert Mason, David Montgomery, Michael Nash, Molly Nolan, Jocelyn Olcott, John Peterson, Frances Piven, Brenda Gayle Plummer, Adam Quinn, Paul Robeson Jr., Bernie Sanders, Ellen Schrecker, Sam Shepperson, Peter Stansky, Jill Stephenson, Hugh Wilford and Marilyn Young.

My literary agent Sydelle Kramer was helpful in helping me get the book into shape, and I am especially thankful to her. I am most appreciative, too, of the outstanding support of Nicola Ramsey at Edinburgh University Press.

Mary, my wife, seems to have forgiven me for writing more books in my retirement. My love and thanks go to her.

Rhodri Jeffreys-Jones

Chapter 1

THE REPUTATION OF THE AMERICAN LEFT

The American left has a reputation for failure. Explaining its failure has occupied the minds of intelligent observers for more than a century. This book challenges the validity of that field of inquiry. It sets out to show that the left has belied its reputation, and has had many successes. The initial challenge, then, is to explain not failure itself, but the reputation for failure.

Understanding the reputation for failure is a step in the direction of infusing credibility into the notion that the left succeeded. It is instructive to begin by considering the issue of free speech. In America, this has not always been available to the lower ranks in American society. That deficiency has had a bearing on the left's reputation for success or failure.

The impact of free speech restrictions on the left's reputation needs to be considered in the context of other factors, as we shall see. But it was real enough. For one illustration, we can look at the case of Jack London.

By 1898, the young writer had already lived the life that shaped his views. It had been a hard one. Abandoned by his natural father and brought up in poverty in the San Francisco Bay area, London scraped a hand-to-mouth living in the manner of so many other child laborers in the United States. Writing to a publisher in 1900, he recalled a "long sordid list of occupations, none of them trades, all heavy manual labor." He had been an "oyster pirate" who stole from offshore shellfish beds. Then at the age of seventeen, he had enlisted as a deck hand on a Pacific sealing schooner.

All the while, he "was never without a book." In due course, London passed the entry examinations for the University of California at Berkeley, only to be "forced, much against my inclinations, to give this over just prior to the completion of my Freshman Year." So he joined the Alaska Gold Rush of 1897, the database for his later, totemic work, *The Call of the Wild* (1903).[1]

London differed from more privileged artists who romanticized the West – the novelists Owen Wister and Zane Grey, and the painter Frederick Remington. Unlike them, he experienced the rugged side of Western life not as an experimental departure from the middle class comfort zone, but out of necessity. This may help to explain why he was by 1897 a confirmed socialist. He told a friend that he took his inspiration from Eugene Debs, who had led the American Railway Union strike of 1894 and served a prison sentence for his pains.[2]

In the aftermath of America's brief war with Spain in 1898, London wrote an essay analyzing US foreign policy. Titled "The Question of the Maximum", it offered a left-wing critique. But although it was a brilliant piece of writing, he could not find a publisher who would commit to it. He said a respected editor initially accepted it with great enthusiasm, but "became afraid of its too radical nature, forfeited the sum paid for it, and did not publish it." Not until 1905 did an updated version of the essay finally appear in the novelist's *War of the Classes*. Disrespectful views expressed by a literary genius from the wrong side of the tracks had failed to find their way into print in 1899, when they would have been a more timely contribution to the contemporary debate over whether America should have an empire.[3]

The media at the time were already largely in the private possession of men who were critical of the left because they disagreed with it, and because adoption of its policies would have threatened their wealth and power. Fond of asserting that socialism would destroy free speech, such men themselves withheld that right from critics of their preferred political system.

The situation has not greatly improved over the years and may have worsened. Back in the 1890s, America had 1500 weekly newspapers, but that diversity has now shrunk resulting, in the words of Columbia University professor Todd Gitlin, in the media of the "consolidated corporate economy."[4]

The resultant absence of competition means more power for press and media barons, such as Rupert Murdoch, the sponsor of Fox News with its support for Tea Party politics. Complaints about rich people's suppression of free speech and abuse of media power have been legion. For example, in 2011 a *New York Times* journalist charged that Glenn Beck's Fox News Channel program was inciting violence against another Columbia University professor, seventy-eight-year-old Frances Piven. Her crime in the eyes of Murdoch, Beck, and their sympathizers – campaigning against poverty and defending the social security system.[5]

Potentially, the federal government could have compensated by intervening to ensure that political candidates received free time on television. Between 1960 and 1997 there were 163 free time proposals in Congress. In 1998 the Advisory Committee on Public Interest Obligations of Digital Television Broadcasters (the "Gore Commission") recommended minimum standards of public interest requirements. However, opponents of the idea of universal free speech defeated free time.[6]

The affluent media backers of the Bush, Jr. administration can be defended up to a point. There was more fairness and diversity in the American media than in, say, Iran, China and Eritrea, respectively 166th, 167th and 173rd out of the 173 nations that Reporters Without Borders ranked for press freedom in 2008. Yet the United States was no higher than equal 36th in that ranking. At a time when the Bush administration was brandishing the flag of liberty, America had less press freedom than almost every European nation, and in its own hemisphere yielded to Jamaica, Costa Rica, and Trinidad and Tobago.[7]

The rich not only owned the media, but could also use the coercive power of advertising to promote their cause. Not every rich person is conservative, and vice versa. Nevertheless, rich patrons did withhold advertisements from media that voiced dissident opinions. More proactively, they ran political advertising campaigns. In the two years following the passage of President Barack Obama's health care law in March 2010, the US Chamber of Commerce and other private interests spent $235 million on attack ads – supporters of the provision could muster only $69 million. President Obama, a man of the left or not depending on your view, was openly critical of the media's treatment of his social and economic policies.[8]

The list of charges against moneyed conservatives has included the assertion that they suppressed free speech in the nation's universities. In 1917, for example, Columbia fired two professors for their left-wing antiwar views. Prominent colleagues spoke out in their defense. The socialist philosopher John Dewey expressed his outrage and America's leading historian Charles Beard resigned his post in protest. But it was all to no avail. In 1918, the angry Beard lamented the decline of "higher" learning into "hire" learning. In the 1960s, the New Left revived the issue. It raged against the "military-industrial-university complex." Berkeley students launched the Free Speech Movement because they were being denied free speech on campus.[9]

Since the 1960s the pressures against free thinking have in some ways become more oppressive. Whereas students in the booming universities of the Sixties demanded and often obtained courses that were "relevant" to political and social issues, college campuses since then have veered in the direction of vocational courses. This put a squeeze on posts for professors in the humanities who might express left-wing views. Furthermore, a casualization of labor in the name of flexible management has meant fewer tenured posts, and instructors on temporary contracts are vulnerable to intimidation.

There has been a well-funded witch-hunt against professors who challenged the conservative viewpoint. Edward Said was an authority on the Middle East who inspired the left. An article in *Commentary* in 1999 called him a "professor of terror." The neoconservative organization Campus Watch attacked eight professors and fourteen universities because it disapproved of their views on Islam and Palestine. The conservative polemicist David Horowitz mounted a campaign against left-wing scholars and in 2006 published a book on the 101 "most dangerous academics in America." There were still plenty of left-wing professors who defied the pressures. But, in light of the pervasive atmosphere, if you wanted an academic job or desired to be re-appointed to one, it was sometimes best not to express certain opinions.[10]

Rich men defended their version of free speech by destroying other people's access to it. This contributed to the stifling of the American left. It has also diminished our appreciation of the contributions of the left to American society. All this is undeniable and needs to be stated. However, it is far from being a full representation of reality.

For the left itself helped to diminish the repute of the left. Because they feared persecution or because they thought it would help their political campaigns, a string of people who once called themselves socialists chose to discontinue that practice, though in a good number of cases they continued to fight for the same reforms. To anticipate some examples developed later in this book, Selig Perlman drew up the plan for a welfare state that came to fruition over the years, but then he became a virulent anti-socialist. The Mattachine Society that pioneered gay rights in the 1950s forgot its communist associations and sought an image of conservative respectability. There was no mention of socialism in Betty Friedan's *Feminine Mystique* (1963) in spite of her previous socialist connections. In the same era, the socialists Michael Harrington and Martin Luther King were discrete about the use of the "s" word. For a while, socialists took to calling themselves "liberals" until that, too, became a too-hot-to-touch word. In recent times, in the words of historian of the left Michael Kazin, even "'liberals' took refuge in the 'progressive' label."[11]

This nomenclative flight could be regarded as an admission of weakness, or even as cowardice on the left. In reality, though, it was a sign of two things, a broadening agenda – the word "socialism" is too narrow to describe the expanded aspirations of the modern left – and pragmatism. To the practical and dedicated reformer, what is likely to be more important, the rigid adherence to left-wing labels like "socialist" even if they alienate potential supporters, or the achievement of, say, federally-supported medical provision for senior citizens?

Whether one chooses to be critical of or sympathetic to the flight from labels, one thing is plain – reformers did not chalk up their victories as triumphs for the left. How could they? They had typically abandoned the word. It may be an improbable partnership, but the left teamed up with media tycoons in undermining the idea that the left could in any way have contributed to the improvement of American society.

The left's pessimism reached epidemic proportions in President Obama's first term in office. There were those who anticipated the demise of the left and its kissing cousin, liberalism. Pulitzer Prize-winning journalist Chris Hedges depicted Obama as "weak" and saw an underlying problem, the "death of the liberal class." He accused post-1980s liberals as a whole, not just Obama, of having failed to protect the working and middle classes against corporations that undermined democracy, looted the public purse, and "waged imperial wars that can neither be afforded nor won."

Another dose of pessimism came from former *Harper's* editor Roger Hodge. Playing on the title of Obama's manifesto *The Audacity of Hope*, he called his book *The Mendacity of Hope: Barack Obama and the Betrayal of American Liberalism*. Hodge thought that Obama had ruined the prospects for reform by chasing the "elusive will-o'-the-wisp of bipartisan consensus." He had merely "changed the wallpaper and rearranged the furniture in the White House," continuing the disastrous policies of his Republican predecessor.[12]

This left/liberal pessimism brings us to a further reality. It is this. The faction in American politics most responsible for recognizing and preserving the left's reputation for effectiveness has been the conservatives, the anti-left. Conservatives representing the interests of the affluent may have denied free speech to the left, but they did give it the oxygen of publicity.

The Tea Party phenomenon is an example. This movement was a short-lived attempt to destabilize the early Obama presidency and represented itself as grassroots. Billionaires funded it, notably the brothers David and Charles Koch. Fox News promoted it.

Tea Party activists fastened on President Obama'a alleged socialism. In a Google-driven digital search of the *New York Times*'s text for the twelve months leading up to the mid-term elections of November 2010, the term "Tea Party" links to phrases in frequencies that suggest a scale of antipathies. The term "budget deficit" crops up 391 times, and "big government" on 635 occasions. On a slightly higher plane, there are seven hundred links with the term "progressives."

However, by far the strongest Tea Party links were with the terms "socialist" (16,800 hits) and "liberal" (19,400 hits). These were the dirty words in the Tea Party lexicon. One tirade of September 2010 in the business magazine *Forbes* attracted attention for its bitter take on the title of Obama's memoir, *Dreams From My Father*: the president, "a socialist – not an out-and-out Marxist, but something of a European-style socialist, with a penchant for leveling and government redistribution," was truly enacting the dreams of his father, a "philandering, inebriated African socialist."[13]

That choice of words is a reminder of how unreasonable the right can be. Over the last century, conservatives have irrationally confused democratic socialism with communism, and labeled as socialists those who prefer to be called liberals or progressives. Such confusion is understandable in a way, as the distinction between words like socialism, the left, liberalism and progressivism are blurred, and change over time. While every democratic socialist is on the left, not all left-wingers and very few liberals or progressives would call themselves socialists. This book reflects contemporary debate by introducing the words left, liberal and progressive with greater frequency in relation to later decades, but it is always an open question, and there is an appendix that considers some of the semantic-pedantic issues.

If the right has sometimes been unreasonable about the left, the left for its part has gone too far in behaving as if conservative opinions are just stupid and must be always rejected wholesale. Thus the left creates for itself a danger. The right claims that the left poses a real threat to what it stands for. In denying that reality, the left denies its own potency.

One needs to distinguish between unreasonable conservative charges against the left, and complaints that have a basis in reality. When the moderately conservative Republican Party campaigned in 1950 and 1952 on the premise that the New Deal had been essentially socialist in character, this was a reasonable thing to say.

Equally, when the celebrated conservatives Milton and Rose Friedman observed in 1980, "almost every plank in [the Socialist Party of America's] 1928 presidential platform has by now been enacted into law," they were culpable of only minor exaggeration. Indeed, they were able to list fourteen significant areas in which SPA policy had been implemented, ranging from the public administration of water and transportation assets to the termination of child labor.[14]

Reasonable conservative estimates will be a vein running through this book. It is possible to disagree with conservatives' premise that the left was wrong, while agreeing with their observations about the left's impact.

So far, we have identified two reasons for the left's reputation for failure. First, the conservative media both denied the left a hearing and denounced it – paradoxically, its denunciations publicized the left, so they were to a certain degree counter-productive. Second, the left was compliant with the idea that it had been martyred and thwarted.

There are other reasons, too. To begin with an obvious reason, the electoral defeats of labor, socialist and left parties in American history have contributed to an impression of failure. In spite of the fact that its Founding Fathers drafted a Constitution designed to avoid "faction", America has always been fascinated by party politics. There has been a tendency to dwell on the failure of left-wing parties to make major breakthroughs on election day – the most successful left-wing political party, the Socialist Party of America, elected only two of its candidates to Congress. It is not surprising that the left's election-day failures have distracted attention from the left's political and cultural impact.

The logic does not hold up. Labor or socialist parties are not always all that transformative. For example, Australia has a successful Labor Party with a socialist ideology, yet in the opinion of some analysts shares some of America's more conservative characteristics. Outcomes do not necessarily depend on political parties. After all, as the historian Martin Sklar points out, nobody ever voted for a Capitalist Party of America yet few would dispute that capitalism is a prominent feature of American life.[15] Nevertheless, appearances can be deceptive. Many have succumbed to the temptation to look at the American left and say, no electoral success, total failure.

Prejudice is another factor militating against the left's reputation. It is widespread and by no means limited to American politics. While the word "right" also means "correct", a left-handed person in any nation might be discriminated against, even forced as a child to use his/her right hand. Muslims use their right hands for food, their left to clean their anuses. Deriving from the Welsh *cachu* (shit), the term cack-handed refers to a person who is a left-hander and clumsy, or clumsy like a left-hander. In many languages, right-handers exert a bullying majoritarian influence – in spite of the reverse myth, "Lefties are the best lovers."[16]

The prejudice is more than trivial. Protestant bigots refer to Catholics as left-footers. The Latin for left is *sinister*, a word that translates very well into conservatives' take on socialism and the left. In a word borrowed from the French language, a *gauche* person is clumsy or socially inept, and France has something else to answer for, too. In political usage, the term "left" derives from the seating arrangement the French National Assembly established for itself in 1789 – supporters of the Revolution sat on the left of the chamber. And the French Revolution degenerated into a bloodbath.

Sticking with the foreign theme, still another reason for poor reputation was European observers' habit of patronizing and even deriding the American left. We can begin with followers of Karl Marx who noted the failure of American workers to develop a sense of class-consciousness, and tried to explain that as if it were a measurement of socialism's rise or fall. In 1906, the German economist Werner Sobart published his oft-cited *Why Is There No Socialism in the United States?* Ignorant of the debate on poverty then being fomented by socialists like Robert Hunter, Sobart singled out prosperity as the cause of no socialism. Moving to a later example, the socialist historian R. H. Tawney asserted in 1942 that the American labor movement had only recently acquired a social agenda, and was retarded compared with its English counterpart.

Writing in 1949, the former Labour Party chairman and political scientist Harold Laski inaccurately observed that the American labor movement was "marked by violence" – it lacked the qualities necessary to take "the decisive step of forming a workers' party." Oxford University historian Henry Pelling thought the British left had been positive about America in the nineteenth century, negative in the twentieth. He showed some appreciation of the American left, but his book was still called *America and the British Left* (1956), not vice versa. Prejudice – shared by the present author until he experienced America in the 1960s – ran too deeply to accommodate sympathy. Snobbery about America in the European socialist salon combined with a failure to look beyond party politics in assessments of the US left. In an era when the special UK–USA relationship still mattered, European and especially British leftist belittlement undermined the American left's faith in itself and in its historical achievements.[17]

A homebred "why the left failed in America" industry has been even more demoralizing. Its toilers can be found across the political spectrum. Selig Perlman and Martin Lipset have been prominent amongst those who have set out to explain the institutional and electoral demise of the left, and of socialism in particular. They wrote as if institutions and processes count for all, and outcomes for nothing. In 1955, Louis Hartz, a Harvard professor of government and one of the most influential political scientists of the Cold War era, welcomed what he thought was the triumph of liberal capitalism, and measured that in terms of the ideological demise of the left. He failed to anticipate that the left would become more cultural than ideological.[18]

The shortcomings of the illuminati invite explanation. Why so many flashes of inspirational darkness? The quest for reasons leads back to the issue of academic independence. But there were other factors at work, too.

In the 1970s, literary critic Alfred Kazin wrote of a gentler but still potent process. He noted the disposition of some to modify their views to help them climb the "greasy pole" of academe. Still later, interviewed in 2009, Columbia professor Frances Piven thought that rising scholars make an unconscious psychological adjustment as they ascend the scale. They express their views more cautiously; sometimes they involuntarily blind themselves to the truth.[19]

To recognize the achievements of movers and shakers is not always a good idea if you want to join an establishment. In any case, why threaten the stability of an elite to which you intend to gain entry?

Gloom and doom have not, however, been universal. In 1978, UK Secretary of State for Energy Tony Benn addressed the European Committee of the US Republican Party at the American Club in London:

> In the United States socialist policies have long been adopted by Administrations of all parties, and by state and municipal authorities. Indeed socialized education in America long preceded socialized medicine in Britain and each of us has influenced the other to adopt both.[20]

Benn was, unusually, a British optimist about the American left. Over the next few years American scholars, too, began to note that their country was not quite so free enterprise and self-made man as one might imagine.

American society was developing in unexpected ways. As advocated by Marx though not in the way he intended, workers came to own much of their nation's industry – through their pension funds. These workers did not object when the great American corporations in which they had invested stifled competition in order to boost profits and dividends. But they could not see themselves as self-made men. Social mobility was grinding to a halt. Defeat beckoned the American Dream as defined by James Truslow Adams in 1931: "Lincoln was not great because he was born in a log cabin, but because he got out of it."[21]

Today, there are increasing signs of skepticism about the failure of the left hypothesis. The socialist historian Norman Markowitz noted the assumption of repetitive resurrection in stories of the left's demise: "The Left, broadly defined, has been proclaimed dead so many times that such proclamations are for historians a guidepost to historical periods."[22]

In some quarters there was optimism not just about the past, but also about the present state and future prospects of the left. The Harvard-trained economist Richard Wolff thought that the left had declined in the past and was disorganized, but was "strong and getting stronger by the minute." Reacting to a Pew Research Center poll that indicated young Americans were disenchanted with both capitalism and socialism but preferred the latter, a former British Member of Parliament argued that a "re-energized US left" had "much to teach its dismal European counterparts."[23]

Setting aside the crystal ball, the time is ripe for a re-assessment of the historical effectiveness of the American left. The process has already begun. For example, Pittsburg University historian Richard J. Oestreicher has noted how left-wing activists played a role in social reform movements ranging from labor organization to antiglobalism – they "forced mainstream politicians to respond to their arguments."[24]

Peter Dreier, a politics professor at Occidental College (where Barack Obama studied) notes that "progressives" in the past had achieved an enormous amount, including votes for women, environmental protection, the prevention of lynching, labor union rights, income tax, shorter working days, the minimum wage, pensions for seniors and now federally-underpinned health care. Denounced by the conservatives of the time as "utopian" or "socialist", the reforms became part of the fabric of America's civilized society to such a degree that, according to Dreier, Americans now "take these ideas for granted", which is why there is little recognition or knowledge of how hard progressives had to fight for the reforms in the first place.[25]

In his book *American Dreamers* (2011), Michael Kazin traces the left's contribution to the equalities: equality for women, minorities and homosexuals. The left, he argues, helped Americans to celebrate sexual pleasure, advanced the cause of multiculturalism, and contributed to America's antiauthoritarian tradition. Kazin's left was against "inherited hierarchies and identities." His emphasis was on cultural impact. Like Oestreicher, he credited the left with political influence and with being at least a "junior partner" in influential reform coalitions such as that behind the New Deal of the 1930s. However, the left's victories "never occurred under its own name."[26]

Kazin's nomenclative point is another reminder that officially titled socialist organizations did not achieve left goals directly. Changes did take place in American society that were socialist or otherwise left-wing in character. The left itself did not directly engineer them. But they were still triumphs for the left, and the more responsible right-wing critics had reason on their side when they denounced them as socialist or leftist.

With these points in mind, here is a prospectus for left achievements as discussed in the rest of this book. We can begin with the assault on racism. In 1909, socialists were prominent in the creation of the National Association for the Advancement of Colored People, and they remained in the vanguard of the civil rights struggle throughout its history. The SPA took the lead, amongst political parties, in demanding the vote for women, achieved through the Nineteenth Amendment in August 1920. In the same year, socialists were to the fore in the creation of the American Civil Liberties Union. Not every supporter of civil rights, civil liberties and feminism was on the left. But the great majority of them were.

In the 1920s, through the "Negro" or "Harlem" Renaissance and more broadly, writers and other artists on the left helped to define both American culture and democracy on the one hand, and its main enemy, fascism, on the other. The left's impact on literature and the arts was to endure, and is very evident when one looks at individuals. To name a few on the fiction front: Jack London, Upton Sinclair, John Dos Passos, Theodore Dreiser, Dashiell Hammett, Lillian Hellman, John Steinbeck, Arthur Miller, Norman Mailer, Walter Mosley, and Barbara Kingsolver.

Rebel/folk/classical music? Take your pick from Joe Hill, Woody Guthrie, Bob Dylan, Pete Seeger, Joan Baez, Aaron Copland. In the movies, we can start with Charlie Chaplin, remember about Jane Fonda and move forward to the more recent manifestations of the "Hollywood Left" featuring the Right's bugbears George Clooney and Michael Moore.

In the depression of the 1930s, there was a powerful left contribution to the framing of social security legislation. The program was the brainchild of socialist researchers engaged by the US Commission on Industrial Relations in 1913. It was just a matter of time before one of the two major parties adopted the social security program, to gain an advantage within the two-party system as well as to resist challenges to that duopoly. In the event, the Democrats were the first to realize that social reform was the road to both power and justice, and it was the main feature of their New Deal – imperfectly achieved, but a statement of principle. Defenders of the New Deal poured scorn on conservatives who argued that the 1930s reforms were socialist in character, and today people collect their pensions and benefits without thought for their left-wing provenance. But the conservative perception of a socialist revolution was not divorced from reality.

Public ownership was a reform that the left characteristically demanded. Americans had always embraced the principle – after all, it was President George Washington who established the Post Office in 1792. But the issue has become more prominent over the last century, with many examples of successful municipal and collective ownership, as well as conspicuous large-scale examples like the Tennessee Valley Authority and Amtrak. Such enterprises succeeded where private ventures had failed, but without undermining the workings of the free market that determine rational price levels, and without throttling private initiatives in the larger portion of the economy.

The New York and New Jersey Port Authority is the world's largest public body, bigger than anything achieved in Europe, India or China. But it is simply part of the fabric of public life in the most populous area of the United States. Commuters may gripe about fares, delays, graffiti and crime, but they accept the business model inherent in the Authority, a model for a planned, publicly owned and integrated transport system. Yet, as Long Islanders and Brooklynites commute, perhaps transfixed by the latest Walter Mosley novel, they are unmindful, and few would care to remind them, that they are participating in a collectivist enterprise.

The Port Authority has not limited its activities to subways and bridges and tunnels and airports. Take the Twin Towers, completed in 1970 and 1971. They were the Port Authority's creation, and housed many government agencies. When the *Washington Post* portrayed Al Qaeda's destruction of those edifices on September 11, 2001 as an attack on an "icon of capitalism", it perpetuated and no doubt shared with the terrorists themselves a misunderstanding about the nature of American society.[27]

The Constitution's opening words "We the People" ring down through the ages, and over the last century the left has helped to insert the People into foreign policy debate. Socialists – such as Jack London, W. E. B. Du Bois, Charles Beard, William Appleman Williams, Noam Chomsky, and Edward Said – offered the main critique of American diplomacy. They argued that foreign policy was too often built on racial illusions and conducted in the interest of elitist minorities such as munitions makers, financiers, multinationals and the military.[28]

The socialist and left arguments have generated conspicuous controversy and policy outcomes, for example in the cases of American neutrality in the 1930s, and withdrawal from the Vietnam War. Few academic debates have been so vigorous as that of the last twenty years revolving around Said's critique of US policy in the Middle East. The left/progressive critique was at the root of the rejection of the Iraq War. In the realm of foreign policy, perhaps there has been greater public recognition that the left has been able to generate effective dissent.

There has been a major leftist influence on family life. Historically, the left promoted birth control as a means of improving the welfare of women. Fanny Wright, to her critics the "red harlot of infidelity", promoted contraception in the 1830s.[29] Against the background of improved technology, three other socialists gave the campaign a decisive boost in the early years of the twentieth century. These were Emma Goldman, Rose Pastor Stokes and Margaret Sanger. Betty Friedan, who in the 1960s helped to reshape the politics of American family life, was likewise the product of a left-wing background.

The left/progressive battle for gay and associated rights resulted in significant legislative victories. The Hate Crimes Prevention Act of 2009 afforded federal protection to lesbian, gay and transgender citizens and was the latest stage in a campaign that had its origins in the drive for antilynching legislation, first called for in 1901.[30] Just as importantly, the campaign led to more enlightened private attitudes and to the acceptance of the fact that non-straight people were not pariahs but contributors to the enviable diversity of American society.

The left's impact on the America of today then, is variegated in nature and the product of decades of campaigning. Its effective outcomes provoke counter-attacks by the right, but are often accepted just as commonplaces. The latter state of affairs is a tribute to the left's success, even if it amounts to an erasure of memory.

Today, there is continuing ambition in political circles. To take an example, there is a cross-party determination to improve transportation. President Obama called, in the fall of 2010, for a six-year plan to upgrade US transport in a way that would boost jobs and improve the economy's infrastructure. An estimated $350 billion would be poured into the reconstruction of runways, roads, and rails. The president called for a federally run bank to finance the more innovative transportation ventures.

Planning and major public investment have for the past century been associated with the left in politics. The Democratic Party has often accepted the principles, but has not been alone in doing so. There was, for example, bipartisan support for Obama's call for a public bank. Amongst the bank idea's prominent endorsers were California's Governor Arnold Schwarzenegger, a Republican, and the independent mayor of New York City, the billionaire Michael Bloomberg. Historical statistics demonstrate that the United States has been increasingly keen on public investment, with levels of government expenditure edging ever closer to those in Europe.[31]

We have seen that the reason for the left's reputation for failure is not failure itself – it has other causes. A convincing list can be made of the left's achievements, especially if one includes triumphs for as well as by the left.

Some qualifications are in order. Some reforms, for example universal medical insurance, took longer to achieve than others. Another poignant example has to do with equality and equality of opportunity. A fairer distribution of wealth is one goal of the left. One critic of the British Labour Party's use of progressive income tax to achieve this goal concluded that the desired outcome had not been achieved. Similarly in the United States, the picture is one of defeat bordering on rout. The middle class defined as the middle 60 percent of American households received 53.2 percent of the nation's earned income in 1968, but only 45.7 percent in 2011, while the top 5 percent of households took home 16.3 percent in 1968, and 22.3 percent in 2011. As for your chances of escaping from poverty, they are lower in the USA than in most other countries.[32]

The left has failed here, and one can paint an even darker picture. Not every impact of the left has been benign. At different times in its history, factions on the American left supported Stalin and spawned neoconservatism.

But for better or worse, the impact itself cannot reasonably be denied. We can begin by looking, in Chapter 2, at the left's formulation of an American welfare state.

Chapter 2

THE SOCIALIST ORIGINS OF SOCIAL SECURITY

America's present-day social security system takes care of people who are in their senior years, or unemployed, or sick. Not everyone would agree with those conservative critics who say that this amounts to social-ism. The enactors of the relevant legislation in the 1930s and in our own day saw themselves, in ascending order of preference, as leftists, liberals, progressives or just plain Democrats.

An examination of those who planned social security on the eve of World War I nevertheless suggests that the conservatives' labeling of social security as "socialist" is correct.

At the same time, there is a need to explain why the social security blue-print emerged when it did. It was at least partly because of the impact of an event that had little to do with socialism.

At one o'clock on the morning of October 1, 1910, around a hundred people were at work in the stone-clad edifice of the *Los Angeles Times*. The explosion that ripped through the building a few minutes later sent the entire south wall tumbling into Broadway Street. Heavy linotype machines crashed through the floors and broke the plumbing in the basement. Gas escaped from the ruptured pipes and caught fire. Storage barrels full of ink exploded. The damage came to a gross sum of $509,900. Twenty workers lost their lives.[1]

What went through James McNamara's mind as he laid the charge that led to all this devastation? For one thing, there was the motivation that prosecution lawyers stressed in his trial – a determination to get even with Harrison Gary Otis. For the proprietor of the *Times* was hostile to organ-ized labor, especially the bridgemen's union in which James's brother John was a senior official. James was a seasoned saboteur for the union, which for years had been conducting a "national dynamite campaign" against antilabor employers in the steel erection industry.

There is a just-as-strong possibility that the work-shy James McNamara dynamited simply for the money, to fund his chain-smoking, womanizing, liquor consuming habits.

Other explanations can be safely laid to rest. A conservative-minded Catholic, the bomber had no revolutionary intent. And whatever was passing through his non-too-acute mind as he primed the lethal charge, he certainly was *not* thinking, "If only I can destroy this building, it will bring about an American social security system."[2]

But events can have unintended consequences. Within five years of McNamara's detonation, a federal industrial commission had drawn up a blueprint for social security, a blueprint that ultimately transformed the fabric of American life. The *Times* explosion itself did not achieve this, but the panic over class war that it triggered did pack a political punch. In the ensuing debate policymakers ignored the conservative, non-socialist, non-revolutionary character of the McNamara brothers. They acted instead on the assumption that their nation faced a social cataclysm.

After months of panic in business circles and the press, it fell to the monthly journal, *Survey*, to demand a federal investigation of violence in industrial relations. Reacting to the McNamaras' confessions, *Survey*'s editor Edward T. Devine had expressed the fear that French-style revolutionary socialism would break out in the United States. In the wake of his appeal, the social reformers Jane Addams and Rabbi Stephen Wise were amongst those who petitioned President William Howard Taft.[3]

Momentum for the demand increased when the Progressive Party's "Bull Moose" platform for the 1912 presidential elections called for social security reforms in the areas of unemployment, old age, and sickness insurance. Formed in that year, the Progressive Party consisted of Republicans who were discontented over the selection of Taft as their party's presidential nominee. They wanted Theodore Roosevelt instead. Though he had retired from the presidency in 1909, Roosevelt now agreed to stand on the Progressive presidential ticket against the Republicans (for whom President Taft was the candidate), the Socialists (Eugene Debs), and the Democrats (Woodrow Wilson, the ultimate victor).

The Progressives had extensive support and Roosevelt was an impact politician. Notably, his espousal of conservation in his terms as president (1901–09) had given international stature to the environmentalist cause. Now, in common with the Socialist Party of America (SPA), he called for a minimum wage, an end to child labor, social insurance – and a "national industrial commission." Though unsuccessful electorally, Roosevelt's

Progressive Party campaign of 1912 was a real fillip for those on the left of American politics.[4]

In spite of being portrayed as a conservative by his opponents in the other three parties, President Taft was to play his part. He endorsed the industrial commission proposal. Congress authorized the United States Commission on Industrial Relations (CIR) on August 23, 1912, and it fell to Taft and his successor President Wilson to set up the inquiry.

To represent the public on the commission, President Wilson chose John R. Commons of the University of Wisconsin (Madison). Commons's Quaker family had fled the North Carolina slavocracy, and he spoke of how his father had regaled him with stories of the underground railway, the slaves' secret escape route. His sympathy with the less fortunate contributed to his becoming a Christian socialist. John Commons was the prime intellectual mover on the nation's prime reform campus, as well as being the nation's leading expert on industrial relations. Though he did not direct it, he would be the dominant influence on the CIR's Division of Research and Investigation.

The bulk of the CIR's budget went on public hearings. Its final report of 1915 pointed to what the commissioners considered to be at the root of discontent, the fact that 2 percent of the nation owned 60 percent of the wealth. It recommended a million-dollar cap on inheritance.[5]

The CIR's Research Division cost less, but achieved more. Under Commons's guidance it set forth a case and blueprint for social security. Commons and the young researchers in the division in this way diverged from the revolutionary path being followed by many socialists in Europe, where followers of Karl Kautsky dismissed social reform as merely a way of propping up capitalism. The American architects of social security were very much social democrats, rather than social revolutionaries.

Commons's researchers, several of whom were or had been his students at the University of Wisconsin, called for federal solutions to the nation's social problems. Take, for example, the Research Division report on "Feeble-Mindedness as a Cause for Homelessness." The language in this report sounds archaic to the twenty-first century ear, but it was a thoughtful document. It listed the problems: the "feeble-minded" too often ended up in prison because there was no other institution that could care for them. They succumbed to alcoholism in disproportionate numbers, and they ended up homeless because they could not handle money. The report considered public opinion on eugenics and concluded that people were actually not prepared to segregate and sterilize "morons." In terms of public policy, the anonymous author condemned the irresponsible attitude of local and state authorities. The often interstate vagrancy of the educationally challenged hobo played into the hands of these buck-passers. But it also brought the problem within federal jurisdiction. In fact, only Washington could supply a remedy: "We can look forward to the day when this subject will be a matter for Federal treatment."[6]

William M. Leiserson contributed significantly to the analysis of social welfare. Born within the Jewish community of Tallinn, Estonia, Leiserson had grown up in New York City, where he worked in a shirt factory and studied evenings. Like Commons, Leiserson was a socialist, as is revealed in his correspondence with his friend Oscar Ameringer and with another Research Division socialist, Edwin Witte. After graduating in economics from Wisconsin, he took a PhD at Columbia, his research for that degree inspiring the model for the New York Employment Service System. He went on to head Wisconsin's employment office, and then got the number two job at the Research Division, running its day-to-day operations after it had moved from Washington to Chicago to ease the commuting problems of its Wisconsin-based researchers. He argued passionately in favor of an investigation of unemployment and for social-insurance solutions to that problem: ". . . it is the fear of losing a job that jeopardizes a man's rights."[7]

A CIR conference on unemployment in February 1914 reviewed attempts to tackle the problem in the Scandinavian countries and in Britain. The latter country had adopted legislation in 1902 and 1909 that established a national system of 430 labor bureaus and these had helped seventy thousand people find jobs.

Those at the conference showed a prescient awareness that employment exchanges alone would not solve the problem they were trying to address. Professor Henry Seager of Columbia University noted the European experience showed that "labor exchanges *could not create work*." There was an awareness at the CIR conference that government might have to play a role in the area of job creation. The Chicago economist Herbert J. Davenport had suggested the government might borrow money to fund public works and jobs in times of depression, with debt-repayment taking place in more prosperous years. An embryonic enthusiasm for public works now seemed to exist, for when Maria Sanford (emeritus, University of Minnesota) revealed that Duluth was digging sewers to promote employment, her statement met with "prolonged applause." Anticipating the economic recipes of the future, Leiserson proposed "saving public work for dull times and thus regularizing [the] labor market."[8]

Leiserson nevertheless pressed the need for employment exchanges, and his reports emphasized the role the federal government should play. President Taft had approved a law establishing a cabinet-level Department of Labor, and the Bureau of Labor Statistics (dating from 1884) was one of its divisions. Leiserson proposed there should be a bureau of employment, too. He explained in one report that this bureau would lay down rules and regulations. These would govern public employment exchanges. They would also regulate private employment agencies operating on an interstate basis, some of which exploited more vulnerable workers. They would bar job applicants from lying about their qualifications, and prohibit employers from misrepresenting the nature of the work involved.[9]

In a further report, Leiserson explained that the principle behind a federal system of employment exchanges was "to bring the workers and the work together in order that the fullest application of the labor force of the country may be secured." To achieve that goal, it would be necessary to create "uniform systems of registers and records and uniform methods of doing business." Leiserson aimed not only to improve the work situation, but also to end or at least combat the injustice of the blacklist. Under his scheme, no applicants could be refused work on the ground that they had previously participated in a strike.[10]

Because of his efforts in framing the Social Security Act of 1935, Leiserson's Research Division colleague and fellow socialist Edwin Witte is routinely referred to as the "father of social security," and scholars have assumed that the program was born in the 1930s. In terms of practical outcome, this is a fair assessment. But the *ideas* behind American social security germinated two decades earlier. Witte was closely familiar with them, and in 1914 his legislative expertise was already sufficiently well developed for him to be entrusted with the task of formulating laws that the CIR might propose. However, in the formulation of social security thinking Witte came a distinct second to one of his Research Division colleagues.[11]

Selig Perlman was born in the medium-sized textile-manufacturing town of Bialystock, in northeastern Poland. Russia had administered the area since Poland's partition in the eighteenth century. Almost two-thirds of the city was Jewish, and Perlman grew up with strong principles that blended Judaic and democratic-socialist ideals. Prejudice and poverty excluded the young idealist from higher education in his native province, and he moved to Italy in the hope of doing better there. Then in 1905 when he was seventeen, his fortunes changed – all because his aunt had won the job of arranging Anna Strunsky's wedding trousseau.

Formerly in a relationship with the novelist Jack London, Strunsky had recently attached herself to William English Walling. Her latest socialist was a millionaire, hence the elaborate trousseau. Perlman's aunt learned that the Wallings were traveling to Italy. She told Walling her nephew had a brilliant mind, and arranged an introduction. The meeting was a success. Perlman impressed Walling with his knowledge of the writings of Karl Marx (of which Walling was ignorant), and the affluent American arranged for his new protégé to study at the University of Wisconsin.

Discussing his relationship with Commons forty years later, Perlman noted that they were both socialists, but remembered his rationalist reservations about a man who was imbued with Christian "moral fervor." The immigrant scholar was also convinced that Commons had reciprocal reservations. Perlman was poor, shy, and depressive. He spoke with a painful stutter in a heavy Yiddish accent. Relying on what his father told him, Selig Perlman's son Mark said that these characteristics irritated Commons. It is also possible that Commons, so long the master of his domain and prone to nervous breakdowns himself, felt threatened by Perlman's abilities.

But Commons was too professional to neglect the talents of a colleague. He and Perlman collaborated in the Research Division. In his reports for the division, Perlman flayed the capitalist class. For example, he investigated conditions in Lawrence, Massachusetts, where in 1912 there had been a militant strike organized by the revolutionary Industrial Workers of the World (IWW, or "Wobblies"). In his report of 1913 he found that the local employers used labor spies – in fact, until they discovered a comradely letter from Walling in one of his pockets, a group of Wobbly shoemakers thought that with all his questions Perlman was a spy. The local newspapers ran a disinformation campaign against the IWW. To keep the union weak by diminishing its bargaining power, the manufacturers advertised for labor outside Lawrence even at times of high unemployment. They shut down local textile mills to punish the union while running at full tilt the plants they owned in other cities. They played divide and rule with the multi-ethnic workforce, buying off the Irish by giving them special treatment.[12]

In a series of reports in the fall of 1914 Perlman's tone was both militant and thoughtful. He argued that in the 1880s a "revolutionary labor movement" of English-speaking Americans had forced employers to come to terms. Now, it was the immigrants' turn, and employers were responding with devious measures:

The extraordinary growth of the movement for welfare work by employers for the benefit of their employees during the last five years may be said to be directly traceable to . . . revolutionary strikes.[13]

Perlman accused employers of using welfare as a means of subjugation. He took his cue from a book by the socialist William J. Ghent who had denounced employers' schemes as a form of "benevolent feudalism" with pensions and other inducements offered only in exchange for the "faithfulness and obedience" of the "villein class." Perlman said employers were setting up "establishment funds" ostensibly to insure their employees against accidents, sickness, death, invalidity and old age, but really to create a distinctly unbenevolent "feudal" dependency on the part of the workers. For example, in most schemes if a worker left to take up another job he would lose the death benefit to which he had contributed his own dollars and cents. He might also lose the house provided for him by his paternalistic employer. Under most welfare plans, the employer could "muzzle" recalcitrant employees by threatening to withhold old-age pension benefits, and could force them to agree not to sue as a condition of accident insurance. Employers' welfare schemes were just "American makeshifts for social insurance."[14]

Perlman asked, "Is [employers'] welfare work intentionally used as a prophylactic against industrial unrest?" He recommended instead a thoroughgoing federally run system of social security. He had calculated the running costs of such a scheme in Germany, and concluded that the private employer in America could not in any case afford to emulate a proper state-run program.[15]

The Research Division investigated America's needs in the area of medical insurance and health care. Perlman's guiding hand is evident here, too. Two specialists helped him. Benjamin S. Warren was a forty-one-year-old surgeon in the US Public Health Service. With a history stretching back to 1798 and traditionally concerned with improving the health of sailors, the service had expanded its remit in 1912. Warren monitored its experimental vaccination program for public employees, and worked on public health aspects of infantile tuberculosis. His Research Division colleague Edward Sydenstricker was not medically trained. Born to missionary parents in Shanghai and an economics graduate of the University of Chicago, he drew on other experience and would be a pioneer of public health statistics.

Together, Warren and Sydenstricker produced for the Research Division a paper on sickness insurance that pointed to the costs of not having a universal scheme. They calculated that on average, each of America's thirty million employees lost nine days' work each year because of sickness. Existing insurance schemes focused on accidents, but these were "insignificant" as a cause of poverty and suffering, compared with illness. In a separate paper, Warren cited a US Public Health Service estimate that Americans spent half a billion dollars annually on medicines, most of them "consumed haphazardly and not under the direction of a physician." When other medical expenses such as doctor's bills were taken into account, it was clear that a compulsory insurance plan would on average cost the American citizen just half of the current amount, and for "a much better service."[16]

In August 1914, Devine and a group of like-minded reformers published in the *Survey* a plan for sickness insurance reform. Insurance should cover medical services and supplies, nursing, and hospitalization. They thought both workers and employers should contribute, but that compulsion should apply only to those earning very low wages. There should be a "voluntary supplementary system" for poor people who were not at work.[17]

In an annotated summary of the Devine article, Perlman indicated that he wanted to go further. He argued that there should be an additional funding input by "both the state and the community (municipality)." But his disagreement was more profound than this. He really wanted to destroy a system based on what he thought was the pervading principle behind employers' medical insurance schemes, namely "prophylactic" amelioration aimed at subduing the workforce. In a memorandum to McCarthy, he dismissed as "incorrect" the view "held by some people" that existing employers' compensation schemes could be "the logical entering wedge for sickness insurance." Employers' schemes tended to compensate only for occupational diseases. He recommended "we should attack the problem of sickness by a straight forward system of compulsory insurance."[18]

Warren and Perlman drafted a plan for the implementation of such a system on the state level with federal supervision. They envisaged universal sickness insurance for individuals between the ages of 16 and 65 who were in employment and had an annual income of $1,000 or less. There would be compensation for loss of earnings, death benefits and comprehensive medical and surgical coverage. There would be federal and state supervision with enforcement of proper standards of care. Individual states would be entitled to call on the expertise of the US Public Health Service.[19]

Warren addressed the issue of finance. He suggested a bond flotation to launch the scheme. In the case of interstate schemes, the federal government would issue the bonds, but locally state governments would float their own. In a separate report, he spelled out how the scheme might be administered, proposed specific cash limits on what beneficiaries should receive, and recommended who should pay what for continuing funding. Workers, he thought, should make at least 50 percent of the insurance contributions, with employers paying a smaller sum and the taxpayer contributing as little as 10 percent. In a rhetorical flourish, Warren anticipated the bitter attacks that would follow, and issued a pre-emptive justification:

> The compulsory membership in some fund will probably meet with some criticism as being un-American and contrary to the spirit of America's free institutions. The reply is that this is a social problem and that individual rights must be limited for the social good.[20]

Such arguments did not prevail in the short term, and it took a considerable time for the analyses and recommendations of the Research Division team to register with policy makers and change American society.

One reason for this was a debilitating spat within the CIR. On March 17, 1915 Commons wrote Helen L. Sumner, a campaigner for children's and women's rights who also collaborated with him in the field of labor history: "We had quite a blow up in our Commission . . . which means that practically all the staff that I had selected to write up the reports, recommendations and constructive program will have to go within a week or two."[21]

The Wisconsin professor had wanted to secure publication of the Research Division's reports. The CIR did publish under its own imprint Luke Grant's study of industrial relations in the steel construction industry, thus fulfilling the original intention of those who saw the investigation as a response to the dynamiting of the *Los Angeles Times* Building. But although other publishers in due course brought out numerous books and articles informed by the federal inquiry, Commons was unsuccessful in his immediate goal of verbatim publication of his team's reports. Congress even ordered the destruction of the unpublished records of the Research Division, and only two incomplete sets survive today.[22]

World War I was another setback for social security. Europe embarked on its self-immolation just as Perlman and his colleague were formulating their proposals. At home, the inevitable surge in patriotism before and during American entry to the war meant that Ben Warren's scheme for health bonds gave way to war bonds. World War I drained resources and diverted attention from potential social security schemes. Members of the medical profession circulated leaflets equating health insurance schemes with "Teutonic tyranny." In the summer and fall of 1918 President Wilson opposed proposals to widen the federal provision of health services beyond workers in strategic industries – for him it was "an inopportune time to suggest to Congress the expenses and elaboration of such an instrumentality."[23]

In spite of the delay, the Research Division's work on social security ultimately had a major impact on American society. Its key researchers were young, and implemented its ideas as their careers developed. Leiserson chaired the Commission on Unemployment Insurance in Ohio, and beginning with the Wagner-Peyser Act of 1933 his ideas on employment exchanges came to fruition as the federal government rolled out a national network.

In the 1920s, Witte also acquired practical experience on the state level, when he had an opportunity to influence Wisconsin's social insurance provision. When Witte drafted the 1935 federal Social Security Act, he had another Commons protégé to help him – Arthur J. Altmeyer had been an undergraduate at the time of the Research Division's deliberations, and already had an interest in social insurance. Other students of Commons and Research Division veterans influenced a wide range of social policies, both directly and by becoming professors and training new generations of scholars, administrators and politicians. Witte's own student Wilbur Cohen, for example, worked on the Social Security Act.[24]

Even after the passage of almost a hundred years, issues defined in the Research Division's reports continued to prompt discussion. In 2009, two-thirds of America's juveniles in custody had at least one mental illness. "Jails and juvenile justice facilities are the new asylums," lamented a child psychiatrist at the Texas Youth Commission, echoing the words of the Research Division report on the "feeble-minded" and homelessness. In the same year, other data indicated you could get cataract surgery for $12,712 privately, or for $584 under Medicare, suggesting that Ben Warren's questions on costing were still a live issue.[25]

Although the Research Division was instrumental in establishing the bases of US social security, its work has gone largely unrecognized, an example of how the left's contribution to American history has been ignored. Historians have preferred to explain the origins of the welfare system in terms of theories of citizenship, of the impact of "maternalist" feminism, and of New Deal reforms that improbably sprang out of the blue.[26]

One reason for the blind eye turned toward the Division was its socialist character. Those associated with it were already aware of the potentially damaging nature of the socialist label. As early as 1903, Commons had shown caution when he warned social critic Henry Demarest Lloyd against joining the SPA. If he did so, the media would shun him. Best to articulate his views as an independent, Commons advised, and let the SPA exploit them. Leiserson's appraisal of the situation confronting socialists was similar. He contributed to the socialist press, but anonymously.[27]

The oppressive atmosphere worsened with the approach of World War I. The Department of Justice sent special agents into Wisconsin to identify socialists and to arrange, in secret, for their persecution. "Precautionary visits" took place. At the university in Madison, agents interrogated students for the flimsiest of reasons, for example one Jessica Colvin who did not oppose the war but who expressed "sympathy" for pacifists. Professors rushed to conform, and senior administrators were at pains to establish their loyalty. In one case, they helped special agents identify those who had invited the socialist philosopher John Dewey to speak on campus.[28]

With the Bolshevik takeover in Russia in the fall of 1917, intolerance entered a new phase. By 1919 the "Red Scare" was in full swing, with real and suspected socialists being harassed, investigated, arrested, imprisoned and deported.

Against this background of long-running intolerance, Commons and other Wisconsin socialists gradually dropped the socialist label. It was difficult enough already to achieve meaningful reform, without the additional encumbrance of the word "socialism." The historian Leon Fink suggests the reasons also had to do with personal survival: "The radical social scientist . . . had his own career (and ultimately, family) to look after."[29]

The most spectacular exemplar of this change of attitude was Selig Perlman. For he would ultimately be remembered, not as the architect of American social security, but, rather famously, as the author of *A Theory of the Labor Movement* (1928). This was a diatribe against socialism. The most gifted champion of social reform had become its enemy. It was an indication of how the socialist label had become too hot to touch, and helps to explain why socialist/left contributions to social reform are underecognized in accounts of America's past.[30]

There was another reason, too, for the unsalutory neglect. For although the invention and gradual introduction of social security had profound implications for America, it was by no means the most charismatic aspect of left-wing activity. It is more exciting to remember the left for other things. However worthy and effective they may have been, Wisconsin's researchers fell under the shadow of more charismatic innovators and personalities.

Chapter 3

EARLY ACHIEVERS ON THE AMERICAN LEFT

Left-wing personalities had a major impact on American history and society from the late 1890s through to 1920. Their contemporaries were aware of their achievements, yet sometimes unaware of their socialist leanings. Historians have sometimes been blinkered, too. In a few cases, though, left-wing personalities had socialism bolted into their charisma in a way that nobody could ignore. They dazzled in ways that Wisconsin's studious reformers could not.

A time-line of some of the more imaginative contributions illustrates these points. It shines a light on the input of the American left in the years when at least some leading citizens dared to call themselves socialists.

1898. Jack London writes "The Question of the Maximum." As we saw in Chapter 1, this essay was significant for the delay in its publication, a delay that prompts discussion about free speech in America. At the same time, though, it did signal the contribution of the left in two spheres, the critique of American foreign policy and the shaping of American culture.

In "The Question" London noted that British trade was "falling off," and predicted "The Capitalistic Conquest of Europe by America." But America had its own exports problem. That explained the Open Door policy of 1899–1900, Secretary of State John Hay's attempt to obtain the China market for US exporters. Yet this attempt, too, was doomed, for "the East itself is beginning to awake." America would have to tighten its belt. There was a danger that living standards would fall. Workers would find it impossible to save for old age. The competition for mastery in commerce was "the first struggle to involve the globe." The same applied to investment opportunities: "Predatory capital wanders the world over, seeking where it may establish itself." With globalization, "capitalistic exploitation of the planet approaches its maximum." London's analysis had a prophetic ring, and anticipated the foreign policy critique of later left-wing writers.[1]

"The Question" examined foreign policy and also heralded the left slant in London's later fictional writings. Jack London was one of several pre-1920 left contributors to American culture. The historian Michael Kazin detailed their achievements in his *American Dreamers*, a book that challenged the failure-of-the-left hypothesis by setting forth the left's contribution to US culture and thought. He noted that there was a "long and distinguished" roster of artists and intellectuals who belonged to the Socialist Party of America (SPA) before 1920. Those he had in mind ranged from Jack London to the dancer Isadora Duncan. His list included the multiculturalist critic Randolph Bourne and America's greatest defense lawyer, Clarence Darrow.[2]

1899. John Dewey publishes *The School and Society*. Together with William James (who had similar socialist leanings), Dewey had a claim to being the leading American philosopher of his day. Both he and James advanced that characteristically American school of thought, pragmatism. In *The School and Society*, Dewey identified other touchstones of Americanism. He argued that even in elementary school, teachers should emphasize the distinctiveness of American history. He further urged that education should not be a process of adults thrusting their values onto a younger generation. Instead, education should be child-centered.[3]

Dewey's school would be a microcosm of society. The philosopher stated that "individualism and socialism are at one" in an ideal school. There, children from all classes would be taught side by side, with no distinction between vocational or "manual training" on the one hand, and "science and history" on the other. These apparently different aspects of learning were integral to each other. The Industrial Revolution had reshaped society, and the school should mirror that fact. Dewey's outlook was egalitarian, and ran counter to a trend toward private education for the American old-money elite. It would have an enormous impact on the shaping of twentieth-century education.[4]

1899. Florence Kelley agrees to head the newly formed National Consumers League. Her League used consumer education and the threat of consumer boycotts to achieve reform. Kelley agitated for the restriction of child labor in the manufacturing of consumer goods. With Eleanor Roosevelt joining the campaign in the 1930s, Congress finally agreed to place at least some restrictions on the use of child labor in passing the Fair Labor Standards Act of 1938.

Kelley had a privileged yet uncompromisingly socialist background. She was the daughter of a man who had taken the precaution of becoming rich before taking an interest in reform. William D. "Pig Iron" Kelley had represented Pennsylvanian steel interests in Congress. The family affluence opened doors for Florence Kelley, who attended Cornell University and, in the manner of the privileged, did the European tour. She witnessed German education at first hand, at the university in Zurich.

In that city in 1884, Kelley joined the local socialist party. Shortly afterwards, she married the Russian socialist and medical student Lazare Wischnewetzky, bearing his child in the course of what would be a short marriage. She now entered into correspondence with Friedrich Engels, Karl Marx's patron and collaborator, and undertook what would be the first translation from the original German of Engels's classic exposé, *The Condition of the Working Class in England in 1844*.[5]

1904. Robert Hunter publishes *Poverty*. In his first message to Congress, President Theodore Roosevelt demanded action to address what he termed the nation's "very serious social problems."[6] It was a shock to conservatives, who just could not believe that their affluent country could have such a thing. Three years later, the publication of Hunter's book had begun to strip away people's illusions about universal American wellbeing.

Hunter was no son of the proletariat. The well-educated progeny of an Indiana manufacturer, he knew the people who mattered in American social reform. Florence Kelley was a friend. He married Caroline Phelps Stokes and thus into a family known for its philanthropic interests and sympathy with the African American cause – Caroline's brother J. G. Phelps Stokes was a founder of the NAACP. Like Stokes, Hunter became a socialist, joining the SPA in 1905, the year after he published *Poverty* and at least partly because of the research he did for it.[7]

Hunter's immediately acclaimed tome introduced the "poverty line" into American political discourse. It was not an entirely objective tool of analysis. The line varies over time, according to which nation is being discussed, and according to political expectations. Hunter's poverty line of $460 annual income in 1904 would today be absurdly low in America yet a figure only to be dreamed of in parts of Africa. However, as a propaganda tool the poverty line proved to be effective.

1906. Upton Sinclair publishes *The Jungle*. A nominally fictional description of conditions in the Armour meat packing company, the novel told the story of Jurgis Rudkus, a Lithuanian immigrant who worked in the stockyard area of Chicago known as Packingtown. Jurgis loses his job after an injury, takes to drink, loses his attractive wife to a bullying foreman, and sees his little boy drown in Packingtown's unregulated effluence. Sinclair spared no sensibilities in his description of the unhygienic meat canning processes, with rodent and human remains turning up on the American family's dinner table.

Pursuing his campaign, Sinclair bombarded the White House with messages and telegrams. President Roosevelt pleaded with his publishers, "Tell Sinclair to go home and let me run the country for a while." Still, the president was impressed, and so was Capitol Hill. Congress passed the Meat Inspection Act.[8]

As Sinclair wryly acknowledged, he "aimed at the public's heart, and by accident I hit it in the stomach."[9] *The Jungle* is a gripping story, but the socialist epilogue is boring and probably few people managed to struggle through it. Unwittingly, Sinclair had struck a blow for a different kind of left-wing cause, consumer power.

1909. W. E. B. Du Bois helps to form the National Association for the Advancement of Colored People (NAACP). Influenced as he was by his reading of Henry George, Jack London and John Spargo, Du Bois was probably already a socialist by the time of the NAACP's formation. In a book devoted to the thought of this leading American intellectual, the historian Adolph Reed reviewed the literature on Du Bois's leftward leanings and noted, "everyone agrees that Du Bois died a socialist, but few agree on when he became one or what kind of socialist he was." He mentioned the view of another student of African American history, Manning Marable, that Du Bois was far from being a revolutionary socialist on the lines of the IWW's leader, William D. Haywood. Rather, he was a gradualist socialist like Jane Addams – a woman with a claim to being the greatest American of her day, Addams had the courage to risk her reputation by opposing American entry into World War I, but if, as Marable suggests, she was a socialist, she did not trumpet that fact.[10]

Du Bois's attitude to organized socialism indicated the scope for individualism and variety on the left. He did not join the SPA until 1911, and resigned the following year. It is true that half a century later at the age of ninety-three he joined the communist party and emigrated to socialist

Ghana, but even this signified no sudden advent of confidence in party apparatus. Rather, it was a defiant gesture against continuing racism in the USA. In the words of one of his biographers, it was an act of "Homeric nose-thumbing."[11]

There were reasons for Du Bois's reservations about the SPA. While it may have been an improvement on the governing Republican Party (Du Bois detested the racial policies of President William H. Taft) and while socialists like Mary White Ovington, William English Walling and Charles Edward Russell had helped form the NAACP, there were racially unenlightened elements within the party.[12] Also, there was the question of optimizing black power. The reason Du Bois gave for his resignation from the party was that it expected members to toe the SPA line. This was no good for African Americans, who had to preserve the option of tactical voting. They "could not afford to have a man in the White House whose election was not due, at least in part, to their [tactically cast] vote."[13] So Du Bois continued to register as a socialist voter but, like other black socialists, kept open the option of putting his own people first.

This tactical reservation enhanced Du Bois's socialist critique of American foreign policy. His 1915 essay "The African Roots of War" added a racial dimension to the analysis of imperialism. His economic argument was similar to Jack London's, but he stressed the way in which corporations could corrupt white workers in colonizing countries not just with economic bribery, but also with rhetoric about their racial superiority. Speaking in racial terms, Western elites promised rich pickings for "laborers" as well as middle and upper class people through the exploitation of areas of the world where labor unions and inconvenient questions did not exist, "where 'niggers' are cheap and the earth is rich."[14] The Du Bois critique contributed to the struggle against white colonial exploitation that continued for decades, and finally prevailed.

1915. Joe Hill dies by firing squad in Salt Lake City. The poet-songster of the IWW had endured an unfair trial for the murder of a grocer and his son. This was not quite the same thing as being palpably innocent (rarely a good thing for a revolutionary's image), but it was enough to make him a martyr. His songs became a staple of left-wing protest in America. Bob Dylan, the poet-songwriter so emblematic of the rebellious, described Hill as "a Messianic figure."[15]

Hill knew how to make an impression. He behaved as if the guys on death row get the best girls. He wrote to one of them as he awaited his execution, telling her he did not deserve her attention, as he had spent the last few years "among the wharfrats on the Pacific Coast."[16] This was Elizabeth Gurley Flynn. The novelist Theodore Dreiser remembered Flynn as she had appeared in a socialist meeting a few years earlier, "a girl just turned sixteen, as sweet a sixteen as ever bloomed . . . [she] electrified the audience with her eloquence, her youth and her loveliness."[17] On the eve of one of the days scheduled for his death (there were several stays of execution), Hill confirmed that Flynn was the object of his affections, even if he could not embrace her: "Good-bye Gurley, not because you are a girl but because you are the original Rebel Girl."[18] He confirmed that his soon-to-be-famous poem "The Rebel Girl" was dedicated to her.

Hill's relationship with Flynn was unconsummated, and more appealing for that reason. Yet he was no virgin. The gunshot wound that led police to assume he had exchanged fire with the dead grocer may well have been inflicted by the jealous alternate lover of a young woman in Hill's lodgings. Hill refrained from calling the witnesses in his defense. He was stubborn and proud, writing to Flynn following an appeal for clemency by President Woodrow Wilson: "Now I'll tell you Gurley; – I never did like the ring of the word 'pardon' and I think I'd rather be buried dead, than buried alive."[19]

Joe Hill's poems conveyed in simple words some of the left's main messages. His song "Casey Jones" was about a "union scab," a locomotive driver who belonged to a railroad brotherhood whose skilled workers carried on working when the humble track laborers went on strike. Another savaged the message of Christians (in this case the Salvation Army) who promised heavenly reward to obedient workers: "You'll get pie in the sky when you die."[20]

Songs about Hill became legends in their own right. They were sung by his contemporary T-Bone Slim, and then by others ranging from Woody Guthrie to anti-Vietnam War protester Phil Ochs. Immortalized by the bass-baritone son of a fugitive slave, Paul Robeson, and by another Vietnam rebel Joan Baez, the best known of the songs summed up the dead poet's appeal. Alfred Hayes and Earl Robinson wrote it in 1925: "I dreamed I saw Joe Hill last night."[21]

Hill arranged his own life and death as if they were a poem. He became a long-term inspiration for rebels and freedom-lovers on the left.

1916. Emma Goldman and Margaret Sanger go to prison for upholding sexual liberation. The Nineteenth Amendment met one of the demands of the SPA and permitted women to vote nation-wide for the first time in 1920. But another revolution was under way that would profoundly affect the lives of the female half of the population and many others besides. It heralded a century-long debate on family values and prefigured the culture wars of the present day.

Sexual prophylaxis had been a political issue since Fanny Wright spoke out for it in the Jacksonian era. But its opponents carried the day in the nineteenth century. The Comstock Act of 1873 categorized information on the subject as "obscene literature", and banned it from the US mails. One reason for contraception's controversial nature was its relationship to the eugenics debate. Assuming that the white middle classes would be the first to afford and use condoms, some supporters of the ban feared the passing of the "superior" race.

Socialist advocates of contraception changed the framework of this debate. They advocated it as a means to gender equality. They saw counter-pregnancy technology as a means of emancipating women from the tyranny of endless infant-nurture. They advocated it also as a way of fighting poverty, and finally as a right for women who longed to enjoy sex free of the worry that they might conceive.

Margaret Sanger's mother, Anne Purcell Higgins, was a devout Catholic who endured eighteen pregnancies before dying of cervical cancer. After giving birth to three children herself, Sanger moved to New York with her husband. There, she witnessed the deadly effects of frequent confinements amongst the poor of the East Side. She joined the IWW and moved in radical circles in Greenwich Village. She befriended the feminist socialist Rose Pastor Stokes, a Polish-Jewish-American who had married NAACP founder and "millionaire socialist" J. G. Phelps Stokes.

She also met the legendary anarchist Emma Goldman, a woman for whom marriage meant the "death of sexual passion" and who saw no need to conform to any laws, even the rules of socialist parties: "If I can't dance, I'm not coming to your revolution."[22]

This triumvirate launched a campaign for what they began to call "birth control." Sanger wrote and disseminated "how to" literature. After publishing a tract called *Family Limitation*, she fled to Europe to avoid arrest, there meeting sister feminists and learning about the diaphragm method. Back in the USA, she illegally circulated information about the diaphragm, and in 1916 brought out another leaflet, *What Every Girl Should Know*. February found her speaking publicly on the issue with Goldman, Stokes and Anna Strunsky Walling. At this point, the authorities clapped Goldman into Queen's County jail, where she served fifteen days for disseminating practical advice on contraception.[23]

On May 5, there was a public meeting in New York's Carnegie Hall to welcome Emma Goldman's return from prison. Max Eastman took the chair. He was the brother of Crystal and editor of *The Masses*, a magazine that featured socialism and the arts.

Goldman rose to speak. "In the cause of motherhood," she announced, "I am still proud and glad to be a criminal." At this point, Stokes tried to hand out birth control leaflets to the married women present. But instead, according to one reporter, she was mobbed by "men, girls and boys," who "rushed up the aisles en masse to reach her."[24] In their enthusiasm, they half-tore her shirtwaist from her body, and her husband had to step in and whisk her away. Men as well as women wanted to be informed. A Virginian wrote Stokes in December 1916:

> Since the birth of my last child in 1915, my wife's health has not been good, and we both feel it would be a calamity to have any addition to our family. Therefore, not knowing any contraceptive methods we are forced to forego the pleasures of matrimony. This is a great hardship on both of us, and as it takes every cent of my small wages to support my family of six, I am writing you as a Socialist comrade to please give us, in strict confidence, one of the pamphlets you gave out in New York.[25]

The need for discretion must have seemed very evident. For by this time Sanger, whose pioneering birth control clinic had opened in October only to be raided and closed by the police, had served thirty days in prison. The socialist campaign for birth control was appealing not only in itself, but because its leaders were sufficiently principled to go to prison for their cause.

1919. Eugene Debs goes to prison for protesting the pointless slaughter of men. Debs was a left-winger through and through. Though his personal relationships with women were flawed, he supported the female franchise campaign. He had been brought up to admire the abolitionist John Brown, and demanded fair and equal treatment of African Americans. At the 1903 SPA conference, he insisted on that principle.

The former labor leader ran for president on the SPA ticket in 1904, 1908 and 1912. In the last year, he won over nine hundred thousand votes, 6 percent of the popular vote. Running again in 1920, Debs received 913,693 votes. This was the highest-ever tally for a socialist candidate, but at 3.4 percent a diminished percentage as the US population had increased, and women had just joined the electorate – apparently they did not vote in significant numbers for the party that had fought for their rights. The SPA's vote tally in 1920 was a reminder that if the American left helped to shape America, it was not through its success on election days.

At the same time, the 913,693 votes were a tribute to Debs considering that he was in prison from April 13, 1919 to Christmas Day, 1921. He was there for protesting American entry into World War I. Debs did not subscribe to the view, fashionable in both left and business circles, that America suffered from surplus production, therefore needed to export, and thus had to join in the great expansionist game, with its resultant wars, being played by leading powers. Excessive profit-taking explained, in his view, the apparent economic constipation of American capitalism, and profiteering was rampant as the USA began its preparedness campaign.

Debs had been appalled by European socialists' use of Marxist sophistry to justify desertion to the cause of sanguinary nationalism after 1914. International socialism being in disarray, he couched his opposition to war in terms drawn from Washington, Jefferson, Franklin and Paine. In the words of one historian who sees him as having helped to create a strand in US foreign policy thinking, "he epitomized [an] essentially American form of liberalism."[26]

In an address to the Ohio state convention of the SPA on June 16, 1918, Debs urged a people's foreign policy that would be antimilitaristic:

> In all the history of the world you, the people, have never had a voice in declaring war and strange as it certainly appears, no war by any nation in any age has ever been declared by the people . . . . You . . . have nothing to gain, and everything to lose – especially your lives.[27]

This was the speech that led to Debs's arrest and imprisonment under the oppressive Espionage Act of 1917.

It did not take long for disillusionment with World War I to set in. Americans would in future demand more of a say in foreign policy, and would take a critical stance toward militarism. The tradition stretched back to Tom Paine, but its resurrection as a left-wing cause can be attributed in measurable degree to Eugene Debs. He was an inspirational character. Not an intellectual, he was an intelligent politician who was a born communicator. And it is not every day that a politician sacrifices his personal welfare for the sake of a principle. Prison took its toll on his health. When he died in 1926, the non-socialist press hailed him as a great American. His antimilitarism had made its mark.[28]

1920. Roger Nash Baldwin helps to found the American Civil Liberties Union (ACLU). The Debs case had a further significant repercussion. The charge in his case arose in connection with the speech he delivered in Canton, Ohio, on June 16, 1918. John Lord O'Brian, a special assistant to the attorney general, at first delivered a benign verdict on the contents of the speech. He thought the socialist sailed close to the wind in denouncing the ruling classes who "have always taught you that it is your patriotic duty to go to war and slaughter yourselves at their command," but "all in all the Department [of Justice] does not feel strongly convinced that a prosecution is advisable."[29]

O'Brian's view was overtaken by the hysteria of the time, but the authorities' treatment of Debs inspired a civil liberties campaign. Roger Baldwin worked for the creation of an organization that would be known as the American Civil Liberties Union (ACLU). An IWW supporter, pacifist, and admirer of Emma Goldman, Baldwin received support from the admired feminist-socialist Crystal Eastman and SPA stalwarts Norman Thomas and John Haynes Holmes. He remained in charge of the ACLU until 1950. Though some conservatives credibly claim to be libertarians, civil liberties has been a chiefly leftist cause ever since the Debs prosecution and the Red Scare of 1919–20 made the ACLU a necessity in America's democracy.[30]

Although the political use of the term "left" was not yet even in its infancy in the Progressive Era, it is legitimate for the historian to identify, in addition to those listed in the time-line, some influential figures on what might be termed "the non-socialist left." Thus, for example, the historian George Mowry depicted President Roosevelt (bizarrely a hero to neoconservatives in a later age) as a politician who saw himself as "left center" until 1908, and then moved further to the left. The Populist presidential candidate William Jennings Bryan was part of the left ambience. So was Senator Robert M. La Follette Sr. (R-WI), who opposed World War I and in 1924 accepted the presidential nomination of the SPA when running as the candidate of a revamped Progressive Party.[31]

Between 1898 and 1920, American socialists and others on the left inspired new attitudes. There were also, however, some concrete reforms that could be represented as left inspired. The Newlands Reclamation Act of 1902 encouraged irrigation in arid and semi-arid states and was a major intrusion of federal government into the private domain. The Meat Inspection Act of 1906 was testimony to pressure from the left. Milwaukee elected a socialist administration in 1910, and was one of several American cities to introduce public ownership of local services. The adoption of the Sixteenth Amendment in 1913 met one of the SPA's fundamental demands by legitimizing a federal income tax. The La Follette Act of 1915 was doubly leftist in that it protected the rights of crews as well as the safety of passengers on US-flag ships. The same can be said of the Adamson Act of 1916 that improved travelers' safety by limiting to eight hours the shifts worked by locomotive engineers. Finally, the ratification of the Nineteenth Amendment in 1920 satisfied the SPA's demand for the vote for women.

So the establishment of a social security agenda was not the only achievement of the American left in the first one-fifth of the twentieth century. The left's input is visible in culture, education, consumers' rights, antipoverty campaigns, food hygiene, African American rights, women's political and sexual liberation, antimilitarism, civil liberties, workers' rights, and public planning, both agricultural and urban. Yet the traditional argument has been that socialists failed to achieve because they failed at the polls. That assumption rests on a narrow definition of politics, and on the shaky premise that social change stems only from political process. Equally, it invites a re-examination of the socialists' role in Congress.

Chapter 4

SOCIALISTS IN CONGRESS

The theory that socialism failed in America is based on a premise regarding political outcome. The premise defines failure as an inability to capture the presidency or Congress. Socialists never came remotely near achieving an official majority in Congress. Yet there is a conundrum here. For conservatives, including front line Republican politicians, repeatedly insisted that Democratic legislators passed one socialist measure after another to the severe detriment, in their view, of the American way of life.

The difference in perception reflects different ways of counting. Strict constructionists who see socialism as a failure refer to the mere handful of declared socialists who have served on Capitol Hill. There is a double oversight here. First, the socialists may have been few, but they had an impact – not only directly, but also because the major parties stole their programs in order to pre-empt their electoral success.

Second, the strict constructionists have neglected to look at the broader picture. They could learn from conservative rhetoric. Those on the right (like those on the left) engage in hyperbole and exaggeration, but they can also be moderate and accurate in their observations. Worried conservatives look not just at how legislators label themselves, but also at what they said and did. Repeatedly and sometimes credibly, conservative Republicans have argued that certain influential Democrats were socialistic wolves in sheep's clothing.

Instead of absorbing or accepting such charges, left-inclined politicians tended to go into denial. They accused their accusers of hysteria. Even more defensively, they resorted to serial label changing. They sought to escape from the liability of being regarded as socialist or leftist. They called themselves liberals, then fled from that term, too, in recent years plumping for the term progressives. They shielded their eyes from the phenomena of socialism and leftism in Congress and denied to others that they existed.

A historical profession in thrall to failure-of-socialism myth has followed meekly in their wake.

All this is understandable. Imagine yourself to be a member of Congress. You want to support the passage of a reform that conservative opponents are already labeling socialist and "unAmerican" in character. Do you say, "yes, it's socialist, so what?" and lose the fight? Or do you deny it is socialist, denounce the conservatives as unscrupulous scaremongers, and increase the prospects for the passage of your cherished reform?

There was another reason why left-inclined politicians disavowed socialism and distanced themselves from its advocates. This was that the officially labeled socialists in Congress were in some ways inappropriate icons for modern left-wingers, liberals, and progressives. To be sure, they were innovative and "politically correct" in some ways. But in other ways, they were not. Indeed, socialist-labeled congressmen could be just as fallible as anyone else.

Take the following extract: "Not right for Mama. She never did get proper calling cards. And she only had one go-calling sort of dress. But Papa assured her that was right for a Socialist's wife." That was what Doris wrote in an unpublished biography of her father Victor Berger, recalling the time when he arrived in Washington, DC as America's first congressman elected on a socialist ticket, and sought to do the social rounds associated with political success. According to Doris, Victor and his wife Meta were tightly sealed as a couple. Yet at times Doris expressed the anger she felt her mother must feel. In contrast to his penurious wife, she wrote, her father could afford to dress "neat with just a touch of nattiness." He had plenty of suits, "all the right canes and luggage," and, thanks to Meta, fresh underwear daily.[1]

Doris had plenty more to say. She recalled how in a courting letter sent to Meta in 1895, Victor demanded sympathy for his hemorrhoids. Later, he let it be known that he would have preferred a son to a daughter. In public he took a puritan line on sex and opposed birth control; in private he was a womanizer. As a child Doris knew that her father "was two-timing Mama or three- or four-timing her." Listening through the bedroom wall, she heard her father justify his ways with women to her relatively uneducated mother. He did so by referring to the writings of the sexually promiscuous French novelist Anatole France.[2]

In a synopsis of her intended biography, Doris referred to her father as "intelligent, arrogant, genial, and yet lonely." Mrs. Berger's lack of calling cards was no accident. Most of America's policy makers shunned her husband, as well as her. And the shunning was not just because the media and political establishment were prejudiced against socialists. People did not warm to Berger because he did not warm to them. As his daughter put it, he was intellectually committed to the brotherhood of man, but "didn't take naturally to brotherhood."[3]

Gifted and relatively successful though he may have been, Victor Berger was a man of limited human sympathies. He had grown up in an imposing house in Leutschau, a small town in the eastern part of present-day Slovakia. In that corner of what was then the Austro-Hungarian Empire, his father ran a prosperous inn with its very own gypsy band. Victor had studied at the universities of Vienna and Budapest and according to one student of his life, had developed an "aristocratic" outlook by the time he arrived in America. It was an unpromising trait in such an egalitarian nation.[4]

A social democrat, Berger treated the far left with a superior disdain. He supported the "recall" (i.e. expulsion) from the SPA of IWW members like Bill Haywood. This was on the ground that they advocated violence, a hot issue in the wake of the *Los Angeles Times* bombing.

More upsetting to many of his contemporaries as well as posterity was Berger's appeal to the racial prejudices of American workers. In part, it was opportunism. He was one of those who thought that the SPA might be more popular with white workers if it refrained from demanding black rights. However, his civil rights inaction also reflected his personal bigotry. He subscribed to a racial table of merit that put whites on top, yellows second and blacks bottom. As a later biographer put it, "he favored the exclusion of the Oriental and the neglect of the black American."[5]

These attitudes show that while socialism may have been a philosophy of the left, individual socialists sometimes lacked the full panoply of leftist principles. His prejudices impaired Berger's appeal to future generations – with the passage of time, he was in significant ways less and less relevant to a left with a broadening agenda that included women's rights, revised family values and civil rights. They reduced his standing as an icon of the left, and help to explain why historians have not been attracted to the task of assessing the role of socialists in Congress.

At first sight, this neglect is justifiable. The number of party-affiliated socialists in Congress has been tiny. The voters of America only ever elected two SPA candidates to the House of Representatives, of whom the unsympathetic Berger was one. This was out of the 10,700 who served between 1789 and 2009.[6]

But socialists in Congress did exert influence, and are worth studying more closely. In spite of their weaknesses, they made a qualitatively strong contribution. They contributed to social security and antimilitarism. They were backed by allies on the left both inside and beyond Congress, and by the campaigns of fellow socialists in presidential and municipal elections.

Two persons could not have achieved all this, and the subject of enumeration needs to be revisited. There has been a chronic tendency to underestimate. Greeting the election of Vermont's Bernie Sanders in 2006, Raja Mishra described him in the *Boston Globe* as "the first self-proclaimed socialist to serve in the Senate." But the accompanying table shows that at least five earlier senators had socialist credentials. Mishra was even wider of the mark, though not alone in his assumption, when he went on to observe that when Vermonters voted Sanders into the House in 1980, he was "the first identifiable socialist elected since Victor L. Berger of Wisconsin."[7]

For a start, there are the obvious examples. There was New York's SPA congressman, Meyer London. There was Vito Marcantonio, who represented East Harlem for a lengthy period in the 1930s and 1940s and followed the communist party line.[8] Then there was Ron Dellums who sat in the House for twenty-seven years representing a poverty stricken district on the opposite coast of America. A long time socialist, Dellums was vice-chair of the Democratic Socialists of America (DSA) in between quitting Congress and becoming mayor of Oakland in 2007. Representing a left-leaning district in Brooklyn, NY, Congressman Major Owens was another African American member of the DSA.[9]

On top of this, you could use wider definitions and identify larger numbers of socialist legislators. You could even follow the practice of President Truman's ambassador to Guatemala, Richard Patterson Jr., who courted notoriety when he explained that he identified communists by applying the "duck test" – if it looks like a duck and swims like a duck and quacks like a duck, it's probably a duck.[10] Applying such impressionistic criteria and picking up on the rhetoric of right-wing politicians vilifying reformist opponents, you could in fact identify hundreds of additional "socialists" in Congress.

In the accompanying table, the criteria are more cautious. Individuals are included not just because they advocated public ownership, federal control of the economy or welfare state legislation, but because they also expressed sympathy with socialism, or were labeled socialist by more neutral observers. The criteria exclude some interesting characters, for example Congresswoman Bella Abzug (D-NY). Abzug played a pivotal role in congressional opposition to the Vietnam War, was a major figure on the feminist left, and had been active in Hashomer Hatzair, a youth group that blended Zionism and socialism. But in Congress she was neither an avowed socialist, nor generally regarded as one, and for this reason does not appear on the list.[11]

Senator Robert M. La Follette is in the table because he accepted the nomination of the SPA in 1924, but his son Senator Robert M. La Follette Jr. is not because, in spite of his championing of labor and civil liberties, he had no observable socialist connections. Senator Paul Douglas was in later years a conservative-style supporter of the Vietnam War, but is in the table because in addition to working for a left agenda in his youth he supported the SPA presidential candidacy of Norman Thomas in 1932, and in the same year proposed the creation in the United States of an equivalent of the British Labour Party.[12]

No definition can be perfect, and there are bound to be marginal examples. For this reason, all but five of the entries in the list are italicized to indicate that they are marginal candidates for inclusion. The exercise shows that outside of Berger, London, Maverick, Dellums and Sanders, any list of socialists in Congress must be regarded as a prompt to discussion, not as the final word. Yet to exclude all marginal candidates would surely be to distort political history.

The Populists, for example, were no trifling group. In alliance with the Democratic Party and with William Jennings Bryan as their joint presidential candidate, they became a major force in American politics, ultimately failing at the polls by a much narrower margin than the later SPA.

The eighteen Populists on the list were the first People's Party wave in Congress, all serving in the sessions from December 7, 1891 to March 3, 1895. Many more were elected later, and could have been listed. Equally, some of the eighteen could have been excluded for being less interested in social reconstruction than in other issues like the gold standard, the tariff, and white racial supremacy. Tom Watson is an example. Watson supported Eugene Debs when the socialist was in jail for opposing World War I. He demanded "Debs in the White House and [President] Wilson in Prison." But, in marked contrast to Debs, Watson was already a racist. By the time he became the Populists' presidential candidate in 1904, he had turned his back on his former championing of racial equality.[13]

So one can quibble. But the eighteen are included to represent the whole because of the way in which they were labeled at the time. Anna L. Diggs, a Kansas advocate of votes for women who lectured on the Populist circuit, noted in April 1892 that the "office-holding class" and

Socialist Members of Congress (marginal cases in *italics*)

Name	State	Years in House	Years in Senate	Affiliation
William Baker	*KS*	*1891–6*		*People's Pty*
Benjamin H. Clover	*KS*	*1891–2*		*People's Pty*
John Davis	*KS*	*1891–2*		*People's Pty*
John G. Otis	*KS*	*1891–2*		*People's Pty*
Jerry Simpson	*KS*	*1891*		*People's Pty*
William A Peffer	*KS*		*1891–6*	*Farmers' All.*
James H. Kyle	*SD*		*1891–1902*	*People's Pty*
Omer M. Kem	*NE*	*1891–6*		*People's Pty*
William A. McKeighan	*NE*	*1891–2*		*People's Pty*
Kittel Halvorson	*MI*	*1891–2*		*People's Pty*
Thomas E. Watson	*GA*	*1891–2*		*People's Pty*
William V. Allen	*NE*		*1893–1902*	*People's Pty*
Thomas J. Hudson	*KS*	*1893–4*		*People's Pty*
William A. Harris	*KS*	*1893–1902*		*People's Pty*
Haldor E. Boen	*MI*	*1893–4*		*People's Pty*
John Bell	*CO*	*1893–1902*		*People's Pty*
Lafayette Pence	*CO*	*1893–4*		*People's Pty*
Marion Cannon	*CA*	*1893–4*		*People's Pty*
Robert M. La Follette	*WI*		*1906–25*	*Republican*
Victor L. Berger	WI	1911–12, 1919, 1923–8		Socialist Pty of America
Meyer London	NY	1915–18, 1921–2		Socialist Pty of America
Fiorello H. La Guardia	*NY*	*1917–20, 1923–32*		*Republican*
Thomas R. Amlie	*WI*	*1931–8*		*Progressive*
Gerald J. Boileau	*WI*	*1931–8*		*Democrat*
Vito Marcantonio	NY	1935–6, 1939–50		American Labor Party
F. Maury Maverick	*TX*	*1935–8*		*Democrat*
John T. Bernard	*MI*	*1937–9*		*Farmer–Labor*
H. Jerry Voorhis	*CA*	*1937–46*		*Democrat*
E. Hugh DeLacy	*WA*	*1945–7*		*Democrat*
Paul H. Douglas	*IL*		*1949–66*	*Democrat*
Ronald V. Dellums	CA	1971–98		Democrat
Major Owens	*NY*	*1983–2006*		*Democrat*
Bernard Sanders	VT	1991–2006	2007–	Independent

"corporation-serving press" no longer considered farmers to be "solid yeomanry" but instead accused them of being "hayseed socialists" who sought "class legislation."[14]

In scholars' accounts, the reform-bent farmers of the 1890s acquired the less condescending label "prairie socialists." They were not limited to the prairies, though. Kansas, it is true, became a hotbed of socialism. But so did the Rocky Mountain states, where hard rock miners voted Populists into office before becoming disenchanted with politics and launching the IWW. When the Populists were on the rise, radicals like the Rev. W. D. P. Bliss, founder of the Christian Socialist Society, were keen to join them. When the Populists collapsed, the SPA was a logical point of refuge. Eugene Debs declared himself to be "an out and out People's party man" before he went on to join the socialists.[15]

Eventually it became plain that although Populists set up banking cooperatives and public granaries and fought for railroad regulation, many of them also had a pro-property, pro-business mindset. At the time, that was enough to put an end to their putative alliance with urban socialists in Illinois.[16] In retrospect, however, their preference for a mixed economy looks like a precursor to the twentieth-century social democratic outlook. The Populist members of Congress merit at least partial inclusion in the socialist fold, and for all their blemishes can be numbered among the pioneers of left reform.

In the era of the New Deal, one could argue that, by international standards, at least half of both houses of the US Congress was socialist. Majority votes were required to pass laws establishing social security and the Tennessee Valley Authority. In other countries, such legislation was considered on all sides of political debate to be socialist.[17] The nomenclative situation in the United States was different in that, with the exception of Marcantonio, American legislators voting for social security did not describe themselves as socialists. However, critics of the New Deal called them precisely that.

One sympathizer with the New Deal has also pointed to the presence of socialists in Congress. Sally M. Miller offered a list of 1930s legislators who were socialist in all but name. The author of a book on Victor Berger, Miller wrote the entry on "Socialism" in *The Encyclopedia of the United States Congress* (1995). She argued that, in addition to Marcantonio, four 1930s congressmen pursued the socialist agenda. These were Thomas R. Amlie, Gerald J. Boileau, H. Jerry Voorhis and Maury Maverick. Additionally, she said that there was wide support for "democratic socialist" objectives from progressively minded legislators such as Fiorello La Guardia.[18]

The FBI operated on a similar assumption about the presence of socialists in Congress. The Bureau was not supposed to conduct political surveillance, but did. For any self-respecting political reformer, it became almost a badge of honor to have an FBI file.

The FBI file on Gerald Boileau indicates that several members of Congress were subject to political surveillance because they were suspected of being socialists. In 1937 the Bureau recorded that the communists' *Daily Worker* was sympathetic not just to Boileau, but also to Caroline O'Day (D-NY), Voorhis and Maverick. A 1938 FBI report listed those who had endorsed the American League against War and Fascism. Recently renamed the American League for Peace and Democracy, this organization worked through the Christian churches, but had a communist input. In addition to Boileau, the congressional endorsers included John T. Bernard (Farmer-Labor Party-MN), John M. Coffee (D-WA), Nan W. Honeyman (D-OR), Jerry J. O'Connell (D-MT), Byron N. Scott (D-CA) and Henry G. Teigan (Farmer-Labor Party and formerly secretary of the North Dakota State Socialist Party-MN).[19] The FBI file on Boileau confirms that suspicions about socialism/communism in Congress were not confined to the rabid right, but were to be found also in an institution that was attuned to politics even if it acted in defiance of its declared remit.

As for the 1930s, so for the 1960s. Those who in 1964 voted for the amendment establishing Medicare were, in European terms, socialists. A similar labeling issue persists for later years. Representatives Dellums, Sanders and Owens called themselves socialists, but they were neither the only ones, nor necessarily the most socialist. Arguments have been made for politicians such as Barney Frank (D-MA), Neil Abercrombie (D-HI), and 2008 Democratic nomination contender Dennis Kucinich (OH). According to former student radical Todd Gitlin, the Democratic Socialists of America had ten followers in Congress in 2008.[20]

All this illustrates that any estimate of how many socialists sat in Congress at a given time depends on a particular definition of what makes a socialist. Taking the modern European definition of democratic socialism, ever since the nineteenth century there have been substantial socialist numbers and sometimes majorities on the Hill. Taking the strict-construction definition that requires a person to label him/herself a socialist and act like one at all times in a nation where the label has been unfashionable at best and dangerous at times, the number is much smaller. But then, the strict-construction definition would yield different results also in other countries, where people sometimes called themselves socialists while holding complex views. The modern "socialist" legislator, whether in Austria, Argentina, Australia, or indeed America, doubles up as a capitalist as well, simply arguing for a pragmatic and humane public-private policy mix.

Quantitatively, the socialist presence in Congress has been more extensive than left-wing pessimists might think. Qualitatively, too, the contribution has been significant. The cases of the two SPA congressmen illustrate the point.

In spite of his shortcomings and isolation, Victor Berger did make his mark on contemporary politics. He spoke up for socialist policies in the House. He had started advocating governmentally facilitated old age pensions in 1908. He continued to press for them to the very end of his days in Congress, in 1928 introducing a bill to provide a means-tested pension for all those over sixty years of age.[21] In his fairly lengthy congressional career, he also pressed for improved conditions for workers, the promotion of public works, and shorter working hours.

On foreign policy, Berger spoke not only to his contemporaries but also to future generations. The very first resolution he introduced in Congress tied the socialist movement to the peace issue. Backed by a ninety-thousand-signature petition organized by the SPA, it demanded the withdrawal of US troops that had been posted on the Mexican border in the wake of Mexico's revolution. As Sally Miller put it, his action represented "the commitment to international solidarity of the socialist movement and served to distinguish Berger from his fellow Congressmen in the area of foreign affairs." Writing at a time when the anti-Vietnam War movement was on the brink of success, she added that Berger's protest was a "portent of future events" and that he was of "contemporary" significance.[22]

Then came the "Great" War, that four-year slaughter of millions caused, in the SPA's analysis, by Europe's "ambition-crazed monarchs, designing politicians and scheming capitalists."[23] To the SPA's dismay, the socialist movements in Germany, France, and Britain lined up behind their governments' World War I military programs. In contrast, the great majority of American socialists stuck to their principles and opposed the involvement of the United States in the conflict. In so doing, they identified a popular theme, but without benefiting from it. For the Democrat Woodrow Wilson stole the socialists' thunder by proclaiming a similar peace message from his high pulpit in the White House – only to lead the country to war in 1917.

Austria-Hungary, Berger's place of birth, lined up with Germany in

World War I, and that prejudiced Berger's plausibility as an antiwar leader. The voters of Milwaukee who sent him to Congress were also of largely Germanic origin. Milwaukeeans who opposed American entry into the war on the side of Britain and France were accused of being more pro-German than pro-peace. A defiant Berger nevertheless contributed to the antiwar message. He attacked "preparedness", the gearing up of the American war machine. He helped form a socialist-led People's Council designed to co-ordinate the pro-peace campaign.

On March 18, 1918, the federal government indicted Berger and four other SPA national officers for conspiracy to violate the Espionage Act. Berger was convicted of conspiracy, and only later did the Supreme Court quash that verdict. In Milwaukee he continued to do well, being twice elected to the House of Representatives. The House on both occasions refused to seat him, leaving Milwaukee unrepresented in Congress for the duration of the war. With America in the war and the fighting in Europe at a bloody climax, Berger decided to run for the Senate as a peace candidate. He received 110,487 votes out of 423,343 cast, the best-ever showing by a socialist candidate in Wisconsin. Whatever Victor Berger's personal short-comings and however much he was isolated, he delivered a message to the nation and to his fellow politicians. He clearly articulated the link between left-wing principles and antimilitarism.[24]

What of the other SPA congressman, Meyer London? His father Ephraim had arrived from Russia in 1888, and the twenty-year-old Meyer joined him three years later. With help from organized labor, he stood on a socialist ticket and took on the corruption-tainted Democratic Party machine in New York City.[25]

Tammany rigged the 1912 result against London. Its thugs beat one SPA poll watcher and tore his tally sheet to shreds in front of his eyes. But London gave as good as he got. The unions afforded him "protection." He deployed his debating skills against Henry M. Goldfoggle, the Tammany candidate whom he finally defeated. Goldfoggle had referred to London as "un-American" and to himself as "a one hundred percent American." The SPA candidate replied that Goldfoggle was "an ordinary Tammany jade, a zero without a circumference."[26]

Like Berger, London was the lone socialist in Congress – their terms there did not coincide. Like the Milwaukee man, he was gifted. On the Hill, he rivaled in erudition the scholastically vain Senator Henry Cabot Lodge (R-MA). In addition to his facility with the English language, Meyer spoke Russian, Jewish, German, English, French and Italian.

Where Berger was a backroom politician, London was at ease with the common man and a gifted communicator. He had a wider spectrum of human sympathies. For example, his attitude toward women was more in tune with left/liberal aspirations than that of the Wisconsian. Speaking for female franchise in the fall of 1917 he urged a wavering Congress to accept that a woman is a "human being", and laid into those Southern Democrats who saw universal enfranchisement as an infringement of states rights. In the Civil War a million men had died to establish the Union, he reminded them, and "the States are mere geographical conveniences."[27]

On February 19, 1916, Congressman London introduced to the House of Representatives a resolution proposing the setting up of a national insurance fund to help mitigate the effects of unemployment, disability and sickness. His action furthered the American socialist campaign in this area. The SPA had been the first party to advocate social insurance, Selig Perlman and his socialist colleagues had drawn up a blueprint for the welfare state, and now another socialist had launched the first federal legislative initiative.[28]

Like Perlman, London rejected voluntary schemes and advocated a universal, compulsory arrangement that would cover every American, including the poorest. When a congressional committee considered London's proposal and heard evidence, Isaac Rubinow, a socialist and author of a 1913 book on social insurance, explained how European nations were moving in that direction.

However, American Federation of Labor president Samuel Gompers opposed the plan. Gompers wanted to steer the labor movement away from politics, especially left-wing politics. He believed that labor unions existed to serve a privileged minority of wage-earners, namely those white workers whose skills were difficult to replicate and who could go on strike without having to worry about being replaced by strikebreakers. While the labor movement contained other more broad-minded people, Gompers set the tone. He aligned labor with business, demanding only that unionized workers received fair recompense for their labor.

Gompers was both a cause and a symptom of American labor's rejection of socialism. He objected to the compulsory and universal elements of Perlman's scheme, arguing that they ran counter to the American principles of freedom and voluntarism. Equating compulsory insurance with socialism, he took up more than half the committee's time to express his disapproval. He did so from an erudite standpoint, as he was well acquainted with the writings of Karl Marx and other socialists.

This opposition by the official tribune of organized labor damaged the social security campaign. Significantly, Edwin Witte took handwritten notes on Gompers's opinions and learned from the experience. He could see that from the political standpoint, the socialist label was an albatross slung over the neck of the social security campaign. When he pushed through social security in the 1930s he took care not to mention his socialist background.[29]

London's social insurance proposal went down to defeat by 189 votes to 139, and then a second time by a wider margin, 199 to 133. One can pause here to note how remarkable it was that he persuaded 139 congressmen to vote with him. If it is too bold to call those 139 legislators socialists, they were certainly on the left of the political spectrum on a vital matter in the same way as those who voted in social security in other countries, and in America in the 1930s.[30]

In the realm of foreign policy, London promoted a left-wing internationalist agenda. Speaking as a Jewish immigrant, he declared, "I do speak on behalf of all the oppressed races." A champion of the underdog, he opposed policies that smacked of imperial exploitation. For example, when the Jones Act of 1917 gave US citizenship to only 25 percent of the inhabitants of Puerto Rico, he saw it as a recipe for revolution and demanded that all should be treated equally. In parallel vein, he feared that Zionist ambitions might trample on the rights of Palestinians. In making that point he alienated the Zionists in his constituency, and they helped to block his re-election in 1918.[31]

London brought his debating skills to the antiwar cause. In a 1916 speech in Congress, he articulated what would be the standard 1930s critique: "This war is the direct result of a serious clash of economic interests of nations." He opposed the military draft: "They talk about conscription being a democratic institution. Yes; so is the cemetery." He defended the socialists' anticonscription stance:

William F. James (R-MI): The gentleman from New York and his Socialistic friends are against conscription. If Congress should pass a volunteer bill, would there be a wild rush from the Socialists to fight for their country?
London: There would be a bigger rush from the Socialists than from the membership of this Congress.

As his rejoinder hints, London turned into what could be termed a peacetime pacifist. Like so many European socialists, he accepted his nation's role in the war once it had become a belligerent. He helped the war effort. When the 1917 revolution threatened to take Russia out of the war allowing Germany to concentrate its forces on the western front, "as the only Socialist member of the American Congress" London urged Prince Kerensky's government to keep fighting.[32]

So London did not have a "perfect" record as a left-wing legislator. Like Berger, however, he made a contribution. That contribution can be better assessed by placing it in the context of the collective impact of socialists on American society in the first two decades of the twentieth century. Back of the SPA legislators, as indicated in the last chapter, were the host of left-wing campaigners ranging from John Dewey to Margaret Sanger, and the Wisconsin crowd had ensured the credibility and future success of London's social security initiative in Congress.

There were other manifestations, too, of socialist impact. To recall a prominent example, there was the stand taken by the SPA's preeminent leader, Eugene Debs. Debs's career is a reminder that the legislators were not the only left politicians who mattered.

Socialist activities on the local level further complemented the efforts of national legislators. The prairie Populists fought Wall Street and the railroads by setting up local co-operative banks and grain elevators. Towns and cities invested in publicly owned gas works and electricity plants. Socialist-type measures were quite common at the municipal level in the 1890s and the following decade.

From 1898, the socialist label made municipal advances. In that year, the Social Democrat John C. Chase won election as mayor in Haverhill, Massachusetts. Once established, the SPA enjoyed a number of local successes, a rush of them occurring in 1910–11, when voters elected twenty-eight socialist mayors in communities stretching from Berkeley, California eastward across the nation. Milwaukee was the largest city affected. Its citizens elected Emil Seidel in 1910, and mostly chose socialist mayors for the next half century.

Thousands of socialist mayors, aldermen, and other elected officials could boast of local achievements. Milwaukee had early stressed the importance of public health, and the city's record was enviable in that regard. The socialist-governed city had an admired police force. Milwaukeeans fondly remember the city's tidiness, its orderliness, and its spacious avenues. The efficiency of Milwaukee's administration was especially conspicuous because it stood out in comparison with Chicago, just eighty miles down the road – in the words of labor historian Henry Pelling, the Midwest's leading city was "notorious for its civil corruption."

As Pelling and other students of local socialism have remarked, there were limits to what could be achieved locally. In the United States, initiatives at one level of government were constrained by the nation's diffusion of constitutional powers. The "cooperative commonwealth" could not be fully achieved on the local level because the state and national governments and the courts retained important powers.[33]

On the other hand, the potency of the socialist challenge is attested to by the efforts made to resist it. Confronted with an actual or potential socialist victory, the Democrats and Republicans would sometimes field a fusion candidate. This tactic failed in Milwaukee after an initial success that saw Seidel unseated in 1912. In other cities, however, it proved effective. Socialism faded in local politics from its peak around 1911. The fusion tactic conveyed the message Anything But Socialism. It illuminated the actual and potential appeal of local socialism, even as it sought to throttle it.[34]

As the historian Richard Hofstadter reminded America at the height of the Cold War, "The moral and intellectual leverage exerted by the Socialist Party and Socialist ideas in the Progressive era has never been sufficiently recognized."[35] American socialists proposing social security were small in number, but persuasive. They studied foreign solutions and devised an American plan. Meyer London introduced the first legislative proposal in Congress. He, Berger and their potential congressional allies offered a potent political agenda. If the two traditional parties had ignored it the SPA might have grown. But the American political system was too pragmatic and flexible for that to happen. It was just a matter of time before the Democrats or the Republicans would seize the prize.

In the event, it was the Democrats who learned how to adopt the socialist platform and consign to the political wilderness not just the SPA but also the Republican Party. If only after delays of varying length, the socialists' plans prevailed. To this achievement, can be added the socialist congressmen's contribution to American antimilitarism and to civil liberties. Too long ignored, the socialists in Congress and their allies need to be given greater credit by students of social and political history.

Chapter 5

THE IDENTIFICATION OF AMERICA AND ITS FASCIST ENEMY

In an article for *Nation* in January 1931, William M. Leiserson once again appealed for a national scheme of social insurance. Casting his mind back to his days as a federal investigator, he revealed his awareness of the sensitivity of the issue then and since. For conservative opposition had continued in the years since his reports of 1914–15 – "one hundred percent Americans" had lined up to denounce proposals for social reform. In an attempt to re-channel the nation's identity Leiserson thus asserted, "government compulsion to protect workers and their families has always been an essential characteristic of real Americanism."[1]

So what, then, was "real Americanism"? In the years between the two world wars, socialists played a significant role in shaping a more inclusive American political identity. The socialist re-imaging of America was by no means confined to the introduction of a welfare state.

Cultural developments reinforced the new sense of identity and had a strong left input. Notably, the "Harlem Renaissance" contributed to a new sense of national character. In harmony with this, socialists challenged racism at home and abroad. By pushing on the civil rights front at home, they signaled the possibility of a national identity for all Americans, regardless of race. Turning to foreign affairs, socialists were largely responsible for identifying the new threat to America and its racially inclusive values, fascism.

Cultural developments both derived from and stimulated the left. Harlem, New York, gave its name to a flowering of artistic talent through fiction, poetry, drama, painting, literary criticism, jazz and blues, and, indirectly, musicals. The term "Harlem Renaissance" is strictly speaking a misnomer. The phenomenon that students of American culture often prefer to call the "Negro Renaissance" or "New Negro Renaissance" affected Chicago and other cities as well as New York. Thus what is popularly called the Harlem

Renaissance had a wider impact than the phrase implies. In fact it had a worldwide impact at a time when America was emerging as a great power. Having flourished in the 1920s, the movement withered in the 1930s partly because its African American protagonists were especially vulnerable to poverty, then revived on a wider canvas and under different labels from the 1940s on.[2]

The term "renaissance" or re-birth was a nineteenth-century description of the cultural flowering that started in northern Italy in the fourteenth century and spread across Europe. It exercised a fascination for Americans. In the Jim Crow era, US literary critics suggested that a white literary American Renaissance was occurring. They linked it to the Greek, Christian and British literary traditions.[3] The Harlem Renaissance was a radical departure from this. It was non-white and proudly American.

Various reasons explain why the Renaissance happened when it did, where it did, and why it was the achievement of black people. By the 1920s, African Americans had enjoyed a half-century free of chattel slavery and were gaining in confidence and ambition. Black fighters dominated the boxing ring; the NAACP was a force in the land; the Harlem Silent Parade of 1917 signaled a rise in African American militancy; the racially flawed peace that followed World War I spelled out anticolonial messages loud and clear and black America listened; a renewed pride in Africa bourgeoned under the leadership of the Jamaican immigrant Marcus Garvey. As Alain Locke put it in a defining essay of 1925 on the "New Negro", "Uncle Tom and Sambo have passed on."[4]

The substantial black population of Harlem found itself located within the cultural capital of white America, New York City. Yet the Harlemites found more that was American within their own black tradition. In fact, they lived cheek by jowl with European immigrants who were a daily reminder that nobody was more American than the descendant of a Southern plantation slave. Yet, at the same time, the Renaissance reverberated beyond America. To quote another of Locke's phrases, "the pulse of the Negro world had begun to beat in Harlem."[5]

The hot spot if not the sole location of the Renaissance, Black Harlem had been fertile soil for socialist ideas. In fact a leading progenitor of those ideas, Hubert Harrison, questioned the very idea of a "renaissance." A charismatic thinker whose plural taste in women was matched by his mastery of six languages (including Arabic but not Russian), Harrison influenced SPA thinking on racial matters and helped to scotch the idea that the party should have segregated locals. He insisted that there had been a stream of cultural productivity in the black community stretching back to 1850. The "Harlem Renaissance" was no more than a tardy recognition of that talent, and moreover an attempt to impress on it the stamp of white cultural homogeneity.[6]

The Renaissance did receive a boost from the white salons of Greenwich Village, literary talking-shops that antedated the 1920s. Socialists who frequented Mabel Dodge Luhan's salon on adjoining Fifth Avenue included the white literary figures John Reed, Max Eastman, Walter Lippmann and William English Walling. In the words of the Harlemite intellectual historian Harold Cruse, these white figures "are to be remembered for their close personal relationship with certain Negro individuals." Black literati frequented the Luhan salon from around 1912. As Harrison noted, they did not materialize from thin air – but they did benefit from salon patronage.[7]

As with any lively intellectual group, there were tactical and ideological fissures. These fissures weakened but at the same time affirmed the vitality of the Renaissance left. The Luhan salon and its equivalents amongst the black bourgeoisie did not command universal support. SPA supporter A. Philip Randolph was that rarity, a successful black labor leader – he led the Pullman porters' union. In 1917 he founded *The Messenger*, a socialist magazine for African Americans. He was soon involved in two splits. First, he disapproved of the Bolshevik takeover in Russia, thus being at odds with the future American communists. Second, Randolph's magazine reflected a split in its dismissal of the Harlem Renaissance, saying "with us economics and politics take precedence to 'Music and Art'."[8]

Randolph was no lightweight protagonist. He had a powerful following and became one of America's most effective civil rights leaders. However, his disapproval still failed to dampen the Renaissance. On a political level, it even inspired it. In a 1919 article for *The Messenger*, Randolph wrote of a "New Negro" who objected to the old ways of shirking radicalism and left politics, thus inventing the phrase that Alain Locke would popularize later on.[9]

The Renaissance flourished and helped to project cultural legends, some of the most gifted of whom – for example, W. E. B. Du Bois, Richard Wright, Claude McKay, Langston Hughes, Dorothy West and a little later Bayard Rustin and Paul Robeson – were socialists. Taking a broader view, just about all the participants in the Harlem Renaissance could be regarded as having been culturally subversive of the existing order. They ranged from blues artist Lead Belly (when not in prison) to poet Countee Cullen. To understate the matter, they were not on the political right.

According to one point of view, the Harlem Renaissance was just an episode in the white patronizing of black America, a moment in history when the white literati acknowledged – and then only temporarily – that the black citizen existed.[10] A parallel grouse is that the black impact in the 1920s was cut short because white men stole black folk's music, then commercialized and sanitized it. Other doubters suggest the Renaissance was an exaggerated phenomenon arising from the impact of shock – black talent having hitherto been suppressed by illiteracy and persecution, it took people by surprise in the 1920s, but they did not think it something to take seriously in the long run.[11]

Of special influence, a whole cadre of historians has castigated and dismissed the Renaissance because of its close association with socialism and particularly communism. The Cold War frightened scholars who, reading history backwards, tarred pre-Stalin communists with the brush of later Stalinist atrocities. They sometimes expressed their arguments as an objection to "integrationist treason", aligning themselves with those African Americans who saw racial pride through separation as a higher priority than the color-blind brotherhood of man. For them, what transpired in the 1920s was less a re-birth than an abortion.[12]

The novelist, literary critic and social observer James Weldon Johnson offered a more optimistic assessment of black accomplishments in an address to the Intercollegiate Socialist Society at Bellport, Long Island in 1917. In remarks reported around the globe, he claimed, "the only things artistic in America that have sprung from American soil, and been universally acknowledged as distinctively American, have been the creations of the American Negro." It was a bold assertion designed to capture the attention of people who had been blind to the talents of the African American. Johnson later issued a qualification, observing that the American skyscraper had not been a black invention. He had tried hard to come up with a list of white cultural contributions, but this was the best he could do.[13]

Johnson's chutzpah is evidence of a more general aspiration to black self-esteem. Du Bois was another Renaissance socialist who articulated ambition. Black citizens, he wrote, did not just want to enjoy the rights of Americans. They also wanted to redefine the American character: "We who are dark can see America in a way that white Americans can not."[14] Today, few would quarrel with his view that race and slavery had played a huge role in shaping American history and that, until the black awakening, white America had been blind to that fact. Du Bois erased American history and started writing it again.

By redefining America past and present, the articulators of the Harlem Renaissance invited reflection by white Americans. Carl Van Vechten was one literary critic who took up the theme that "blackness was an essential feature of Americanness."[15] The Christian socialist F. O. Matthiessen set out to re-define American culture. His book *American Renaissance: Art and Expression in the Age of Emerson and Whitman* served as a modifier to the Africanist views of James Weldon Johnson, but it was also a challenge to the Jim Crow assumption about the European origins of American culture.[16] A white man, Matthiessen identified the years 1850–5 as a time of special fertility, and portrayed his literary figures as American not European in inspiration. He focused on five proto-leftist writers: Thoreau, who opposed taxation because it supported the military; Melville, an enemy of poverty and friend of oppressed workers; Hawthorne, practitioner and upholder of collectivism; Emerson, championed by the socialist John Dewey as "the philosopher of democracy"; and Whitman, whose "emergent socialism" made him such an eloquent champion of the American common man.[17]

Matthiessen had a claim to being the leading literary critic of his day, and to have invented the discipline of American studies – at Harvard, he directed undergraduate programs in both literature and history. Judged by later standards, he was in some ways conservative. Matthiessen paid less heed to female and black writers than to male Anglos, and never came out of the closet as gay. Furthermore, nationalism and exceptionalism permeated the pages of his famous book.

These were traps that would ensnare other writers on national character. In World War II, the anthropologist Margaret Mead set aside her customary cosmopolitanism to write a book called *The American Character* in which she suggested that "we are better fitted than any people on earth today" to produce an improved world. By the 1950s, the search for an American character was part of a Cold War stance, an attempt to present America as homogenous and driven more by consensus than by such debate as might dangerously divide the nation in the face of a foreign foe.[18]

Another reservation about Matthiessen's contribution might be that he was a high culture guru having little if any direct influence on public opinion, or on the socially progressive legislation of the New Deal era. Compensating for this, there were others who had the talent and common touch to convey the socialist message.

Left writers ranged from Clifford Odets to Ernest Hemingway, from Lillian Hellman to her lover Dashiell Hammett. John Steinbeck rounded off the decade with *Grapes of Wrath*, the indictment of agricultural business that won the Pulitzer Prize in 1940. In the wider arts world, left messages came from such individuals as movie actor Charlie Chaplin, muralist Diego Rivera, and composer Aaron Copland, all contributors to American culture even if the first two were English and Mexican respectively. The left-wing balladeers Woody Guthrie and Pete Seeger reinforced the message conveyed by Steinbeck – for example in Guthrie's protest song "Talking Dust Bowl" – and kept alive the tradition of Joe Hill.

Walter Rideout noted the relative popularity of the "proletarian novel" in the 1930s. There were seventy such novels in the decade. Rideout noted that this did not constitute a rush to communism, as around 1,900 novels were published annually in the USA. But there were more proletarian novels than in the prime years of the SPA, and the early 1930s marked a peak for that type of book.[19] One might add that few novels make an overtly political point. Left books were a noticeable presence within the more limited numbers of the political fiction genre.

Writers and artists on the left had a symbiotic association with the New Deal. Established in 1935, Federal Project One of the Works Progress Administration (WPA) through its separate programs for Theatre, Music, Writers and Art gave employment and modest remuneration to numerous creative people who found themselves out of work during the Depression. Only some of the beneficiaries were socialist. Black literati who benefited from the Writers program included Ralph Ellison (anti-socialist) as well as Richard Wright (socialist). But the WPA schemes helped left writers who might otherwise have been stifled by the twin silencers of poverty and media proprietors' censorship. And there were further streams of federal support. The Farm Security Administration (FSA) helped Steinbeck research rural problems. A special FSA photography program took to a new level the visual depiction of social conditions pioneered in an earlier generation by Jacob Riis and Lewis Hine. Images of Depression-era suffering recorded through Dorothea Lange's lens would haunt the American conscience for decades.

All this provoked a furious attack from the right, and in 1938 the House Un-American Activities Committee (HUAC) launched an investigation. On the one hand, outraged conservatives exaggerated the degree of left influence and output, for in fact fewer than 10 percent of the Theatre project productions dealt with social issues. On the other hand, HUAC was not entirely divorced from reality. According to one informed estimate, 106 of the 300 beneficiaries of the New York Writers project were card-carrying members of the communist party. More important than maximizing or minimizing the degree of left infiltration is the issue of how to evaluate the nature of the New Deal-left creative arts connection. It could be argued that by patronizing the arts and refusing to discriminate against the left, New Deal administrators drew the sting from a potentially dangerous group of critics. However the New Deal, Federal Project One included, was in some measure less the driver than the product of an imaginative construct to which the left had contributed.[20]

Any discussion of socialist contributions to American society in the 1920s and 1930s would be incomplete that did not address the activities of the Communist Party of the United States of America. In some ways, the party was a weak contributor and a liability to the American left. Formed in 1919 in the aftermath of the Bolshevik take over in Russia, it was in the 1920s weakened by factionalism. Even at its height in the 1930s, it never matched the SPA's achievements in terms of membership or electoral success.

There were inherent problems. Though American communists showed signs of wanting independence from Moscow, they were usually controlled from afar, and lacked the autonomy to react flexibly to local conditions and politics. To a greater extent than the SPA, the party adhered to Marxism. But Karl Marx had offered only a critique of capitalism, not a blueprint for the improvement of society. Furthermore, Marx's denunciation of religion as the "opium of the people" alienated those many Christians who had in the past seen and potentially still saw equivalences between aspects of socialism and the teachings of Jesus. For these reasons, Marxism was a deadweight mantra hanging around the party's neck. And this was not all. After news of Stalin's atrocities had leaked to the West and when the Soviet Union and the USA squared off in the Cold War, the overwhelming majority of Americans came to see communism as an enemy creed. An endorsement by the communist party became a liability to any American political cause.

However, that was later. In its heyday, communism did make a contribution to American politics and society. Some of America's bravest and most inspiring citizens of the interwar years were communists. Nor could it be said that the US communist cadres were wholly unsuccessful. They had some local triumphs. Moreover, they helped to put the US race problem on the national and international political agenda.

Communists engaged in numerous local labor struggles. In 1929 their party led one of America's most famous labor struggles, the strike by the

National Textile Workers Union in Gastonia, North Carolina. The 3,500 workers who struck the Loray Mill included African Americans as well as whites. The conservative and racially exclusive American Federation of Labor (AFL) would not help. After armed mobs and the police had terrorized women and children on the picket line, there was a gunfight on the night of June 7. In the course of it, the local police chief Orville Aderhilt was shot dead. In another confrontation, the ballad singer and striking mill worker Ella May Wiggins died in a hail of fire. The authorities ignored her death, but arrested and charged some of the strike leaders over the policeman's death – some of them fled to the Soviet Union. The Gastonia strike failed in its immediate goals, but awoke the nation to the ruthless tactics being used by some American employers, and to the need for collective workers' action to counter those tactics.

To pick another prominent example from the many cases of communist impact on the labor union front, on the West Coast Harry Bridges led the waterfront workers. He won national prominence at the time of the 1934 San Francisco general strike. This was a time when Sam Darcy, leader of the California communists, showed independence from the party line. He recalled how the national party boss Earl Browder and his Political Bureau "were driving me nuts." When they sent "three little jerks" out West to enforce party discipline and one of them proved a special annoyance, Darcy ordered, "take [him] by the ass and by the neck and throw him down the stairs." The message traveled East and California's communists even had some impact on thinking in Moscow.[21]

In 1937 Bridges's followers showed another kind of independence when they split off from the nation-wide International Longshoremen's Association (ILA) to form the International Longshoremen's and Warehousemen's Union (ILWU), again under the leadership of Bridges. Offering a contrast to the mobster-ridden ILA, the ILWU commanded respect. It affiliated with the newly formed Congress of Industrial Organizations (CIO) until the CIO expelled it in 1950 as part of an anticommunist purge.

With pressure coming from employers and from anticommunists, there were several attempts to deny Bridges citizenship and deport him to his native Australia. The ground for doing so, if it could be proved, would have been that he was a member of the communist party. Bridges proclaimed himself to be a Marxist, praised the communist party, and readily acknowledged working with it. Documents released in the 1990s indicate he was a member of the party, and indeed sat on its central committee. But in the 1930s as in later years, Bridges denied he was a party member. He later proclaimed himself to be a Republican voter in gratitude to President Eisenhower who allowed him to stay in the country whereas Democrats had tried to expel him. His lie about membership of the party is one of those cases of American socialism in denial, in this instance for pressing reasons of personal expediency.[22]

Communist labor leaders had mixed fortunes. Harry Bridges and his union went from strength to strength on the West Coast but faltered when they tried to organize in New Orleans. The Textile Workers Union of America, a CIO affiliate in which communists were active, failed to match its successes in the North with similar inroads into the South where there were six hundred thousand lower-paid textile industry employees. But the party organizers did help infuse with hope and fighting spirit the millions of American workers who suffered at the hands of exploitative employers and whose welfare the AFL had neglected. Union membership expanded dramatically in the 1930s, especially after the founding of the CIO in 1935. Organized on industrial lines like the earlier Knights of Labor and IWW, the CIO unions were fertile ground for communists some of whom were, in fact, former Wobblies. Communists in the unions not only helped to win gains for workers, but also ensured that the unions in which they were involved stayed free of the graft and gangsterism that was becoming a problem elsewhere in the labor movement.

For a while, the communists seemed set to punch above their weight in politics. In California, for example, they harnessed themselves to the political activism of Upton Sinclair. The novelist twice ran for office on the SPA ticket in the 1920s, then in 1934 made a bid for the Democratic gubernatorial nomination under the banner of his political action group, End Poverty in California (EPIC). Anticipating the new politics of what would be called the Popular Front, the independently minded Darcy wanted to support Sinclair. He brokered an informal agreement with the EPIC team. In the event, this led to a battle with the communist party center, a battle that Darcy lost. The order came for him to run for the governorship himself. Sinclair won the Democratic nomination but lost the 1934 election to the Republicans. By briefly associating themselves with his campaign, the local communists had come close to being part of a movement with political impetus without really being within reach of a significant victory.[23]

In 1938, the California communists participated in the victorious battle against Proposition 1, an antilabor measure advanced by employers who wanted to snuff out an array of union tactics such as picketing. Now setting aside the dogma about supporting only their own candidates, the communists also helped create the surge of votes that elected the first Democratic governor of California since the nineteenth century – Culbert Olson had been a political supporter of the populist William Jennings Bryan as well as the socialist Sinclair, and offered a left-wing agenda in the campaign that propelled him to the governorship in 1939. In his inaugural address, Olson pledged himself to support civil liberties, a color-blind welfare system, free education for all and the restoration of public owner-ship of utilities. The state legislature had drifted leftwards with him, and added near-universal health care to the agenda.[24]

Olson's Democrats achieved few of their goals at the time, but set an agenda for the future. The Popular Front politics at the back of the gover-nor's electoral success arguably prepared the way for the New Left upheav-als of the 1960s, for the election of San Francisco's socialist congressman Ron Dellums in 1970, and for the Californian radicalism of the ensuing decade.[25]

Socialists – and communist party activists in particular – helped to energize the struggle to raise African Americans from their status as an oppressed underclass. English-speaking Caribbean immigrants schooled in resistance to British imperialism supplied some of the inspiration, for example Hubert Harrison (from the Virgin Islands), Claude McKay (Jamaica), and later on C. L. R. James, who arrived from Trinidad via England. There was a strong Caribbean presence in the United Blood Brotherhood, a radical organization formed in resistance to the Red Scare in 1919 that eventually merged itself into the communist party.

Nevertheless, in spite of FBI claims to the contrary, African American communism was mainly indigenous. This truth may still come as a shock to some readers. As Jacqueline Dowd Hall put it in her 2005 presiden-tial address to the Organization of American Historians, many white Americans have been gripped by a "miasma of evasion and confusion" in their understanding of the nature of the origins of the twentieth-century African American struggle for equality.[26]

James W. Ford was one African American who would slip into historical obscurity because of the prejudices not just of Dixie boosters and conserva-tives, but also of pro-civil rights historians who preferred a respectable and safe account of the past. Ford's grandfather had died at the hands of a white lynch mob in Georgia. His father quit agricultural toil to become an ironworker, blast furnace worker and coal miner – Ford was born in 1893 in Pratt City, a mining town near Birmingham, Alabama. Ford worked his way through Fisk University where he was known as "The Rabbit" for his

evasive skills on the football field. He served in the Army Signal Corps in
World War I, played semi-pro at halfback – Paul Robeson had played for
the same team, the Lincoln Athletic Club. Expelled from the AFL when he
attempted to organize postal workers in Chicago, Ford became active in the
American Labor Negro Congress. He joined the communist party, leaving
the USA in 1929 to spend eighteen months in Russia.[27]

In 1932, Ford stood on the communist party ticket for the vice
presidency of the United States. It would be no picnic. His running mate
William Z. Foster had already earned the sour hostility of the media.
Newspaper proprietors and their editors frowned on Foster's leadership
of the 1919 national steelworkers' strike, and his AFL-defying efforts to
organize black as well as white workers in the steel industry. A Detroit
paper warned during the 1932 election campaign, "Foster's Smile Masks
Heart of Dynamite."[28]

Ford was aware that southern blacks, politically demoralized by Jim
Crow, would be slow to flock to the communist party. In 1928, when the
party had no organizer in the South, Ford noted, "we have practically
no Negro party members." In fact, there were just fifty party members
nationwide out of a black population of twelve million. Still mainly disenfranchised in the South, the African American could not hope to make
an impact at the polls. It is estimated that the communist party received
only 2,117 votes in the southern and border states in 1932, compared with
twenty-nine thousand for the SPA. Nationally, the communist vote was
103,307 and the SPA's 884,885. Ford stood again in 1936 and 1940, this
time as Earl Browder's partner, but both the communist party and SPA vote
declined even from the decade's relatively low peak of 1932.[29]

Yet in the 1930s, influential individuals took the red-black equation
seriously. By the 1940s, FBI director J. Edgar Hoover was ordering his
agents to collect data on "Negro Organizations", with a subcategory on
"Communism."[30]

Ford's candidacies were, in fact, testimony to a coming change. There
were those who recognized the significance of his candidacy. Harlem
Renaissance luminaries Langston Hughes and the normally politically
reclusive Countee Cullen supported his 1932 bid.[31] For Ford was the first
fully committed black candidate for the vice presidency or presidency of
the United States. Frederick Douglass had in 1872 been on the Equal Rights
Party ticket, the running mate of presidential candidate Victoria Woodhull
– a feminist who had brought out the first American edition of Karl Marx's
Communist Manifesto. But Douglass had not taken the campaign seriously.

Ford was a pioneer in another way, too. Between the 1930s and the 2008 candidacy of Barack Obama there were twenty-three minor-party nominations of African American candidates. The great majority of these candidates were socialists, several of them women. Through Ford, the communist party had pointed to a racially and ultimately gender inclusive future.[32]

Ford and other American communists picked up the banner of civil liberties that earlier generations of radicals had held aloft. They continued in particular the US tradition of labor-civil liberties struggles arising out of court cases. In the past, such campaigns had arisen out of the indictment of anarchists for the 1886 bombing episode in Haymarket Square, Chicago, and the arrest of Big Bill Haywood on an apocryphal murder charge in 1905. Then there was the Joe Hill case ten years later, immediately followed by outcry over the jailing on the basis of perjured evidence of left wing labor leader Tom Mooney, who with Warren Billings was supposed to have set the bomb that killed ten people at a Preparedness Day parade in San Francisco in 1916. The communist party fought that one hard. Then there came the supreme test of the 1920s, the case of Nicola Sacco and Bartolomeo Vanzetti.

Sacco and Vanzetti were Italian-American anarchists. Police arrested them for their alleged part in a homicidal factory payroll robbery that took place in Braintree, Massachusetts in April 1920. Seven years later, they suffered death by electrocution. Their trial had been patently unfair, as later revelations confirmed. Evidence unsealed in the 1970s indicated that the police and prosecution had knowingly framed Vanzetti with the offence of stealing a guard's gun, and that Bullet 3, one of six extracted from the security guards and the only one tied to the defendants, could not be traced ballistically to Sacco's weapon.

Perhaps because the evidence at his disposal did not at the time lend itself to an exculpatory verdict, Fred H. Moore, the case-hardened socialist lawyer from the West who defended the accused, decided to widen his argument beyond the interpretation of the crime-scene. Moore insisted the trial was part of a political-judicial effort to crush the Italian anarchist movement in America. This line of defense was a recipe for the globalization of protest.

Some "revisionists" have portrayed the worldwide agitation on behalf of Sacco and Vanzetti as a Moscow-orchestrated campaign. However, most Sacco and Vanzetti sympathizers in America, communist or otherwise, simply saw an opportunity for the rectification of injustice. Whatever the preferred interpretation, this was a time when the communists made hay. For them, the issue of race seemed a fruitful area for endeavor.[33]

The days when African students arrived in Moscow full of hope only to leave scarred by racial taunts lay some distance in the future. In the 1930s, Russia hosted visits by black Americans and lionized them. Black visitors included literary figures Langston Hughes, W. E. B. Du Bois, Claude Mackay and Paul Robeson, all of whom used the experience to refine their views on internationalism, antiracism, anticolonialism and social democracy. When a group of African Americans crossed from Finland into the Soviet Union with Langston Hughes they scooped up the soil in their hands and kissed it. Russia seemed a Red Heaven.[34]

At this point, it is appropriate to record the sowing of the seeds of another type of radicalism, black left feminism. A small number of African American women were active in the communist party and would have a long-term influence. Louise Thompson is of special interest. She was a product of the Harlem Renaissance who visited the Soviet Union where she felt liberated, or at least that was her first impression. Back in the USA, she wrote an article, published in 1936, called "Toward a Brighter Dawn." Here, she used the term – she may have invented it – "triple exploitation" to show how you could be thrice oppressed if you were black, a worker, and a woman. While Louise Thompson had been influenced by communism, in this article she took issue with the communist party's male chauvinism and neglect of women. It was a visionary glimpse of the new feminist and left agendas of the 1960s and beyond.[35]

One case the communists took up in the 1930s was that of Angelo Herndon. Herndon had joined the communist party in the wake of the interracial strike at Gastonia. In July 1932, he organized a one-thousand-strong hunger march on the courthouse in Atlanta, Georgia. This was the largest integrated demonstration that the city had ever seen. Dressing smartly in city-style chic, Herndon sported socialist-red neckties and wore owlish glasses that suggested black men could actually read. He struck conservative southerners as the epitome of black impudence. Because of the hunger march, the authorities deployed a Reconstruction-era state law to indict him on a charge of inciting insurrection. The nineteen-year-old escaped the death sentence demanded by the prosecution, but received a twenty-year prison sentence. The US Supreme Court quashed the case against him in 1937, but by this time Herndon had spent years either in prison or in fear of returning to it, and the publicity-hungry communist party trumpeted the injustices of the case.[36]

The communist party's greatest miscarriage of justice case began when the police in Paint Creek, Alabama hauled nine African Americans off a Southern Railroad Chattanooga-to-Memphis freight train on March 25, 1931. The arrestees were aged thirteen to twenty-one. Known as the "Scottsboro Boys" after the nearby town where they went on trial, the nine were accused of raping two white women who had also been riding on the train. A jury moved by the misconceptions of southern white chivalry condemned all the defendants to death after a four-day trial. The judge over-ruled the verdict in the case of the thirteen-year-old making it a life sentence instead. However, the rest seemed destined to die.

That was before International Labor Defense (ILD) intervened. The communist-backed organization started a propaganda campaign and demanded a retrial. In pursuit of that goal and of a new verdict, the NAACP offered the services of the nation's most famous labor counsel, Clarence Darrow. However, in an endorsement of the communist party the nine opted instead for ILD counsel.

The resultant feud between the communists and the NAACP dented but did not disable the effort for the defense. Recognizing that the trial had been political, the communists resorted to political tactics of their own, for example sending the boys' mothers around the United States and Europe on speaking tours. The political pressure forced people to ask new questions. Some of these were about the evidence. Medical examination suggested that Victoria Price, one of the women who claimed to have been raped by six of the nine accused, may not have had sex at all on the day in question. One of the alleged rapists, Willie Roberson, had a mental age of nine and was so far gone with syphilis that he may not have been capable of intercourse.

Pressure from the communists and their allies forced the case up the judicial ladder. In *Powell* v. *Alabama* (1932), the US Supreme Court ordered a retrial on the ground that no proper defense had been allowed at the original trial. Two lawyers had been allocated to the defense of the impecunious accused. The more competent of the two, Stephen R. Roddy, was a real estate specialist, lacked courtroom experience relevant to the case, and had a serious alcohol problem. The other, Milo Moody, was forgetful to the point of senility.[37]

None of the Scottsboro Boys were executed, and after protracted legal battles the last of them emerged from prison in 1951. In the Cold War years when the Soviet Union had become anathema, there were attempts to discredit the communists' efforts on behalf of the Boys. For example, Langston

Hughes retrospectively credited the NAACP with "initial efforts" that were "nullified by the intervention of the Communists."[38] But in the 1930s the communist campaign over the Scottsboro case won widespread support at home and abroad. Hughes himself, who in his earlier more radical incarnation had visited the men in prison and written extensively in their support, had written a one-act play, *Scottsboro Limited*, that culminated with the raising of the Red Flag and everyone singing the Communist Internationale. Other writers flocked to the cause, and effectively. According to one theatre critic reviewing the 1934 Broadway premiere of John Wexley's play *They Shall Not Die*, it lacked in terms of realism only the "rich bouquet of perspiration and the acrid effluvia of stale tobacco juice."[39]

Abroad, everyone got to know that America harbored a deep racial scar, and that a struggle was going on to heal it. There were protest demonstrations in London, Amsterdam, San Salvador, Santo Domingo and Santiago de Cuba. On the other side of the adversarial divide, the southern segregationists also had international support. In South Africa it came from the advocates of apartheid and in Germany from the fascists. However, even in those countries there were pro-Scottsboro Boys demonstrations – in Johannesburg, and in several German cities, including Berlin.

Communist organization was efficient, and this meant that there was a less than spontaneous quality to some of these protests. In Germany, the demonstrations were as much about the desperate fight against the rising Nazi Party as about conditions in far away Alabama. But non-communists like Albert Einstein and the Kenyan nationalist Jomo Kenyatta joined in the protests. In the estimate of historian Harvard Sitkoff, the communist-led fight against the original Scottsboro verdict was "the most searching indictment of Jim Crow yet to appear in the United States."[40]

As well as civil rights, the communist campaigns stressed economic and labor issues. The party and its ILD conducted a campaign against involuntary servitude. Often referred to as "debt peonage", involuntary servitude was a way of tying laborers to their jobs in the rural southern economy and denying them the proper wages paid in the nation's cities. On the plantations and in the turpentine industry employers kept laborers permanently in debt, forcing them to accept payment in kind – food, housing, medicine. Local law enforcement officials helped force workers to stick to their wageless jobs by threatening to prosecute them and putting them to work as convicts in chain gangs. It was a form of virtual slavery, affected mainly those of African descent, and could be found in every state of the former Confederacy.

The effectiveness of the communists' agitation against debt peonage must be kept in perspective. The NAACP also took a leading part in the campaign, and to a certain degree made common cause with the communists over the issue. From 1936 the Workers Defense League joined in the campaign. This was a non-communist organization led by the SPA's Norman Thomas. A further qualification is also in order. While peonage became virtually extinct by the 1950s, it was not entirely because of the campaign against it. The New Deal agricultural policy had taken land out of production in order to limit output and raise prices, and as a result landowners just got rid of their debt-ridden tenants. Then, the labor shortage caused by World War II meant workers had to be treated better. The introduction of new machinery helped to consolidate the system of fewer and better-rewarded workers.[41]

Nevertheless, the communists' campaigns across several fronts did help to raise consciousness and to arouse public opinion. All this finally had an impact in Washington. A determination to combat peonage had been one of the causes of the creation of the predecessor of the FBI back in the days of Theodore Roosevelt. Since then racial justice had slipped down the Bureau's agenda. But in February 1939, there came into being the Justice Department's Civil Rights Unit. The unit's lawyers utilized the opportunities bestowed by the Thirteenth Amendment of 1865, which had made involuntary servitude as well as slavery unconstitutional. They prepared the ground for the FBI to investigate police brutality, voting rights abuses, lynching – and peonage. In one case alone – that of peonage malpractices in the sugar plantations of Florida – the FBI deployed twenty special agents.[42]

Lynching and other intimidation in the South as well as peonage and summary (in)justice began to go into decline, and this prepared the way for a rise in black confidence that would launch the civil rights movement of the 1950s.[43] The left played an essential role in nurturing the new mentality. According to the historian Glenda Gilmore, "in the 1920s and early 1930s the Communists alone argued for complete equality between the races. Their racial ideal eventually became America's ideal."[44]

The left certainly played its part in boosting blacks' confidence and their willingness to be assertive in their own cause. Du Bois argued for the pursuit of equality all along, for example when editor of the NAACP's *Crisis*, 1910–34. In 1935, Du Bois published his *Black Reconstruction*, a book that defied the demeaning portrayals of African Americans in history texts and showed how they had played an instrumental role in their own history after the Civil War. Then the white man Herbert Aptheker, recently a foot soldier in the antipeonage agitation, wrote his book *American Negro Slave Revolts* (1943). It helped to shatter the myth that African Americans had accepted their lot as slaves. The book stirred up a storm in the historical profession. Non-left historians found it difficult to accept scholarship by party members, but eventually had to debate Aptheker's findings and accept them, even if they brushed their leftist provenance under the carpet.[45]

Socialists and communists not only helped to define a more cohesive America; they also identified the enemy that America would ultimately face. There were those in America who believed, as some still do, that international communism should have been the main enemy in the 1930s. Naturally, American communists and their sympathizers took the contrary view. If Russia's pristine experiment with communism attracted their admiration, so, too, did the communist revolutionary movement in China led by Mao Zedong. Edgar Snow's *Red Star over China* (1937) featured interviews with Mao and a vivid account of his "Long March" military campaign. Under the pen name "Nym Wales", Snow's wife Helen wrote another eyewitness account, *Inside Red China* (1939), which depicted communist areas of China in a good light. Even if neither she nor her husband joined the US communist party, they were effective propagandists for Chinese communism. Agnes Smedley – a leading feminist who did join the party – wrote sympathetically about revolutionary movements in both China and India. Such writers illustrate the internationalism of America's socialists. Their support for certain armed struggles is a reminder that the left, though antimilitarist in the case of World War I, could be far from pacifist.

American socialists identified fascism as the main enemy, and they did so early. Italian-American anarcho-syndicalists took the lead. This group had hit the headlines in 1912, when Arturo Giovannitti, the editor of *Il Proletario*, combined with Joe Ettor to organize for the IWW at the Lawrence, Massachusetts, textile strike. To remove them from the scene, the authorities arrested Ettor and Giovannitti on a trumped-up murder charge. They languished in prison for a year before a jury cleared them – the case was yet another in the litany of left-wing grievances.

In Lawrence, Giovannitti and his comrades became aware of a disturbing outgrowth from their movement. Under the influence of European writers like Georges Sorel who thought parliamentary democracy was decadent and advocated violence instead, what had started as a far-left movement spawned a far-right movement. Syndicalism, yielding in America the IWW idea of One Big Union, gave rise in Europe to the idea of the working class as a homogeneous entity synonymous with the nation. This inspired nationalism, then intolerant nationalism, then its racist outgrowth, fascism.

Benito Mussolini had been a contributor to *Il Proletario*. In the course of the Lawrence strike he had also used his own journal, *Lotta di Classe*, to lambaste the US capitalist establishment. Through the journal *Il Popolo d'Italia*, though, he steered Italy in the direction of ideological migration. His thoughts shifted from class solidarity to extreme nationalism. In 1922 he became prime minister with the mission of suppressing those of his former comrades who had joined the Italian communist movement. Mussolini resorted to strong-arm tactics and soon was Italy's fascist dictator. When he made the trains run on time and showed other signs of efficiency together with military ambition, many Italian Americans on the lower rungs of the US ethnic ladder looked at him with pride.[46]

However, the main contribution of the American left was to antifascism. Robert Hunter, the author of *Poverty* (1904) and an influential member of the SPA, made a theoretical contribution. He published a withering attack on Sorelian philosophy – his book *Violence and the Labor Movement* (1914) was a distinctively American contribution to socialist theory and to the defense of democracy.[47]

A more practical attack on fascism came from Italian Americans who had first-hand knowledge of what was happening, and indeed about Mussolini himself. Enrico Parente was an activist in the Lawrence strike and was later East Coast Italian-language organizer for the International Ladies Garment Workers Union. Interviewed in 1972, he remembered his comrades' early suspicions of Mussolini and recounted how by the early 1920s there were street demonstrations in New York against the incipient Black Shirt movement. He and his Italian-American comrades wielded baseball bats against pro-fascist thugs. In Parente's recollection, these were the world's first antifascist demonstrations.

Certainly the Anti-Fascist Alliance of North America, formed in 1923 and led by the ever-energetic Giovannitti, was the first organized resistance to fascism in the United States. In 1925 it started a paper, *Il Nuovo Mondo*, which reached a daily circulation of thirty thousand.[48]

The Italian-American socialists' opposition to fascism was a seed not an oak. Like the antislavery movement of the 1830s, at the beginning it generated only limited support and bitter hostility. Under pressure from Mussolini's government, the State Department prevailed upon the New York district attorney to launch a prosecution of the IWW alumnus and anarchist journalist Carlo Tresca. The charge on which Tresca was convicted was the dissemination of information on contraception in the interstate mails, but it was his antifascist stance that had given offense.[49]

But that was in the 1920s. Within a few years, the antifascist seed started to germinate in America. Events warmed the ground, and drew into the campaign a new and vibrant group, the African Americans. A particular event alerted black Americans to the fascist threat. In October 1935, suddenly and with no declaration of war, Mussolini's troops invaded the independent African nation of Ethiopia. Mussolini wanted to avenge an Italian defeat at the hands of Ethiopian forces in 1896 and to establish a new Roman imperium.

The fascist soldiers entered from Italian-controlled Somaliland. They came to fight the ill-equipped Ethiopians with tanks, poison gas, and aircraft. They bombed with disregard for civilian life and medical facilities. The League of Nations had tried to no avail to contain the conflict. The international community wearily resigned itself to the fact that the League would be no match for fascist aggression, and that the peace settlement of 1919 was in tatters.

From the African American point of view, it could not have been a louder wake-up call. Black citizens in the United States had not only helped to shape a more cohesive American identity; they had also begun to take a particular pride in their African origins. Pan Africanism was alive. Now, a nakedly racist white European regime had engaged in the destruction of one of Africa's most ancient living civilizations, and a Christian one at that. It was an affront to black pride and identity. Socialists were by no means the only ones amongst the black citizenry to express outrage, but they felt the rub even more keenly than others because the fascists were so hell-bent on the destruction of what they regarded as national socialism's enemy, the left.

Du Bois rued the attack on Ethiopia, the "sunrise of human culture." Langston Hughes urged "all you colored peoples" to "be a man at last" and resist Mussolini. Out of a meeting in Howard University in May 1935 had sprung the National Negro Congress. Supported by James Ford, A. Philip Randolph, W. E. B. Du Bois and soon the communist party, it inveighed against the Italian aggression in Ethiopia.[50]

The Ethiopian question stirred African-American memories of how their own nation had pursued racist foreign policies. In the early nineteenth century America had recognized the independence of white-led Venezuela, Bolivia, Argentina, and Peru, but not the Republic of Haiti, the product of Toussaint L'Ouverture's black-slave-based rebellion of 1799. President

Lincoln remedied that deficiency. But his action did not mark the end of the story of racial bias. The segregationist President Woodrow Wilson sent the Marines into Haiti to start a lengthy occupation that led to the revival of forced labor there. When the Marines opened fire on a protesting crowd at Aux Cayes in 1929 killing twenty-five people, the communist party sent press releases to black newspapers all over America.[51]

Paul Robeson followed these events. He sojourned in Russia. He acquired a good grasp of the language, and his son attended a Soviet Model School where he reported that his classmates (who included Stalin's daughter) were devoid of racial prejudice. Robeson declined movie director Sergei Eisenstein's invitation to make a film about L'Ouverture. But in the wake of the Ethiopian disaster he did drive the Haitian memory home by acting in a play about L'Ouverture written by C. L. R. James.[52]

At home, black citizens angered by the rape of Ethiopia boycotted Italian stores, petitioned the Pope through their churches and began to organize militias. It was the time of the Popular Front against fascism, when communists and others worked side by side to promote their cause. The Harlem-based Provisional Committee for the Defense of Ethiopia organized demonstrations supported by both left and non-left African Americans. James Ford said his party was happy to work with racial-pride Garveyites: "However different our ultimate aims for society as a whole we are agreed on all points against imperialism." The NAACP feud with the communists took a back seat, with its organ *The Crisis* refraining from attacks on the Soviet Union between 1936 and 1939.[53]

Poverty, contingency and politics impeded the realization of plans to help Ethiopia militarily. The shocking speed with which Italian forces moved allowed virtually no time for African American mobilization. President Roosevelt tried to play down the crisis and the divisions it threatened to open in American society. Preoccupied with the Depression, he was not yet ready to engage in responsibilities beyond America's shores. However, in a foretaste of future policy and in tacit recognition of widespread indignation in America, he did refuse to recognize the legitimacy of Italy's presence in Ethiopia.[54]

In July 1936, General Francisco Franco started his revolt against the democratically elected government of Spain, the Republicans. The *cortes*, the democratically elected Spanish parliament, had been introducing social-democratic reforms. As in the case of other fascists, Franco portrayed his "Nationalist" cause as a crusade to save his nation from socialism.

Franco received fifty thousand men from Mussolini and dive-bombers from Hitler: in the Basque village of Guernica in April 1937, the combined German and Italian aerial attack introduced the world to the concept of terror bombing, remembered in Pablo Picasso's painting of the event. The world's democracies looked on in dismay but with a paralyzing indecision that allowed the Communist International to seize the initiative. With some material help from the Soviet Union, the communists organized international brigades to fight alongside the Republican loyalists.

One such force was the called the Lincoln "Brigade." This was the American battalion within the six-battalion XV International Brigade. Its creation meant that, if they could raise the money to join it, those of African descent could now fight. Ninety African Americans did so, joining 200 black Cubans in the Lincoln unit. They were a small proportion of its 2,800 volunteers, but symbolically important. Langston Hughes, Richard Wright and Louise Thompson wrote back from Spain saying there was no racial segregation or discrimination in the Republican forces. Oliver Law gave strength to the claim. He was a veteran of World War I and had been a communist activist in the USA. Possibly the first African American ever to be given command of a mainly white fighting unit, he was the military commander of the Abraham Lincoln Brigade until he met his death in battle in Brunete in July 1937.[55]

Writers on the left (and some not on the left) rallied to the cause of the international brigades. Amongst the notable works of fiction the war inspired were *Homage to Catalonia* (1938) by the Englishman George Orwell, and *For Whom the Bell Tolls* (1940), by America's Ernest Hemingway. Though sympathetic to the cause of democratic socialism, these novels drew attention to the atrocities committed on both sides of the Spanish conflict, and Hemingway like Orwell was critical of the communists' dogmatic ideological approach. But through their criticisms Orwell and Hemingway also showed that democratic debate on the left was alive and well.

The Lincoln Brigade was effective in propaganda terms. Yes, it fought on the losing side and Spain succumbed to dictatorship. But it also prepared the way for worldwide resistance to fascism after Hitler invaded Poland in 1939. When Charlie Chaplin's first talkie appeared in 1940 it was a commercial success partly because other socialists had already prepared the ground: *The Great Dictator* was a witty, devastating attack on Hitler.

Yet having identified the fascists as the enemy, America's socialists faced a dilemma: which was worse, fascism or war? World War I had boosted the pacifist wing of the Christian Socialist movement. This came to be associated with the SPA especially when the pacifist Norman Thomas was the party's leader. The movement reached out to other religions in different countries, published its own organ the *World Tomorrow,* and later ran a news service. How should these Christian idealists react to the threat posed by Hitler and Mussolini?

War was to Norman Thomas the greater of the two evils. In a prescient voice, he protested that war would hasten the development of a society dominated by industrialists and by their allies in the military, with dire consequences for civil liberties. Anticipating the analysis "realist" historians offered in later years, he also warned that America would exhaust itself by fighting Japan and Germany, and leave Stalin to "pick up the pieces." Speaking at a Madison Square Garden rally against American entry into the war in May 1941, he touched on a further theme, imperialism. He attacked magazine proprietor Henry Luce's idea of an "American Century" that would follow in the wake of glorious victory. An Anglo-American victory would mean racist imperialism abroad, Thomas insisted, as well as "a century of slavery for us at home to the military machine."[56]

In January 1941, a number of New York socialists attacked Thomas's objection to Lend-Lease, President Roosevelt's agreement to supply the hard-pressed British on a buy now, pay later basis. Left-wing opponents of Thomas's antiwar stance included former *Socialist Call* editor Gus Tyler. Reinhold Niebuhr of the Union Theological Seminary was another critic. A socialist philosopher like Dewey and James, Neibuhr originally shared Thomas's Christian pacifism, but he had moved to a new position, Christian Realism.

In March 1941, three of the SPA's thirteen-member national executive resigned in protest at Thomas's stance. Thomas and the majority of his SPA comrades nevertheless remained unenthusiastic about the war – even after December, when the Japanese attack on Pearl Harbor brought America into the conflict. Challenged from within, already reduced, and with the nation solidly against them, the Thomasites' numbers shriveled further.[57]

The communists were in even worse shape. It finally became clear to anyone who still doubted it that Moscow pulled the strings. Initially, the Soviet communists opposed Hitler. A few days after the outbreak of war in Europe, James Ford accordingly ripped into the earlier attempts by Britain to appease Germany: "[Prime Minister Neville] Chamberlain, unless checked, will turn large sections of Africa over to Hitler who, with his doctrine that 'Negroes are fit only to be slaves,' would make that continent the most horrible concentration camp on earth'."[58] His rhetoric was in line with his own concerns as a socialist African American, and conformed to Moscow's policy as he understood it.

However, just over two weeks earlier, Germany and the Soviet Union had signed a Non-Aggression Pact. Each side promised not to attack the other, and there was a secret protocol to divide northern and eastern Europe into two spheres of influence, one German and the other Soviet. Moscow now required a change in approach by its worldwide followers.

The party faithful would now, instead of urging resistance to Hitler, oppose the efforts of those who sought to war against him. This was evident in June 1941, when left-wing authors and artists convened in New York for a congress sponsored by the CIO and the League of American Writers (established in 1935, the League had taken over from the earlier John Reed Clubs as a forum for communist writers). Erskine Caldwell was present, and Dashiell Hammett and Rockwell Kent addressed the meeting. So did Richard Wright, whose trademark novel *Native Son* had come out the previous year. Still a communist (though he would split with the party by the war's end), Wright delivered an address on the theme "Not My People's War." He reminded his audience of the bad treatment of African Americans in World War I and its aftermath, and stated "the current war is nakedly and inescapably an imperialist war, directed against the Negro people and working people and colonial people everywhere in the world." It was the communist party line as dictated from Moscow.[59]

But the instructions from headquarters would change yet again. Just five days after Wright's speech came Operation Barbarossa, a blatant breach of the Non-Aggression Pact. Seventy-nine divisions of the German army launched a surprise attack on the Soviet Union. Congressman Vito Marcantonio, a follower of the communist line if not a party member, rose in the House to address the issue: "from the standpoint of defense of our nation, the liberties and national interests of the people of the US, the invasion of the Soviet Union transformed that war, which was predominantly imperialist, into a war which is essentially one of defense."[60] Once more, subservience to Moscow's latest line.

The communists' vacillating approach to the war was not even doctrinaire. It was subservient to the nationalist and imperialist aims of Moscow. Those who had shown loyalty to Moscow in the past had been able to present their actions in an internationalist light, arguing that international socialism would make the nation state defunct and war obsolete. Stalin's ambitions were a betrayal.

The heroic wartime resistance to fascism by European communist resistance movements and by the Soviet Union's Red Army would impress some Americans. But, even before stories arrived in the West of the Soviet dictator's purges resulting in millions of deaths, and even before the USSR became America's Cold War rival, Russian nationalism had harpooned American communism. The communist party USA was dead in the water as a political and moral force.

However, this book is not about the fate of political parties. Nor is it about the failings of American socialists, even if these are listed for the sake of context. It is about socialist and leftist achievements. In the interwar years those achievements included a substantial contribution to the forging of a new, more inclusive, more convincing definition of what America should be about. In turn, this led to the identification of fascism as a creed that stood opposed to the best American ideals.

Chapter 6

THE NEW DEAL'S UNDECLARED SOCIALISM

Starting in the spring of 1933, the Democratic administration of President Franklin D. Roosevelt introduced reforms intended to address the causes and consequences of the terrible depression that had engulfed the nation. By mid-1934, the immediate political crisis was over. Critics on the right now felt free to let rip at the policies of Roosevelt's "New Deal." Some of these critics, for example the former presidential candidate Al Smith, were Democrats. More characteristically, though, they were Republicans such as the recent president, Herbert Hoover. The conservatives launched a rich vein of attack that would continue through the presidencies of Harry Truman, Lyndon Johnson and Barack Obama. They complained about over-regulation of business and Washington-centered Big Government. They resisted governmental efforts to plan society and the economy. They portrayed President Roosevelt and his supporters in Congress as socialist or even communist betrayers of the American Dream.[1]

Some of the rhetoric was emotional and extreme. In reality, hardly any New Dealers would have described themselves as socialists let alone communists. As they were interested in political survival and effectiveness, there was no chance that they would do so. Nevertheless, what is undeclared can still be potent. It can reasonably be argued that some of the main architects of the New Deal believed in and put into effect policies with a socialist hue.

The same can be said on the basis of an examination of the background, thoughts and actions of some of the individuals involved in promoting the social reform policies of the 1930s. Gerald J. Boileau was one such individual. He was a person who might easily be taken for a socialist, and some people did.

Boileau had experienced hardships that helped to shape his political outlook. His father had a weakness for the commodity he sold, liquor.

When the twenty-five-year Boileau marriage came under scrutiny in the circuit court at Oneida County, Wisconsin, the judge heard that John Boileau had taken to beating his wife. On the occasion of one attack, the barely-teenaged Gerald had joined his older brother and sister in dragging their violent father away from his intended victim.[2]

The divorce left Sophia Boileau and her children in poverty, and Gerald Boileau had to strike out on his own. He enlisted with the American Expeditionary Force and fought in the Meuse Argonne campaign of October 1918.

In politics, Boileau opposed Prohibition and supported Robert M. La Follette Jr. The younger La Follette was in 1925 elected on the Republican ticket to occupy the Senate seat left vacant on the death of his father. La Follette Jr., would go on to found the Wisconsin Progressive Party. When Boileau ran for Congress in 1930, a local paper called him "a 'wet' La Follette supporter."[3]

Just after his thirty-first birthday, the successful candidate arrived in Washington, the youngest member of the new Congress. Boileau became the leader of the Progressive bloc that consisted of the Wisconsin Progressives, the Minnesota Farm-Labor Party, New York's American Labor Party, and like-minded members of the Republican and Democratic Parties, about forty representatives in all.

It was a significant group. By 1937, Democratic congressional majorities achieved earlier in the New Deal had been eroded, but Boileau's following was strong enough to help pass legislation and to achieve cloture, the blocking of filibusters. He was able to shape legislation. For example, he forced an increase in the budget of the Works Progress Administration (WPA) in 1938. According to an article in the communist party's journal *New Masses*, Boileau also threatened to support a movement for a national third party, a ploy designed to deter the Roosevelt administration from moving to the right.[4]

Boileau did not describe himself as a socialist, but perhaps in reality he was one. The communists thought he was with them. In conformity with the party's Popular Front approach, the *Daily Worker* in 1937 reported favorably on his activities, for example his appearance at a Workers Alliance of America pro-WPA rally together with Representatives Caroline Day (D-NY), Jerry Voorhis (D-CA) and Maury Maverick (D-TX).

The FBI agreed with the communists' perception. The bureau had a secret file on Boileau that is now available in redacted form. An agent had reported on an appearance by Boileau, along with Vito Marcantonio, at a

Workers Alliance mass meeting in Madison Square Garden. A socialist, David Lasser, was the leader of the Workers Alliance antiunemployment movement and Marcantonio's communist inclinations were evident. At the Garden, bands struck up to the tune of a new song on the theme of unemployment, "Pink Slips on Parade." Boileau demanded a "revamping" of the economic order. The FBI also reported on Boileau's support for the Lincoln Brigade, his wider opposition to fascism, and his political associations with such people as Victor Berger's widow and the communist party's presidential candidate Earl Browder.[5]

The activities of Boileau and his confederates did not convince everyone of their socialist credentials. There were those on the left who regarded the whole New Deal enterprise as too timid. Their denunciations complemented and reinforced the efforts of the New Dealers themselves to shun the socialist label.

Norman Thomas, for example, was unmoved by 1930s reforms, of which he offered a long-running critique. In 1934 he depicted the New Deal as a "reformist" attempt to save capitalism that discriminated against whole segments of society, such as African Americans and child laborers. Two years later, he derided the president's attempt to cure the nation's ills with "pale pink pills."[6]

Marcantonio would denounce the reforming mid-1930s Congress as "hopelessly reactionary." In July 1940, at a time when the Popular Front had been consigned to the dustbin of expediency and it was the policy of the communist party to denounce Britain and America, he declared that President Roosevelt had sold out his own reform program. He told Rockwell Kent that FDR "was the world's greatest betrayer of his own New Deal," and the artist agreed.[7]

Conservatives in contrast talked up what they regarded as the very real menace of domestic socialism. Some of them accused the president of being a communist. More credibly, others commented on the socialist hue of New Deal legislation. Congressman Harry C. Ransley (R-PA) deplored the Tennessee Valley Act (1933) on rational if partisan grounds: "Continue along these lines, and you will have a socialistic government, destroying the initiative that has made this country great."[8]

The American Medical Association's journal denounced the proposed program of universal health insurance in an editorial of 1935. The health reform was "socialism and communism" and an incitement to "revolution." According to a more levelheaded account in the *Washington Post*, doctors recognized the nation's deficiency in insurance provision, but were opposed to "socialized medicine." Such was the force of this campaign that Roosevelt and his advisors Edwin Witte and Secretary of Labor Frances Perkins decided to withdraw the proposed program. The accusations of socialism were just too virulent and potentially damaging. Best to reject not just the label but also, in this case, the policy.[9]

The debate over whether the New Deal was socialist and over whether it went far enough to reform society continued after the war. Conservatives argued that the New Deal had been socialist and ineffective. In the 1960s,"New left" historians criticized the New Deal for not being left enough, and for being ineffective for that reason. Although historians and politicians turned their attention to other interpretations and issues, the familiar fault line ran through into the twenty-first century. In 2008 the conservative African American US Court of Appeals judge Janice Rogers Brown criticized the Supreme Court for upholding New Deal legislation. Her reason? It marked "the triumph of our own socialist revolution."[10]

So was the New Deal socialist? In terms of intention, it was to a certain degree anti-socialist, an effort to prop up capitalism by enacting reforms that would pre-empt the need for more radical solutions. It was furthermore a Democratic effort to capture socialist ideas whose time had come, in a manner that would put the Republicans in the political wilderness for decades. All that was needed was to wriggle out from under the actual label "socialist" in order to escape Republican (and conservative Democrat) opprobrium. The few socialists who still accepted the label had little alternative but to support a program that enacted their planks under another name. They complained that the New Deal did not go far enough, but they supported such measures as went through. After all, their comrades had drafted the blueprint for social security twenty years earlier.

Socialists had kept the social insurance issue alive in the intervening years. This was so in the state of Ohio, where municipalities cherished their ownership of public utilities ("gas and water socialism"), where the state legislature created an accident compensation scheme, and where there was an efficient system of employment offices. Additionally, when the financial crash of 1929 and ensuing economic depression devastated their state along with the rest of America, Ohioans turned their attention to social insurance.[11]

The Buckeye State turned to a professor at Antioch College for help. William M. Leiserson obliged. Drawing on his CIR experience, he contributed to the drafting of a bill that went to the state legislature in January 1931. A year later, with the Great Depression threatening to unravel

American society, Leiserson reiterated his support for a national scheme. In an article for *Nation*, he encapsulated the main thrust of the CIR Research Division's finding – that business would have to pay its share, and "compulsory action by the government is necessary."[12]

Leiserson served in the Roosevelt administration as executive secretary of the National Labor Board and as chairman of the National Mediation Board. He and Edwin Witte were voices from the Wisconsin school of socialism at the federal policy making table. But it was not just a question of voices. New Deal legislation was substantively socialist in character. Socialism inhered in the New Dealers' approach to planning, public ownership, the welfare state and "Big Government."

Otis L. Graham, a student of the history of planning from the 1930s to the 1970s, defined such planning as federal intervention "to touch all fundamental social developments" and as "anticipatory" rather than reactive in character. In 1928, the Soviet dictator Joseph Stalin had introduced a "Five Year Plan," the first of many adopted in Moscow. Just before that, Stuart Chase and Rexford G. Tugwell, respectively a journalist who coined the "New Deal" slogan and an economist who helped shape New Deal policy, had visited the Soviet Union and came back convinced of the advantages of economic planning.[13]

US socialists like Norman Thomas, John Dewey and the future senator Paul Douglas (a "quasi-socialist" according to Graham) promoted the idea of planning. So did influential figures like Charles Beard and journalists such as *New Republic* editor George Soule. Father John A. Ryan, a priest who was famous for his public advocacy of curtailments to the power of capitalism, was a pro-planner. Businessmen potentially supported the idea, some of them having profited from the planning measures introduced in World War I.[14]

To increase their chances of success, planners argued for their ideas in what Graham called "a decidedly American way." For example, Harvard economist and leading New Deal adviser Alvin Hansen distinguished between American planning and dictatorship. The US version, he wrote in 1941, "means a system under which private, voluntary organizations function under general, and mostly indirect, government control."[15]

On account of its socialist pedigree, planning still made enemies. Invited to contribute to a planning forum in the *New York Times*, AFL president William Green contended that higher wages and shorter hours were better goals to aim for. However, planning had its devotees at the heart of government. Edwin Witte was a keen student of the idea. He compiled a survey of the literature on "Planning conceived of as an advisory function of experts reporting to the President or Congress" (his trust in "experts" was typical of the Wisconsin intellectuals). Witte noted that the planning idea had been "carried furthest in integrated programs for extensive governmental intervention in the economy to maintain purchasing power or eliminate depression." He was thus aware of the crossover, in economic policy, between socialist concepts of planning and a market-linked emphasis on consumption as an engine of full employment.[16]

Secretary of the Interior Harold Ickes opened his contribution to the *Times* forum with a quotation purporting to show how the president had been a planner since his Albany days – Governor Roosevelt had called for "better planning of our social and economic life." Ickes, a commanding personality of the New Deal, rounded on planning's opponents. He accused them of being "un-Christian" adherents of the "dog-eat-dog" theory who hid behind the semantic cloak of "rugged individualism."[17]

While a variety of motives affected the array of New Deal legislation, planning was an important element in much of it. It is discernible not just in the rhetoric, but also in policy – in the attempts to boost consumer purchasing power, in the imposition of regulations on private industry and in attempts to assuage the effects of the depression, especially unemployment.

Federal efforts to boost employment rested, in part, on the stimulation of purchasing power. There was support for the labor movement, with an eye to buoyant wages that would increase the demand for goods and stimulate production. There were also direct efforts to create jobs. Established in April 1933, the Civilian Conservation Corps in the period through 1942 gave work opportunities to 2.5 million youths. These young persons labored mainly to create environmentally helpful assets like public parks.[18] In the same vein, the Civil Works Administration of 1934 and its successor the Works Progress Administration (WPA, 1935) put people to work on public projects. WPA beneficiaries built thousands of hospitals, schools, playgrounds, and airport landing fields, and participated in the Federal Arts Project. The Emergency Relief Appropriations Act of 1935 made $5 billion available for such projects. It was peacetime's largest ever appropriation. The WPA put four million to work and thus to spend, boosting demand for the nation's products.[19]

Some measures simply put dollars into the pockets of those who needed them, individuals who were likely to spend quickly on life's necessities rather than save up to buy luxury goods. Into this category fell the Federal

Emergency Relief Administration of May 1933, which dispensed $3 billion to the needy via the states.

The New Deal's intervention in the housing market was both humanitarian and a means of planning a way out of the recession. The Home Owners Loan Corporation pumped money into the economy from 1933 by lending money to homeowners faced with foreclosure. The National Housing Act of 1934 widened the availability of mortgage loans, helping poorer people to find secure shelter. From 1938 the administration of the scheme fell to the Federal National Mortgage Association (known since the 1960s as Ginnie Mae, with its offshoots dubbed Fannie May and Freddie Mac). The injection of liquidity into the housing market allowed homeowners to think of spending money on both houses and other things. It helped the construction industry, creating jobs and boosting consumer demand in that way.

Although the boost to urban growth was leftist in character, there was also a left critique of the urban sprawl. A movie of 1939, *The City*, stated the case. Aaron Copland wrote the score of this iconic film, and the script was the work of another socialist, Lewis Mumford. Mumford served on the board of *New Masses*, a journal that would fall under the control of the communists in the 1930s.[20] He was, however, anti-Stalinist and anti-Marxist. Very much against regimentation, he sought to humanize people's living environments in a way that heralded the green and environmental movements of a later era. *The City* told the story of Greenbelt, Maryland, an architecturally innovative community that gave priority to children, families, and their relationship to living spaces. It is a sign of the left's strength in the 1930s that its imprint is visible both in the housing policies of the time, and in their antidote.

The government had a further package to help the economy, especially industry. For yet another law of 1933 established the National Recovery Administration (NRA). The NRA encouraged big business to fix prices in a manner that stifled the cutthroat competition that had led to depression-era deflation. When such agreements went into effect, there would be exemption from the terms of the Sherman Antitrust Act, a law of 1890 designed to prevent anticompetitive practices. In return for this exemption, the industries that signed up to the agreements would have to accept codes of fair practice. These codes protected the rights of consumers, the welfare of children who would not be allowed to work in the designated occupations, the right of workers to organize into unions, and the living standards of employees in the favored industries, who would receive a minimum wage and a forty-hour week. The corporations would then stamp their products with a blue eagle denoting their federally approved standing and inviting consumers to buy with confidence and a clear conscience.

To its conservative critics, the NRA was the heavy hand of socialist bureaucracy throttling American enterprise. The automobile manufacturer Henry Ford was bitterly critical and refused to sign up to the blue eagle. On the left there were supporters of the NRA, but also those who had reservations. In spite of the unionization of semi-skilled industries like the non-Ford section of automobile manufacturing, and in spite of the creation in 1935 of the Congress of Industrial Organizations to encourage and represent those labor unions, the majority of American workers were left outside the enchanted circle. This applied to many African Americans, and to the great majority of women. If you were a white man working for General Motors, you might end up (after some turbulent labor troubles) OK. If you were a black laborer or a Southern child or a white housemaid, you could forget all about those fancy rights.

The big planning push came in Roosevelt's first administration, especially in the years 1933–5. By the later 1930s, his Democratic Party could count on Boileau and his cohorts, but was still a reduced force that operated on slender congressional majorities. The Supreme Court had thrown out the NRA. Portions of the enabling legislation found their way back onto the statute books, but the momentum had diminished and resentment was rising against Big Labor and its exclusive privileges. It now seemed more important to create a sense of social justice by delivering minimum levels of income for all.

For the time being, the idea of planning was losing its appeal. Minnesota, North Dakota, Ohio, Oregon, South Dakota and Texas abolished their state-level planning boards. The economist Alexander Sachs, who had worked for the NRA in 1933 but quit to become vice president of the investment firm Lehman Brothers, attacked the planner as a social entity. Planners came from "academic and theoretical backgrounds." They lacked "knowledge of human nature or practical politics." They were the creatures of "self-seeking pressure groups." Unlike businessmen, they could not be held accountable for their mistakes. Against the background of such criticism, Alvin Hansen feared a return to the "atomistic order" of the pre-planning era.[21]

Hansen need not have worried. In World War II, planning returned with a vengeance, together with levels of appropriation that vastly exceeded New Deal expenditures. Now back in the University of Wisconsin as chairman of the Department of Economics, Witte kept tabs on developments, such as proposals to extend into peacetime the activities of wartime's National Resources Planning Board. In spite of ferocious conservative attacks on its socialist character, federal planning had come to stay and would be bipartisan – the Republican administration of President Richard Nixon, for example, planned for economic growth.[22]

Public ownership stands out as another socialist aspect of the New Deal. The idea of public ownership was by no means new. George Washington's Continental Army of 1775 was a public federal enterprise as have been the US armed forces ever since. Benjamin Franklin started the federal public postal service in 1775. Alexander Hamilton favored the public funding of internal improvements in order to help America's nascent industries. Prominent statesmen like Henry Clay continued to advocate federal engagement in internal improvements.[23]

Toward the end of the nineteenth century, socialists and Populists advocated nationalization. The initiatives of the Founding Fathers and their successors had affected only those areas unclaimed by private business. The new demands for nationalization went further. They involved the assumption of public control over assets hitherto in private ownership. The Populists demanded federal ownership of the railroads and of communications systems like the telegraph, as well as public alternatives to private banking, a postal saving scheme, and a subtreasury plan to help with agricultural credit. Out of this grew the idea that natural monopolies like water should be in public ownership.

If the American left was here in step with its European counterpart, it was also distinctive in being more pragmatic. In a manner replicated in other countries later on, the US left understood that there was a limit to the amount of public ownership people would ultimately accept or desire. Its program was less sweeping than that of its British counterpart. In 1918, the Labour Party in the United Kingdom adopted as clause four, part four of its constitution a plank that came to be widely regarded as the essence of British socialist aspiration. It advocated "the common ownership of the means of production, distribution and exchange." The SPA's 1928 platform was more realistic and yet in its own way more visionary. Rather than making a sweeping statement, it listed its nationalization targets – and it embraced environmentalism. Its opening call came under the heading "Public Ownership and Conservation." It wanted "nationalization of our natural resources," starting with "coal mines and water sites." It advocated a "giant" publicly owned system of electrical power generation and distribution. Railroads were on its nationalization agenda. It demanded the federal administration of "flood control and flood relief, reforestation, irrigation, and reclamation."[24]

The New Dealers took a long stride in the direction of public ownership. The establishment of the immensely powerful Tennessee Valley Authority (TVA) was a notable example. The idea to harness the power of America's mighty rivers had been around for a while, and focused on Muscle Shoals in Alabama. Here, the Tennessee River descended 149 feet through a 30-mile series of rapids. With a view to using the fall to generate electricity that would be exploited to manufacture military explosives, the federal government acquired adjoining land in 1916. After World War I, there was a return to narrower aims such as flood control and the improvement of navigation.

Peacetime attempts to revive the broader federal initiatives sparked a public-private confrontation. Nebraska's Senator George W. Norris pressed the federal government to widen its activities in the area. Private suppliers of electricity resisted his campaign. They opposed governmental competition with industry except in times of national emergency such as war. Norris offered the rejoinder that profiteering private interests were overcharging consumers, a charge that the capitalists vehemently denied.[25]

In 1928, President Calvin Coolidge signaled Republican approval of a parallel scheme when he signed legislation authorizing the construction of the Boulder Dam on the Colorado River. It would be the world's biggest civil engineering project of its type, and when the English left-wing writer J. B. Priestley visited the construction site he called it "the soul of America under socialism." But although Coolidge's successor President Herbert Hoover signed supplementary legislation and the Boulder Dam would come to be known as the "Hoover Dam", Hoover held back from going further with such projects. He feared they might be depicted as socialist, and thus undermine business confidence in the wake of the 1929 stock market crash. Hoover vetoed the Norris bill providing for a Muscle Shoals/ Tennessee Valley scheme.[26]

In the course of the 1932 election campaign Norris acquired an ally. In an address at Portland, Oregon, Governor Roosevelt called for the public development of Columbia River proposals in the Pacific Northwest. He also demanded federal action in the cases of the Boulder Dam project in Colorado, the St. Lawrence power project along New York State's northern boundary with Canada – and the Muscle Shoals scheme. He declared it his aim "to prevent extortion against the public" by private corporations.[27]

All of these projects came to fruition. To focus on the largest of them, President Roosevelt in May 1933 signed a law extending the scope of the

Muscle Shoals plan, and establishing the TVA. Viewed in a global context, it was not a unique move. Government initiatives were taking place in other countries. The establishment of the British Broadcasting Corporation in 1927 was a nationalization of radio. Ten years later, France would nationalize the nation's five major rail companies to form what would become Europe's premier railroad system, the Société Nationale des Chemins de fer Français (SNCF).

However it must be emphasized that the TVA was the largest public enterprise of its type anytime anywhere. It dwarfed, for example, anything ever attempted in the Soviet Union.

The Authority engaged in flood control, the elimination of mosquito-infested swamps, soil conservation, and reforestation. Spanning seven border and southern states, it built dams on the Tennessee and its tributaries and generated hydroelectric power. In a contribution to America's emerging military-industrial state, it manufactured nitrates for the munitions industry. It constructed a 650-mile navigation canal from Paducah in western Kentucky to Knoxville in eastern Tennessee.

Arthur E. Morgan, the first director of the TVA, was an admirer of the idea of nationalization, and wanted to apply it on a wider scale. He remained in charge at TVA from 1933 to 1938, and later wrote a book about the ideas of Edward Bellamy, who more than any other American had aroused interest in nationalization. If the TVA in this way had a socialist provenance, it nevertheless fell short of satisfying every left-wing aspiration. Notably, it played along with Jim Crow prejudices. Like the Civilian Conservation Corps, it favored white workers (as for the SNCF, in World War II it transported Jews to the Nazi gas chambers – public ownership is no indemnity against such crimes).

Opponents of the TVA depicted it as a socialist initiative. Representatives of private industry complained in congressional hearings that the TVA was undercutting the price regimes of private electricity producers. They claimed that by making coal-fired electricity production obsolete, it was putting miners out of work. The chief executives of private utility companies protested that the public operator had the unfair advantage of not being obliged to make a profit. Wendell Willkie had to sell the Commonwealth and Southern Corporation to the TVA. America's largest utility company, it could no longer compete.

From its initial status as an experiment in uncontested territory, the TVA had changed into an instrument for nationalizing existing businesses. Reacting to this, Willkie quit being a pro-New Deal Democrat and became an ardent opponent of public ownership. No trivial critic, the articulate Willkie would be the Republican candidate for president in 1940.

The TVA had able defenders, not least the young Harvard graduate David E. Lilienthal who was one of its three directors and became its chairman in 1946. He tried to insist, "a river has no politics." This cut no ice with critics who, and surely with reason on their side, dubbed his agency "socialistic." The TVA would become firmly embedded in the rhetoric of American anti-socialism.[28]

In Alcorn, a poor county in northern Mississippi, the farmers formed a cooperative and were amongst the first customers of the TVA. The need for rural electrification was acute. Private utility companies had neglected rural America because the profit margins were low. Fewer than one in a hundred of Mississippi's farmers had power lines, a problem reflected across rural America. The farmers of Alcorn and the 417 cooperatives that formed in America by 1939 followed a model that ran back, via the Populists, to the cooperative socialism of Robert Owen and his antebellum followers in America.[29]

To assist the process, Senator Norris helped secure the creation of the Rural Electrification Administration (REA, 1935). Operating within the TVA to begin with and then independently, the REA pumped $40 million annually into rural electrification. Loans to farmers' cooperatives and the encouragement of mini-TVAs in areas like the Pacific Northwest and the upper Missouri resulted in the running of power lines into rural areas where the costs had been prohibitive for private companies. In Norris's Nebraska, there was a statewide system of public ownership. The privately owned utilities were furious and ran "spite lines" parallel with the cooperatives' cables to try to under price and ruin them. The Eisenhower administration would in the 1950s launch an attack on the REA and its outcomes as an example of "creeping socialism." By this time, however, the program had reached 3.5 million consumers. It eased the lives of farming families, helped them to produce more efficiently, and enabled them to branch out into new ventures.[30]

Another enormous federal initiative in the 1930s was the effort to improve America's port and navigation facilities. The St. Lawrence Seaway project of 1934 linked to the hydroelectric ambitions outlined by Roosevelt in his presidential campaign. Enlarged navigation canals would circumvent the two dams to be constructed on the St. Lawrence River. These and other new links would, in the words of a congressional report, "create a new seacoast for the United States, 3,576 miles in length of shore line, reaching into the heart of the nation and converting 30 American cities located on the [Great] Lakes and connecting channels into seaports."[31]

It is worth emphasizing once again that these New Deal enterprises built on past initiatives. They were not "unAmerican", they were simply on a larger scale than earlier projects, and a target for criticism because they were undertaken at a time of increasing awareness of the clash between individual and collective values. Public help with canals and other internal improvements had been extensive in the nineteenth century. In the 1820s the Erie Canal had established an earlier link to the Lakes, in this case from the port of New York City via the Hudson River. In the same decade, Congress authorized funds for the clearing of the Savannah River, which the British had blocked in the course of the Revolutionary War, and President James Monroe and his secretary of war, John C. Calhoun, commissioned engineering reports with a view to opening up the area from the upper South to the Great Lakes by means of extensive aquatic navigation.[32]

In the New Deal, the Flood Control Act of 1936 authorized civil engineering works such as dams and levees, with the aim of saving communities in the Mississippi delta and elsewhere from the consequences of natural disasters. In terms of scale, though, it was the development of the New York Port Authority that rivaled the TVA.

Established in 1921 under an agreement between New Jersey and New York, the Port Authority oversaw and operated bridges and tunnels connecting the island of Manhattan to the other side of the Hudson River and, eastwards, to Long Island and Brooklyn. Untroubled by any notion that public enterprise meant socialism, the pro-business Republican administrations of the 1920s had passed further enabling legislation – a House report of 1922 envisaged "a detailed and comprehensive plan for the development of the port of New York," and the Authority would issue its own bonds. Tidying legislation in 1924 merged private rail marshalling yards and a federal wartime facility in Hoboken to enable the construction of linking "belt lines" on the westerly bank of the Hudson. The Authority's efficiency was one of the factors that encouraged President Roosevelt to press on with the TVA.[33]

The Authority continued to expand during the New Deal. With construction capital of $75 million coming from the WPA, the Lincoln Tunnel opened in 1937 providing a further link from the New Jersey side, this time to Midtown Manhattan. A public body that prospered from tolls and developed an element of independence from both federal and state control, the Authority went on the build today's Newark, La Guardia and Kennedy

Airports, and in the 1960s the Twin Towers International Trade Center project. Considering that the New York City Transit Authority complements the Port Authority in that it oversees bus, subway and rail transportation in the metropolitan area, and considering that it, too, is a public body, it can be said that public ownership and management have become accepted features in the lives of New Yorkers.

So widespread was public ownership by the end of the 1930s, that Congress adopted the Government Corporation Control Act. The new law applied to 115 federal corporate entities, jointly boasting in excess of $20 billion in assets. Passed in 1945, the Control Act, as its name implied, tried to impose uniform administration on the diverse range of publicly owned enterprises, and to bring them under closer federal control.[34]

Socialism inhered not only in New Deal planning and public ownership initiatives, but also in its enactment of the welfare state. Socialists like Robert Hunter had identified the need for it, socialists like Selig Perlman had drafted the blueprint for it, and the socialist Meyer London had first introduced the proposal to Congress. Now, Perlman's former colleague Edwin Witte, a socialist who no longer called himself one, would earn the epithet "father of social security."[35]

The problems Hunter had identified were still present in the 1920s in spite of the prosperity of many of America's businesses in that decade. A Brookings Institution study indicated that 60 percent of families received an income of less than the $2,000 a year required for the provision of "basic necessities." The rich-poor divide, so humiliating for those on the wrong side of the line, was immense: 12.2 million people received only 0.73 percent of the US Gross National Product. That was before the Depression struck. By the mid-1930s, the output of the American economy had dropped by up to 50 percent. A quarter of the workforce was unemployed. Sixty million people belonged to families trying to get by on less than $1,000. The groups particularly affected included farmers, elderly retired folk, members of female-headed families, the disabled, migrant workers, coal miners displaced by the introduction of machinery, and African Americans. Members of these groups did not qualify for employers' welfare schemes, and the labor movement did little for them.[36]

President Hoover had pondered the benefits of a US employment service and was familiar with the idea of public works as a "balancing wheel" that might provide employment in hard times, but with the onset of the Depression would not go beyond expressions of confidence in capitalism and reliance on local relief programs.[37]

The election of a new president made a difference. So did his selection of Frances Perkins to be secretary of labor. A colleague from his days in New York politics and the first female cabinet member in American history, Perkins served throughout his long presidency and pushed a left-wing agenda: social security, a minimum wage and universal health care. At first, the president was wary about giving these issues his full support, but in August 1934, he charged a technical committee headed by assistant secretary of labor Arthur J. Altmeyer with the task of addressing the plight of American workers. Altmeyer had studied with John R. Commons at Wisconsin and took his doctorate under the direction of Edwin Witte, who now directed his staff and shaped the coming legislation. Witte remembered that at the meeting with Roosevelt, the president had called for attention to be given to old age, unemployment, and health insurance. In light of the economic crisis facing the nation, the president's emphasis was on the first two.[38]

The resultant Social Security Act of 1935 provided for old age insurance giving an income to those aged sixty-five and over. It covered thirty-six million workers. Reflecting the concern of the CIR investigators of 1913–15, it arranged for assistance to those, aged sixty-one or over on January 1, 1937, who could not work long enough to contribute to the insurance fund – for these people, there was "old-age assistance."[39] The Act also insured twenty-one million workers against unemployment, and through the states provided funds for those not protected by a breadwinner: they included the disabled, children and pregnant women.

If the campaign for universal health insurance failed, it was not because doctors opposed it. True, at its annual conference of 1938 in San Francisco that year, the American Medical Association declared itself against "social medicine." But a poll of doctors in that year showed that 37 percent of them believed many people could not afford adequate medical care. Seven out of ten doctors wanted a new health insurance scheme and more than half favored the injection of public funds.[40]

Agitation continued for the extension of social insurance to cover health. Governor Olson was trying to push through a local health care bill in California in the face of resistance in the Republican-controlled state senate. Even more ambitiously, Olson put forward a national plan that would compel all those on a salary of less than $3,000 a year to sign up for health insurance. The House considered it and the Senate Committee on Education and Labor held extensive hearings. Its report noted that Roosevelt had originally intended the social security system to extend to health, recorded dissatisfaction with low expenditure in the states, pointed to scandals such as one million births a year unattended by midwives, and proposed a law setting up a National Health Program. Charismatic advocates like New York's Fiorello La Guardia fought for such a law in 1939 and thereafter. But the reformers' efforts came to naught in Washington as in Sacramento.[41]

A further piece of legislation did, however, round out the New Deal's contribution to the welfare state. The NRA codes had aimed to regulate hours and wages in certain industries, but on a haphazard basis that favored those workers powerful enough to win union recognition. The Fair Labor Standards Act of 1938, for which Frances Perkins had fought, provided for the gradual introduction of a forty-cent-an-hour minimum wage and forty-hour maximum working week for all wage earners employed by businesses engaged in interstate commerce.

In its early years, the law was plagued by exemptions. Southern legislators sought permission for local low-wage employers to be excused. Congressman Martin Dies Jr. (D-TX) filed a deprecating amendment aimed at Secretary of Labor Perkins: "Within 90 days after the appointment of the Administrator, she shall report to Congress whether anyone is subject to this bill." But the Fair Labor Standards Act ultimately held open to all toilers the promise of civilized working hours and a minimum wage. It established this principle sixty-one years before Tony Blair's Labour government secured the first British minimum wage legislation in 1999.[42]

The New Dealers may have been at pains to deny it, but to many observers the New Deal looked like socialism. New Deal policies encouraged them in this belief – but so, too, did the thoughts and actions of a wide range of New Deal supporters.

Gerald Boileau was far from being the only person in this category. Take, for example, the similarly influential figure, Thomas R. Amlie. Of Norwegian stock and a native of North Dakota, Amlie like Boileau served in the army and then, on settling in Wisconsin, became a La Follette supporter. He arrived in Congress in 1931 as a Progressive Republican. Though listed in later years in *The Encyclopedia of the United States Congress* as a pursuer of the Berger-London socialist agenda, he did not describe his beliefs in that way. According to the *Christian Science Monitor*, he was "left-wing", but refused to cooperate with communists. On the other hand, reviewing his career in 1939 the *Wall Street Journal* maintained that Amlie wanted to "put the federal government in control of all industry by practical socialization."[43]

Amlie certainly favored national planning. Revealing the influence of Wisconsin, he introduced in 1932 a bill, the first of several, in which he called for a national economic council whose "experts" would run industry and transportation. Five years later, he joined Democratic Congressmen Robert C. Allen (PA), Maury Maverick (TX) and Jerry Voorhis (CA) in calling for an industrial expansion act under which there would be comprehensive federal planning with a view to the elimination of unemployment. Allen (recently a WPA administrator) admitted the proposal might seem "revolutionary" but insisted that the US economic system was "an anachronism."[44]

Amlie supported also public ownership and the welfare state. In 1936, he proposed a "human rights amendment" to the US Constitution. It would have empowered Congress "to enact laws providing for the ownership, operation, and management, through instrumentalities of the Government of the United States, of business, manufacturing, commerce, industry, and banking, and shall have the power to purchase and condemn by eminent domain such enterprises." The Soviet Union had gone further, and had nationalized industries without financial compensation to their owners. But the Amlie proposal was more ambitious than the SPA's platform, and was as radical as any put forward by socialist parties in the democratic world.[45]

Amlie's amendment would also, if adopted, have prepared the constitutional ground for a welfare state. He had long advocated measures such as pensions for the elderly, and he was aware of constitutional objections being mounted to New Deal legislation. His proposal for a Constitutional amendment envisioned federal funding for a welfare state unimpeded by arguments over states rights.[46]

Although Amlie supported the New Deal's planning, public ownership and welfare state provisions, he thought they did not go nearly far enough. In the wake of the administration's "Second Hundred Days" initiative of new programs in the summer of 1935, he launched a blistering attack on the whole range of New Deal measures. The TVA was "the one bright spot in the whole 'new deal' program." The administration's efforts to raise prices by inducing scarcity had not made an impact on unemployment as the president claimed, as twelve million were still out of work. Instead of running industry properly, the government was engaging in a form of "charity capitalism." Efforts to liberalize international trade meant America was exporting "idle plants" to South America, to nobody's benefit. Recalling what he saw as a main cause of World War I, Amlie argued that pushing for exports to boost domestic employment would merely lead to competition with other nations, "with the inevitable result of war."[47]

Broadcast nationally and then reprinted in the *Congressional Record*, this speech marked Amlie's attempted re-launch of a Farmer–Labor third party. Such a party had been established in 1919 but was troubled in the 1920s by left–right splits. Farmer–labor candidates went under a plethora of labels, and factionalism continued to sap their energies. They made headway in Minnesota, Wisconsin, Iowa, and North and South Dakota, but their efforts to march in tandem with Michigan socialists failed, as did their appeal to industrial workers.[48]

One historian has argued that Amlie's radicalism and his prickly personality did Roosevelt a favor by alienating workers and driving them into the Democratic camp. Roosevelt himself took a more serious view of Amlie. He would ultimately offer him a place on the Interstate Commerce Commission, no doubt with the intention of utilizing his regulatory drive while keeping him quiet. In the mid-1930s Amlie and his followers, together with more eccentric wealth-redistributors like Louisiana's Huey Long, reminded the Roosevelt administration that it would be wise to extend the benefits of the New Deal beyond the labor unions and into new territory, as in due course happened with the Fair Labor Standards Act. Amlie not only thought and sounded like a socialist, but also had a certain impact on policy that extended beyond simply voting for New Deal measures.[49]

Some of those identified in *The Encyclopedia of the United States Congress* as New Deal proto-socialists were too individualistic or isolated to make a difference beyond their individual votes. In spite of his persuasive advocacy of collective policies, even Amlie was something of a utopian individualist. He turned down Roosevelt's job offer because he had enough insight into his own personality to see that he might not be an effective team player. Texas's Maury Maverick was similarly too iconoclastic to play the collective game. As for California's Jerry Voorhis, one of his friends remarked that his work went "unheeded" in Congress. Another example was Vito Marcantonio, a pariah figure.[50]

Fiorello La Guardia was another matter. The first Italian American to be elected to Congress, the New York Republican had persuasive talent in inverse proportion to his diminutive, five-foot stature. Things did not always go his way. He lost elections – the New York mayoralty race in 1929 and his congressional seat in the Democratic landslide of 1932. He was no more able to persuade America to adopt a proper health service than any other person on that long list of the virtuous vanquished that would expire only with President Barack Obama's re-election in 2012. But in Congress La Guardia had supported proposals for unemployment insurance and successfully sponsored pro-labor legislation. Then as mayor of New York from 1934 to 1945, he became a major figure of the New Deal era. He was instrumental in persuading President Roosevelt to invest in the tunnels and bridges constructed for the New York Port Authority.

La Guardia had entered Congress in 1917 to represent the slum-ridden 14th District in East Harlem. He resigned to serve with the US Army Air Service in World War I, then ran for office again on a fusion Republican-Democrat ticket designed to keep out the socialists – in 1920, he wore his army major's uniform on the stump and defeated the SPA pacifist candidate, Scott Nearing, in the New York State Assembly elections. He defeated Nearing again in the 1922 congressional election, but many East Harlemites were, in fact, socialist. Out of a mixture of sympathy and good politics, La Guardia had made known at least his absence of prejudice against the left. In 1920, the state assembly had refused to seat five SPA candidates elected to that body because, in the words of Speaker Thaddeus C. Sweet, "Federal Intelligence officers" had spoken against them. La Guardia stood up for the excluded socialists' rights, pointing out that they were democrats not communists, and saying that the socialists "are right in demanding a radical change in conditions."[51]

La Guardia understood that in American politics you could support socialist policies and stand up for the civil liberties of socialists, so long as you did not say that you yourself were a socialist. Warning that if the five were excluded from Albany a tide of support for socialism would ensue, he nevertheless made it plain that he held "no brief for Socialists."[52] He had mixed success in putting this last point across, especially after the SPA listed him on its slate of candidates in 1924 and after La Guardia endorsed Norman Thomas as candidate for mayor of New York in 1925. At the 1929 mayoralty election, the Democrats subjected him to a barrage of abuse for being, as they insisted, a socialist. La Guardia mentored his fellow Italian-American Vito Marcantonio who worked as chief aide-de-camp, and although they disagreed on important issues, that was another spur to conservative indictment as Marcantonio moved further to the left. The *Daily Worker* was an enthusiastic admirer. Its La Guardia obituary in 1947 said he was "one of the great men of our era." He was "an enemy of the imperialists", an opponent of "red-baiting" and an "encyclopedia of accomplishments for the welfare of the people."[53]

The legislators so far discussed were, even if you allow for the networks supportive of Boileau and Amlie, a modestly sized fraction of the member-ship of the House. But it must be remembered that majorities voted for the bills so widely and reasonably depicted by conservatives as socialist measures. The House vote on the Social Security bill was 371 for, 33 against, and in the Senate the split was 76 to 6. After the New Dealers lost ground in the mid-term and general elections of 1934 and 1936, the House vote on the Fair Labor Standards Act was still 314 to 97 in favor, with the Senate ballot at 56 to 28.

These votes represented contemporary attitudes to a domestic crisis, but could also be viewed as aftershocks of Progressive-era socialism. The historian Otis Graham Jr. calculated that most of the "Progressives" from the 1900–20 period opposed the New Deal, but that a minority were in favor. Significantly, the socialists and social workers whom he counted as being amongst the Progressives were prominent in this minority, pro-New Deal group.

Congressional voting patterns uphold Graham's observation about continuity. Take those who were still in the House and Senate in 1935 having been in Congress at the time of the vote on Meyer London's social security bill of 1916. In the latter year, these survivors had favored the SPA congressman's measure by more than three to one. These same veterans of the 64th Congress (1915–17) voted on the 1935 Social Security bill 24 yea, 10 nay, and 2 abstentions. It represents a modest dilution of commitment, but the pro-social security majority is still clear. Socialist measures advocated by Wisconsin and the SPA had endured in the legislative memory and had now prevailed.[54]

Conservative criticism of the New Deal often focused on the socialist tendencies not of Congress but of the executive. The economist Tugwell, a member of Roosevelt's "Brain Trust" before resigning to serve on the New York Planning Commission, was one target of anti-socialist invective. There were similar allegations against another of the president's economic advisers. They held that Treasury Department official Harry Dexter White had communist sympathies and even passed confidential information to the Soviet Union. Alger Hiss, a lawyer who worked in three New Deal agencies, would face trials in 1949 and 1950, accused of perjury for denying that he had been a Soviet spy. On conviction, Hiss served a term in prison. Some extremists accused Roosevelt himself of being a socialist or communist.

The president's intimates thought that these accusations were silly. Frances Perkins had a lengthy political relationship with FDR. She had advised him on social insurance and other matters when he was governor of New York, then served Roosevelt as US secretary of labor throughout his long presidency. She recalled in her memoir of the 1930s that the president did describe himself as "a little to the left of center." But she insisted that Roosevelt was a defender of the American economic system.[55]

Roosevelt would not have dreamed of describing himself as a socialist. Yet he did preside over a political reform movement that was a receptacle of socialist hopes. The faith placed in him by the American Labor Party (ALP) illustrates the point. The founder of the ALP was David Dubinsky, president of the International Ladies Garment Workers' Union and one of the nation's most powerful labor leaders. Born in Russian Poland, the youthful Dubinsky had honed his socialist beliefs inside a czarist prison. His ALP would give meaningful support to socialist and multicultural candidates elected to political office. Marcantonio ran on the ALP ticket. Other beneficiaries of ALP backing were Oscar Garciá Rivera, the first Puerto Rican office holder in the USA, elected from El Barrio to the New York state assembly, and the black congressman Adam Clayton Powell.

Dubinsky's aim was to support the New Deal without supporting Tammany Hall. For him, Roosevelt merited the left's support. In 1936, the ALP nominated Roosevelt for president and delivered him 274,925 votes, mainly from New York City's garment-trade precincts. In the following year, the ALP delivered 482,790 mayoral votes to La Guardia, over 21 percent of his overall support. What was gain to Roosevelt and his supporters was loss to the SPA, which never recovered its electoral popularity in spite of the continuing failure of American capitalism in the 1930s. In the eyes of Dubinsky and those who followed his lead, Roosevelt was socialist enough without having to say so.

The decade of the 1930s was a prime time for American socialist policies. Measurements are not readily on hand to compare US with foreign levels of public ownership and federal planning. In terms of the welfare state, though, it is plain that in spite of the health insurance lacuna America was on its way to joining the international social democratic club. Keeping in mind the estimate that a nation needs to spend 8 to 10 percent of its income on aid to poorer citizens to qualify as a welfare state, America was spending 8.2 percent of its GNP on such programs by the end of the 1940s, rising to 20 percent by the 1990s.[56]

It had been a sudden transformation. A cluster of laws in 1933–5, in particular, had changed America. Germany had undergone a similar progression in 1883–4 and Denmark in 1891–2; Britain introduced reforms more gradually, in the period from the 1890s to 1911, and then in the years after 1945. What happened in America was not exceptional, but seemed revolutionary in American terms. The historian Henry Steele Commager noted the "breathless rapidity" of New Deal change, though he cautioned that the 1920s had been a particularly static period in terms of reform legislation, so the 1930s stood out in contrast. It is understandable that some conservatives saw the New Deal as a lurch to the socialist left.[57]

The conservatives were in fact correct in their observation of the process. However, they were on less firm ground in assuming that it would continue. For from now on, the mainline history of the American left would no longer be synonymous with the story of American socialism. Out-of-office Republicans seeking reinstatement as a political force disregarded that change as they felt they needed the socialist issue. On more than one occasion, they would try to turn the clock back.

Chapter 7

THE REPUBLICAN RE-INVENTION OF SOCIALISM

After World War II, opponents of the New Deal aimed to stem or reverse what they depicted as America's move toward socialism. Through their act of depiction, however, they restored what they sought to eviscerate. They re-invented socialism in a manner that made it seem more powerful. To the architects of the Red Scare of 1919–20, socialism had been a potential threat to the American way of life. According to the conservatives of the later 1940s, the danger had arrived and was real.

The conservatives' claim reflected opportunism as much as genuine belief. The golden age of American socialist agitation was over, and by the 1960s a modernized American left would be offering a more expansive program. To be sure, throughout the period of America's second anti-Red "great fear", 1945–60, socialists fought on. They continued their struggles for the rights of African Americans and in defense of civil liberties. Also, there was residual evidence of socialism's impact on America, for example the trumpeted survival of the welfare state and, shrouded in contrasting clandestinity, America's foreign-policy courtship of the European democratic left. However, America's socialists could boast of but a limited number of direct, self-evident triumphs in this period of conservative and sometimes reactionary politics. Socialist ideas and policies had impacted on America, but the idea of a socialist surge was just a convenient invention.

The conservatives' identification of a continuing socialist threat had a series of consequences. It helped to weaken the New Deal Democratic coalition and to secure the election to the White House of the Republican candidate, Dwight D. Eisenhower. It contributed to the shaping of American foreign policy in the Cold War. The re-invention of a socialist enemy furthermore spurred the growth of neo-conservatism. American socialists did have a role here, and a bizarre one. Some of the ablest neoconservatives were former socialists or communists who were able to contribute authoritative flourishes to the new portrayal of the alleged menace. Finally and in a perverse twist, conservative exploitation of the issue in the 1940s and 1950s kept socialism in the public eye and breathed life into what might otherwise have been a corpse.

The conservative reaction to New-Deal-style socialism was characteristically Republican. Not all conservatives were Republican, and not all Republicans conservative. But political opportunism meant that, after 1945, the Republicans would push the socialist button hardest, as it seemed such a sure-fire means of dislodging the Democrats from office. There were two strands to their propaganda. One focused on the idea of a communist subversion in America. The other spoke of a more reasonable charge, "creeping socialism."

The notion of communist subversion depended on hysteria and the exploitation of hysteria. This is evident in the case of Charlie Chaplin, an artist of the absurd who became a victim of the absurd.

Chaplin, a socialist but not a member of the communist party, gave offense to the conservative media, to government investigative committees, and to the FBI. As a movie actor he had championed the poor, a stance guaranteed to arouse suspicion in the mind of a certain type of conservative. In 1942, he gave support to the demand for the opening of a second front, a demand motivated by the hope that an Anglo-American invasion of Western Europe would relieve the Soviet Union's strain – the Red Army fought the might of the Nazis virtually unassisted until the western allies' D-Day invasion of France in June 1944. In the eyes of Chaplin's detractors, his demand for a second front made him a communist and fair game for foul play. His friendship with such unsettlers of complacency as Pablo Picasso, Clifford Odets, Bertolt Brecht and Thomas Mann compounded his image in such quarters. When Joan Barry, an actress suffering from mental illness, brought a paternity suit against Chaplin, federal prosecutors preferred charges against him under the antiprostitution Mann Act. Though Chaplin was acquitted and turned out not to be the father of Barry's child, it was the start of a prolonged persecution of the world's leading comic actor.

Conferring a further kiss of death given the prevailing hysteria, the leftist press sprang to Chaplin's cause. In 1944, the communists' *New Masses* pointed to the Hearst press's "smear drive" against Chaplin. Its journalist tempted fate too early when he opined that the actor's acquittal over charges of sexual procurement proved "the old enemies of the West Coast movie industry are having trouble gaining the ground they seek."[1]

With the restoration of peace, Chaplin produced and directed the movie

Monsieur Verdoux, a black comedy that won the 1948 Academy Award (Oscar) for best script. But its critique of war and capitalism was red rag to the reactionary bull. There were protests against the film. A New Jersey war veterans' banner demanded "Send Chaplin to Russia."[2] The FBI intensified its investigation of Chaplin. The Immigration Department interrogated the Englishman and threatened to ban him from re-entry into the United States should he leave the country.

In 1952, having lived in the United States for forty-one years, Chaplin went into self-imposed exile. From being an international symbol of Hollywood's artistic integrity, he became a high-profile example of what happens when a nation's citizens turn to intolerance and start informing on one another. In a purge on the lines of the book-burnings of the Spanish Inquisition, American embassies across the world removed from their shelves books about Charlie Chaplin along with the works of US socialists like Langston Hughes, Dashiell Hammett, John Reed, and Agnes Smedley.[3]

"A nation of informers," Chaplin proclaimed in 1957, "will eventually destroy its own civilization."[4] He was wrong. "McCarthyism" was by then in decline. But along with a variety of other victims ranging from homosexuals to Sinophiles and civil rights advocates, Chaplin did bear the brunt of the short-term injustices imposed by hysteria.

Hysteria's roaming spotlight picked out not just private individuals who deviated from the mainstream, but also politicians. It shone with regularity on the late Franklin D. Roosevelt. For example, the Christian Nationalist Crusade – founded in 1942 by the preacher-politician Gerald L. K. Smith and noted for its tirades against Jews and communism – portrayed the New Deal president as a Stalinist stooge. Its booklet *The Roosevelt Death* suggested that the architect of the 1930s reforms might still be alive in 1947. At the time of his funeral, nobody had been permitted to look inside the casket purporting to contain his remains. Like the ghost of Bonaparte in nineteenth-century monarchist Europe, memories of Roosevelt haunted the children of unreconstructed American capitalism.[5]

A widely cited engine of political hysteria in the era of the 1940s/1950s Great Scare is Senator Joe McCarthy's speech in Wheeling, West Virginia, in February 1950. This was the occasion when the Wisconsin Republican alleged that there were communists working in the department of state. There is no verbatim record of what he said; various accounts have him claiming there were 205, 81, 51, or "a lot" of communists in the department. So far as we know, the allegation was pure invention, for not a single communist has been unearthed so far.[6]

While the Soviet adversary was an important spur to the hysteria, leading historians agree that fear of domestic American socialism was also a significant factor. In her 1998 book *Many Are the Crimes*, Ellen Schrecker acknowledged that national security concerns were a significant cause of the Great Scare, but noted also that the Cold War was an excuse for domestic conservatism.[7] Earlier writers similarly remarked on the domestic dimensions of the 1940s and 1950s scare. Richard Freeland (1971) accused President Truman of whipping up anticommunist hysteria at home in order to ensure support for the cornerstone of his Cold War foreign policy, the European Recovery Program (ERP, or the Marshall Plan).[8] Blending foreign and domestic causation, David Caute (1978) wrote that the National Association of Manufacturers believed Moscow was behind Roosevelt's industrial relations policy and supported the persecution of socialists accordingly.[9] Michael Heale (1990) saw the victimizations of the McCarthy years as part of a domestic program, and went on to write another book (1998) looking at anticommunism on the state and city levels, a phenomenon that was by definition at some remove from the Cold War internationally defined.[10]

Senator McCarthy had domestic preoccupations. It may be true that his targets included the Department of State, the Army and the CIA, all of them involved in implementing America's Cold War policies abroad. But the senator knew little about foreign policy, and cared less. His target was communism in America's government. He ruined many lives by tilting at imaginary domestic windmills. American socialism was a live issue in hysterical right-wing politics.

McCarthy and his acolytes depended on a crude definition of socialism, equating it with communism of the Soviet variety. The inherent improbability that this kind of socialism was an internal threat in the United States meant that McCarthy's star would shine but briefly. Once Eisenhower was safely in the White House, the Wisconsin politician was an embarrassment to the Republican Party and dispensable. McCarthy died a discredited figure in 1954.

However, the political exploitation of the specter of socialism was not confined to Joe McCarthy, nor had it begun with him. The Republicans had never been averse to left bashing, and became officially committed to it as a result of the 1948 presidential election defeat. In that election, their candidate Thomas E. Dewey had narrowly come second to the incumbent Democratic president, Truman. Dewey had been critical of the Republican National Committee's anti-New Dealism and privately expressed the view, "if they believe they are going to stop farm price supports, pensions, unemployment insurance, and social advances, they are crazy." The GOP's old guard interpreted his defeat as a sign that a harder line against the left might achieve better results. The Republican Party launched a "liberty against socialism" campaign.[11]

One example of how this worked in practice is the political use made of the congressional voting record of Vito Marcantonio. To *Newsweek*, Marcantonio was a "Red Darling" who opposed the Truman Doctrine (in Marcantonio's view a policy of propping up anticommunist regimes regardless of their character), the ERP/Marshall Aid Plan (Marcantonio: the policy of giving dollars to war-devastated nations only if they eschewed socialism) and the formation of the CIA (Marcantonio: an attempt to run foreign policy in secret without congressional supervision). Domestically, Marcantonio voted in 1948 to reduce income tax for the poor and increase it for the rich, to protect the levels of social security payments, and to defeat an increase in the appropriation for the House Un-American Activities Committee. In that same year, he supported the third-party candidacy of former Vice President and US Secretary of Commerce Henry Wallace. Although Wallace declared himself to be in favor of "free enterprise", he infuriated the National Association of Manufacturers by defending the TVA, had the temerity to point to the Soviets' vastly higher casualty rates in World War II, and supported the civil liberties of communists in the USA. Wallace had the endorsement of the communist party.[12]

The Marcantonio voting record became a template of doom. Congresswoman Margaret Chase Smith's opponents in Maine's Republican Senate primary in 1948 exploited it. They circulated a letter stating she had voted the same way as Marcantonio on 107 out of 242 occasions. On this occasion, it was to no avail. Smith won the primary and then the election, and would become the first major figure in American politics to challenge McCarthy's anticommunist smear campaign.

But the Marcantonio tactic could pay dividends, and not only in the Republican Party. In the 1950 Florida Democratic primaries George Smathers smeared the left-leaning Senate incumbent, Claude Pepper. Smathers' supporters accused his opponent of being a supporter of "socialized medicine" and of the "welfare state." They circulated a pamphlet comparing Pepper's record with those of Marcantonio and California's Democratic Congresswoman Helen Douglas. The red-baiting Smathers won in Florida by sixty thousand votes.[13]

Supporters of Richard Nixon took their cue from this when he ran for the Senate against the aforesaid Douglas. They issued a "pink sheet" with a Marcantonio-comparison smear against the congresswoman. Helen Douglas was already a perfect target because of her views – she believed in sharing atom secrets with the Soviet Union – and her friends – she had been close to Franklin and Eleanor Roosevelt and was allied to (and in fact having an affair with) the pro-New Deal Lyndon B. Johnson (D-TX). Her opponents claimed she was not just soft on communism, but a communist threat herself. The pink sheet stated that Douglas "voted the same as Marcantonio 354 times." Douglas pinned on Nixon the enduringly sticky label "Tricky Dicky." But Nixon triumphed in the election and was on his way to the upper chamber, as well as later to the vice presidency and ultimately the White House.[14]

Both Smith and Douglas had supported ERP but, no matter, they were lumped with the implied treason of the anti-ERP, anti-Cold Warrior Marcantonio.[15] Against the background of Cold War hysteria there was no way in which Smith (the widow of a New Deal lefty) or Douglas (a left-leaner) could betray any sympathy with socialism and survive politically. As women attempting to achieve political break-through, they were under special pressure to conform and were subjected to patronizing diction.

The opponents of these women found "Red" to be too masculine a term. Just as in the 1920s military expansionists had belittled their feminist critics as "pink sisters", so Douglas was a "Pink Lady" and the victim of the "pink sheet" smear. In an absurd world of topsy-turvy assumptions, the temptation for an ambitious woman was further to blur any distinctive image she may have had by adopting "hard" principles. Smith was the first woman to make an impact in the Senate where in June 1950 she showed almost unique courage in challenging Joe McCarthy at the height of his powers. Yet she would in future court a hardline reputation. In 1954, she joined in the Senate vote to provide McCarthy with more investigative funds. As Minority Leader on the Armed Services Committee, she would oppose the Vietnam War in private – but support it in public. She is still another illustration of how even the most courageous of individuals could privately hold left-of-center views yet not always feel free to express them publicly.[16]

Articulated mainly by the Republicans, the anticommunist hyperbole of the Great Scare has attracted a great deal of attention. But there was a second strand to Republican propaganda. It portrayed post-war social reformers as advocates of "creeping socialism." The propaganda portrayed creeping socialism as gradual, secretive and insidious. It was catching America unawares.

Raymond Moley early articulated the concept of New Dealism as a creeping phenomenon. He had not always been critical. In his youth he admired that scourge of poverty Henry George, and Moley had been a member of Roosevelt's Brain Trust. However, the social-justice reformers at Roosevelt's elbow who in historian William E. Leuchtenburg's paraphrase "recognized class cleavages, accepted deficit spending, disciplined business, and planned a welfare state" increasingly appalled him. Moley quit the Roosevelt administration to become a conservative and Republican. He described the New Deal as "creeping collectivism" and when Roosevelt sought re-election for a third term in 1940 he attacked the move toward "creeping despotism." Other Republicans took note, and by 1943 supporters of presidential aspirant Governor Thomas Dewey were (in spite of Dewey's own ambivalence) denouncing the New Deal's "creeping socialism boys."[17]

Six years later, the term came into its own. Creeping socialism was one of the main concepts in John T. Flynn's *The Road Ahead: America's Creeping Revolution*. Perhaps swayed by his Irish-American identity, Flynn saw the incremental advance of American socialism as an evil reincarnation of the gradualist approach of Britain's Fabian socialists. The word "creeping" conveyed to Flynn a sense of something sinister: Democrats who would "never use the word socialism" were conducting "a sneak attack upon our whole way of life." A *New York Times* reviewer described *The Road Ahead* as one of 1949's two most important books on American politics. Private businessmen and the Republican National Committee bought hundreds of thousands of copies of the book, and distributed them in the hope that they would help sink the Democrats in the 1950 mid-term elections. With their help Flynn's tract sold a million copies in 1949, and four million in the election year.[18]

Ohio's Senator Robert A. Taft seized the moment to announce, "The only way to avoid a creeping socialism is to elect a Republican Congress in 1950 and a Republican President in 1952."[19] Critics of the Truman administration hammered away at the theme. Moley explained to the students of Whitman College, Washington. "In 1884, the Fabian Society was formed and it subtly and falsely proposed only 'the extension of Liberalism.' This, of course, was cunning Marxian strategy."[20] Accusations of creeping socialism were to be a mainstay of Taft's ultimately unlucky but nevertheless powerful and influential bid for the Republican presidential nomination.

On the eve of the 1950 vote in New York, Republicans launched an attack on one of the New Deal's main socialist legacies, expanded public ownership. They charged that by promoting the Niagara hydroelectric scheme, New Dealer Democrats were throttling free enterprise attempts to provide cheap electric power. In furtherance of his (successful) bid for re-election to the US Senate, Senator Herbert H. Lehman offered a reply. He defended the Democratic administration's record from TVA onwards and argued that the public development of Niagara would save the taxpayer $60,000,000 a year that would otherwise end up as corporation profits. He accused the Republicans of resorting to "the same tired old word – creeping socialism."[21]

After the midterms, conservatives invoked the same phrase in their attack on Truman's housing plans. The New Deal having earlier established the Federal National Mortgage Association, the Truman administration had taken a further step with a 1949 act that aimed to supply 810,000 units of federally subsidized housing. Running a gauntlet of anti-socialist taunts, Taft himself had helped steer Truman's housing law through Congress. Now, however, House Republicans with some conservative Democratic allies combined to frustrate plans to boost public housing through a revamped Reconstruction Finance Corporation, again citing their opposition to creeping socialism.[22]

In the Spring of 1952, a blaze of publicity greeted the publication of Moley's *How to Keep Our Liberty*. His new book was a blast against state intervention in business, agriculture, transport and medicine. Moley presented a stark choice between capitalism and liberty, on the one hand, and socialism and despotism, on the other. "Creeping socialism," he told the *Chicago Tribune* in a publicity interview, was the deplorable outcome of the New Deal and of Truman's Fair Deal. His supporters in the media could scarcely contain their enthusiasm for the book. Louis Lacosse of the *St. Louis Globe-Democrat* referred to forefathers "cringing in their graves as they see the slithering fingers of a rapacious central government" stealing the "birthright" of their descendants. Losing his concentration, Lacosse invoked the specter not of gradualism, but of "outright socialism."[23]

On the eve of the presidential poll in 1952, Norman Thomas protested to the *New York Times* about an advertisement paid for by the Standard Steel Spring Company of Coraopolis, Pennsylvania. The full-page display attacked socialism and confused it with communism. General Eisenhower having supplanted Taft as the Republican candidate, the GOP by this time looked set to win the White House. Thomas thought there was more to this impending outcome than Ike's popularity. He maintained that the *Times* had published a thinly disguised form of political advertising in behalf of the Republican party as against not only the small Socialist party but the Democrats. Taft and his candidate Eisenhower have both taken the line that what Democrats have done and will do is a form of "creeping socialism."[24]

The comparatively temperate notion of "creeping socialism" – alongside McCarthy's hysterical claims about communism in government – contributed to the Democratic defeat of 1952, and helped to keep alive the notion that socialism was a force in domestic politics.

According to the right, socialism was a present and continuing force in American life in the Truman and Eisenhower years. In some ways, this contention was self-evidently untrue.

Take the case of universal health insurance. At first, the prospects for this must have seemed bright. After New Deal legislation in other spheres, this was the last unfulfilled ambition of the Wisconsin social-security socialists. President Roosevelt had been sympathetic to the idea that health reform would round out the social security achievements of his presidency, and promised to pursue the matter once the war was over. In the 1930s much thought had gone into the drafting of legislation. Canadian-born Senator James E. Murray (D-MT) in 1939 proposed a "National Health Program." He declared, "making available to all of the people the great life-saving services which modern medicine has to offer is an objective which every right-thinking citizen supports."[25]

In 1943 Murray combined with German-born Senator Robert Wagner (D-NY) and Representative John Dingell (D-MI) to introduce a national health bill. An organization purporting to represent the nation's doctors expressed horror. Formed as a political wing of the AMA in February 1939, the National Physicians' Committee for the Extension of Medical Service had chosen for itself a title that suggested a measure of social commitment. In an address of 1940 its chairman Robert L. Benson had referred to "three generations of debauch under Republican administrations" and claimed to be suspending his judgment on the "socialized medicine" programs in Europe. But this was deceptive.

When the chips were down, Benson and his fellow doctors repudiated the medical profession's responsibility for the estimated forty million Americans who could not afford proper medical care. In reaction to the 1943 proposal, Benson's AMA lobby issued a twenty-six-page pamphlet. It warned against "state slavery" and claimed that the cost of abolishing private medicine would be three billion dollars. It claimed to speak for 140,000 physicians.[26]

In his inaugural address of 1945, President Truman urged the adoption of an economic bill of rights including the right to be as healthy as medicine allowed. In a further message to Congress he noted, "the poor have more sickness, but they get less medical care." Calling for a National Health Program, he proposed meeting the cost "through expansion of our existing compulsory insurance system." In one of those statements that signify the opposite of what they say, he insisted, "This is not socialized medicine." In similar vein Murray asked that the proposed legislation should not be seen as socialism. But the AMA was not fooled and called his plan "socialistic." The whole debate in Congress and beyond revolved around that issue.[27]

The National Health Program was not to be. Driven by fears that federally sponsored medicine would be a back-door assault on segregation, southern opponents rolled out the mantra of states rights. As the Democratic coalition needed the support of the South, this was serious opposition. Then when Senator Murray chaired hearings on his health bill, Senator Taft said the proposed law was "the most socialistic measure this Congress has ever had before it." Murray's reply, expunged from the official record but reported by gleeful journalists, was "shut your mouth up and get out." This exhortation did not work, and Truman found himself having to make passionate pleas for health reform in his 1948 re-election campaign. He won the election, but the AMA lined up 1,829 organizations to fight him. Its propagandists invented quotations to show that Lenin was at the back of socialized medicine. Truman left the White House in 1953 with his most deeply cherished social reform unaccomplished.[28]

Politicians continued to be aware of the need for better health care. President Eisenhower knew there was a problem. Early in his administration, he set up the Department of Health, Education and Welfare. He wanted to do something for the uninsured, and floated the idea of reinsurance – the federal government would help to insure the insurers, so that they could offer cover to more marginal cases. The right (AMA supporters) and left (Murray supporters) combined to defeat this. So in the Revenue Act of 1954, Eisenhower's followers instead went for a policy that commanded support from employers, labor unions and the AMA and was thus sure of enactment. Premiums paid by businesses or workers to health insurance companies would attract tax breaks. The policy was private, or voluntarist, in character. Its promoters called it "The American Way." The idea was to encourage more people to take out insurance policies, and some did benefit from generous corporation-sponsored schemes. However, it was far from Murray's dream of universal insurance. His "socialistic measure" had yielded to a system of more privileges for those who already had them, subsidized by less affluent taxpayers who remained uninsured.[29]

The 1940s and 1950s were a time of institutional retreat both for America's democratic socialists and for the communists. Already reduced by the end of the New Deal, these two groups became less and less significant as organizations making a direct impact on election days. By World War II, the SPA was already a shadow of its former self, with fewer than ten thousand members. The appearance of socialist legislation on the statute books and the defection of socialists to the Roosevelt-led Democratic Party accelerated the atrophy, and the atmosphere of the Cold War and the Great Scare of the post-war years was hostile to a democratic socialist revival.

The communist party similarly declined from the membership peak of sixty-five thousand it had achieved in the 1930s. Joe McCarthy in the Senate and the House Un-American Activities Committee in the lower chamber pursued it. So did the FBI, helped by new laws. The Smith Act of 1940 proscribed those who wanted to overthrow the government by force. The communist splinter group, the Trotskyist Socialist Workers Party, was the first organization to feel the brunt of this law. The main communist party at first escaped the rigor of the Act, as the party upheld the government during the wartime alliance with Moscow. But persecution began in earnest after the war and further legislation ensued. The McCarran Internal Security Act of 1950 required the registration of communist organizations with the US attorney general and established a subversive activities control board to investigate suspect individuals. The Communist Control Act of 1954 criminalized membership in the communist party as well as the party itself. Although portions of these laws fared badly at the bar of the Supreme Court, the tenor of the times was extremely oppressive for communism.

Communism would have lost the last shreds of its appeal regardless of all this persecution. The exposure of party members' engagement in espionage against the United States on behalf of the Soviet Union convinced almost all Americans that communism was a despicable creed. In spite of the blanket censorship imposed by the Soviet authorities, news of Stalin's atrocities against his own people increasingly leaked to the West. It was a savage turn-off. So was Moscow's brutal repression of dissent in eastern Europe. In 1953, Soviet tanks crushed an uprising against the communist authorities in East Germany. The western media did not fully exploit that event, but when the same thing happened in Hungary in 1956, there was massive publicity. In the same year, Soviet leader Nikita Khrushchev acknowledged Stalin's crimes making it impossible to remain in denial about them. Heavy defections followed from communist parties across the world. Against the background of such developments, persecution was all the more likely to succeed. The Communist Party USA shrank to become a shadow of its former not very substantial self.

Yet it would be untrue to say that there were no successes for the left in the post-war years. Americans at that time may have witnessed an attack on the rights enshrined in the Constitution, but they were also treated to the spectacle of a fight back in the name of civil liberties, a fight designed to protect the left and its causes, and supported by the left. So effective was the fight back that, following the Senate censure of McCarthy led by Margaret Chase Smith, "McCarthyism" within a few years acquired pariah status. The American Civil Liberties Union (ACLU) did not entirely cover itself in glory in the 1950s. Its national leadership pursued an anticommunist line in order to save the institution from persecution. However, local affiliates of the ACLU experienced a period of growth in the 1950s and showed more vigor than national officials. As a result of such efforts, America arguably ended the decade better protected against the excesses of state surveillance than a good many other countries.[30]

Though by no means alone in fighting for civil liberties in the illiberal 1940s and 1950s, socialists (and former communists now disillusioned with their party) played a significant role. There was, for example, the determined effort on behalf of Junius Scales.

Descended from Confederate soldiers and a Civil War governor of his state, Scales grew up in a thirty-six-room mansion in Hamilton Lakes. As a child, the only black people he knew were servants. After being active in student politics, he joined the communist party in 1939 becoming an organizer in the textile industry. He coordinated civil rights and labor activities in several southern states, and served as vice president of the Southern Negro Youth Congress, the only white officer of that organization.[31]

In 1947 there was a wave of prosecutions of US communists, with all twelve members of the party's national board indicted under the terms of the Smith Act. As a follow up to the ensuing trials of 1949–50, there was a second wave of arrests of local communist party officials, with dozens going to prison for short spells. In 1954, the FBI arrested Scales in Memphis, Tennessee. The charge against him differed from that against other communists. They had been indicted for subversion, but Scales was held under the legislation that made it illegal to be a member of the communist party.[32]

The case took years to progress through state and federal courts. With the passage of time, Scales changed his opinions. He resigned from the communist party when Khrushchev confirmed the atrocities that had taken place under Stalin. Nevertheless, Scales refused to reveal to the FBI and prosecutors the names of his former comrades. This recalcitrance may have contributed to his unusually severe sentence of six years in prison. With help from fellow socialists he appealed his conviction. The Supreme Court quashed it in 1957, only to reverse its decision in 1961. By this time, the case had inspired support both at home and abroad. President John F. Kennedy commuted his sentence after Scales had spent fifteen months in jail. A *New York Times* editorial reflected changing sentiment in its view that "there is something un-American in having even one political prisoner in the United States."[33]

The outcome of the Scales case signposted a decline in intolerance. An even more significant outcome of communist agitation had to do with civil rights. Closely aligned with the communist party, the Civil Rights Congress (CRC) engaged in anti-anti-Red activities from its formation in 1947 until the US government's Subversive Activities Control Board forced it to dissolve in 1956. It was an outgrowth of earlier leftist organizations such as International Labor Defense (ILD) that had championed the Scottsboro Boys, and by 1950 boasted ten thousand members. It devoted energy to the defense of communists persecuted under the terms of the Smith, McCarran and Communist Control Acts.

The main work of the CRC was in the area of civil rights for black people. It played a role in what was a widening movement. For the civil rights movement was stirring anew in the later 1940s. Toward the end of World War II, a horrified realization of the nature of Hitler's holocaust had cemented the idea in most Americans' minds that racism was evil and that America's war dead had perished for a higher cause. There was a rise in support for the campaign to end the second-class status of the African American. The NAACP had half a million members by 1946.

The environment in which African American activists operated had become slightly less intimidating. Although brutal repression continued in the South, the Justice Department now had its deterring eye on the white terrorists who had for two hundred years enforced the region's mores. The years 1952–54 would be the first lynch-free years since records began back in 1882. To be sure, one interpretation of the lull might be that the racist white establishment had such a grip on the life of the region that unofficial killings had ceased to be necessary. But there were more convincing factors than this at work. The black exodus from the South encouraged white employers to make life more agreeable for those who remained, for fear of losing them, too. And, even as it was being persecuted, the left continued unabated its pre-World War II campaign for justice for the black citizen.[34]

The CRC's executive secretary was William L. Patterson, the son of a West Indian father and of a mother who had been born into slavery. In his youth Patterson had immersed himself in the Harlem Renaissance, the study of law, and such left-wing causes as the Sacco and Vanzetti case. He joined the communist party in 1927 and visited the Soviet Union, where he attended the University of the Toiling People of the Far East. He had worked for the ILD and as a party organizer, and was married to Louise Thompson. A contributor to the cultural left in the interwar years, Thompson had spent time in an Alabama jail for her civil rights activities and would form Sojourners for Truth and Justice (STJ), a black women's auxiliary to the CRC. The Pattersons, then, were a political couple.

The CRC took up a series of civil rights cases. In 1946, police officers in Mississippi arrested Willie McGee, a black truck driver, and charged him with rape. The arrest was in response to a complaint by the husband of the white woman in question, with whom McGee had been conducting a consensual affair. An all-white jury took two and a half minutes to reach a guilty verdict. The labor lawyer and future congresswoman Bella Abzug handled McGee's appeal. The CRC helped legally, conducted mass meetings, and ran press exposés of the idea that sex between a black man and white woman was always rape. In this case its efforts were in vain, and Mississippi executed McGee in 1951.

Next on the agenda was an attack on the notion that white men never violated black women. One case sprang from the violent lust of a white man in rural Georgia. Rosa Ingram received a rifle-butt blow to the head when she resisted the sexual predations of John Stratford. Hearing her screams, Rosa's son came to the rescue and killed Stratford with a rather more effective blow to the head. When police charged Ingram and both her sons with murder, the NAACP and STJ as well as the CRC took up the cause. This time justice prevailed, and the Ingrams were out of prison by the early 1950s.

The CRC entered another case in 1948, the trial of the "Trenton Six." The communists dubbed this case the "Northern Scottsboro." In spite of exculpatory witness statements, six black youths had been convicted of the murder of a New Jersey shopkeeper. Agitation by the CRC resulted in mixed success, with four of the youths being released.[35]

The CRC ran into formidable opposition to its program. Dashiell Hammett went to prison for supporting its objectives. When in 1949 Paul Robeson turned up in Peekskill, New York, to sing at a fund-raising concert for the CRC, he and his cortege ran into a crowd yelling "Dirty Commie" and "Dirty Kike." A burning cross, the emblem of the Ku Klux Klan, lit up an adjacent hill. In its flickering light, thugs attacked women and children who had driven to the venue to hear Robeson sing.[36]

Meanwhile allies were in short supply. The NAACP was purging itself of communist or allegedly communist members. It has subsequently emerged that its influential labor director, Herbert Hill (a former Trotskyist), may well have been informing to the FBI on his left-wing associates.[37] The NAACP distanced itself from the CRC except when absolutely necessary. The CIO did the same to individuals and entire unions, stripping away possible human and financial support from the CRC, and isolating it.

Nevertheless, the CRC persisted with its activities. In 1951, it presented a petition to the United Nations published under the title *We Charge Genocide*. It drew upon previously published NAACP research on racial atrocities, but William Patterson injected extra bite into the indictment. He argued that because the federal government sanctioned private acts of murder against black people, they amounted to genocide. Not only this, but by withholding health care and other protection from African Americans, the federal government contributed to the needless deaths of thirty-two thousand black citizens each year. With the issue of German genocide against the Jews still festering in the world conscience, the charge was potent.

Patterson presented his petition confident in the knowledge that the propagandists of international communism would exploit the issue. The Scottsboro precedent indicated this, and the Soviet Foreign Minister Andrei Vishinsky had already attacked the USA over a 1949 incident in Florida where a white mob burned black children alive and the police response was to kill three black men in cold blood. Vishinsky also took a swipe at the NAACP, which was distancing itself from communism and the CRC by defending America's racial record in the international forum. The State Department responded to *We Charge Genocide* with the argument that the UN Convention on Genocide did not apply in the United States because America had not signed up to it. Critics retorted that America had refused to sign for a nefarious reason: southern politicians feared that it would be a backdoor means of making lynching illegal.[38]

At the time of the launch of *We Charge Genocide*, Patterson wrote to communist party USA chairman William Z. Foster noting that it would be of "organizational value" to the party.[39] The charge against Patterson and the CRC is that they were unpatriotic and weakened America's moral authority in the Cold War. With reinforcement from other incidents, for example Indian diplomats being refused service in Maryland's segregated restaurants, developing nations began to have second thoughts about the nation that had presented itself as a beacon of liberty. The USA lost its majority in the General Assembly of the very international forum it had created, the United Nations. The nation famed for its devotion to law would in future years succumb to the temptations of unilateralist and illegal foreign policy.

This was quite an outcome to which, in spite of being on the verge of extinction, American communists had contributed. From Patterson's perspective the destruction of America's reputation was at least partly accidental. He did not intend to put the party's interests above those of the USA. But, fighting for black rights with his back to the wall and deserted by allies turned critics, the CRC and communist propaganda were his only weapons.

So how effective was Patterson in advancing the African American cause? As the 1950s wore on, others were to take up the civil rights cause and the CRC like other socialist organizations became marginal. But it would be perverse to argue that the Civil Rights Congress was not about civil rights and did not advance the case for racial justice in America. The federal government's gradually increasing if reluctant support for racial equality was a response to the gathering momentum of the African American protest movement in America, but it was also in part the product of international pressure which the CRC had helped to facilitate.[40]

To dwell on the demise of socialist institutions like the CRC is not only to overlook their achievements, but also to underrate the contributions of individuals who defied the conservative tenor of the times. A number of these, like Milwaukee's socialist mayor Frank Zeidler, held aloft the banner of an earlier age. Into the same category fell W. E. B. Du Bois, who continued to advance his well-honed socialist arguments. Urging African Americans to turn to socialism and fight for the "advancement of the welfare state", he noted that "nearly all civilized nations" had introduced public ownership of railroads and communications, built public housing and recreation facilities and supplied education and hospitals for all. America was also going down that road, and would have progressed further but for the evils of war and private profit.[41]

A. J. Muste, too, had a radical past as a labor organizer and a founder of the Congress of Racial Equality (CORE, 1942). In the 1950s he set out to demonstrate that while red scares may come and go they do not frighten septuagenarians. The co-founder in 1956 of *Liberation*, an antiwar forum for the non-Marxist left, he campaigned against nuclear weapons and intercontinental ballistic missiles (ICBMs). In the latter cause, he engaged in civil disobedience tactics. By the time the seventy-four-year-old scaled the perimeter fence of an ICBM park in Omaha, Nebraska, in 1959 to protest what lay within, he had a growing band of followers who were prepared to question the sanity of nuclear policy. One of them was Erich Fromm, a distinguished refugee from Nazi Germany known for his Marxist-Freudian approach to psychoanalysis. In 1957, Fromm helped form the Committee for a Sane Nuclear Policy (SANE). These activities were not futile. They helped to arouse public consciousness in a way that led to atmospheric test bans, strategic arms limitation, and, indirectly, opposition to the Vietnam War.[42]

Ideas such as those articulated by Du Bois, Muste and Fromm had a greater impact because others popularized them. Some of those who helped rejuvenate the left had a specialist appeal. The songs of "bloodstains on my tie" Tom Lehrer reached university-educated audiences – a minority, but an expanding one that would have increasing influence. Singing with deadpan black humor, the Yale math instructor satirized everything from Harvard University to nuclear fall out, and took a swipe at racism and consumerism.

Woody Guthrie was blacklisted and had concerts cancelled, but his folk style appealed to a wide audience. "If I Had a Hammer" demanded social change at the time of the Peekskill riot – in which Guthrie's wife and three-year-old son were both injured. In 1955 Guthrie had to testify to HUAC. He took a defiant stance. Next year, he produced his haunting rendition of the song, "Where Have All the Flowers Gone?" It asked why young men died in wars, leaving their girlfriends lonely. Because of similar antiwar views, Guthrie's father had in 1918 lost his job at the University of California, Berkeley. Thanks in no small measure to popular artists like Woody Guthrie, the fortunes of the antiwar left were about to improve.

We can now turn to manifestations of government leftism that are apparent even in an era of anti-socialist rhetoric. One such manifestation would have stretched the credulity of many onlookers, had they known about it at the time. From the later 1940s, the United States pursued a foreign policy initiative that would come to be known as the "Opening to the Left."

National security historian John Prados suggests the term is a translation of *apertura della sinistra*, coined to describe the split between the Italian communist party and democratic socialists in 1956. The policy (if not the phrase) was of earlier origin. William Colby, director of the CIA, explained how the Opening to the Left operated from shortly after the CIA's creation in 1947. The idea was that America would court the democratic left in countries like Italy and France. To uphold the right would have been to court the danger of driving Europeans of moderate socialist convictions into the arms of the communist parties and thus into the Soviet orbit. Drawing on his experience as a CIA officer who had served in Italy, Colby recalled how his colleague Cord Meyer worked to recruit the adherents of "democratic socialism."[43]

In Britain, where the CIA secretly subsidized the left-wing but anticommunist magazine *Encounter*, the left moved in a direction that would have been satisfactory to the agency's strategists. OK, the Clement Attlee-led Labour government of 1945–51 had nationalized the coal and rail industries and set up the National Health Service. But it was anticommunist, and the two governments trusted each other enough to set up the "UKUSA" intelligence exchange agreement. When Hugh Gaitskell succeeded Attlee as leader of the Labour Party in 1955, he committed British socialists to a "mixed economy", signaling an end to the nationalization program. There were by the early 1960s some dark mutterings on the British left about the source of the funding behind the Gaitskellite publicity machine. As the historian Hugh Wilford has shown, Gaitskell reflected the wishes of the British people regardless of any secret funding he may have received from the CIA. The American willingness to court its chosen vehicles on the British left is significant nevertheless as an example of US left-leaning foreign policy.[44]

Senator Joe McCarthy suspected that the CIA was left-inclined. According to one of his biographers, he wanted a major congressional investigation of the agency, an inquiry that would have "interested him more than any other." But CIA Director Allen Dulles refused point-blank to cooperate. Vice President Richard Nixon had to broker a face-saving deal. Congress would be accorded the right to subpoena CIA personnel to testify before its committees, in exchange for a promise that it would never do so. Thus the Opening to the Left remained secret. The American left (with the exception of some of its members who had been recruited by the CIA) did not realize what was going on. A matching international unawareness meant that the CIA carried the reputation of being an instrument of conservative US policy.[45]

Yet if people had chosen to observe them, there were other very clear signs that US diplomacy did not always cleave to the right. US policy toward Israel is a prime example.

From a socialist perspective, the creation of the Israeli state on May 14, 1948 was a triumph, and so was Washington's recognition of the new nation within fifteen minutes of the event. It fulfilled the dream of America's socialist Zionists. One of the early leaders of those US left-wing Jews had been David Ben-Gurion, who became the first prime minister of the new nation. With the formation of Israel, some American Jewish socialists moved there, especially to participate in the idealistic cooperative communities, the *kibbutzim*. They did so in sufficient numbers to drain and weaken the Jewish socialist movement back in America. That draining process no doubt contributed to America's loss of memory about the first thirty years in US-Israeli relations. Israeli politics also contributed to the amnesia. For since the Israeli election of 1977, conservatives have been more prominent in that country's politics. This has made it easier to forget the time when America's prime ally in the Middle East was a socialist polity.[46]

The picture just painted does need modification. Some American socialists, including Jewish socialists, had reservations about the Zionist ambition. They worried about its chauvinism and its disregard for the rights of displaced Palestinians. It would also be misleading to suggest that American socialist Jews alone accounted for the creation of the new Zion. Other forces were the moral impact of the Holocaust, the hope that a Jewish nation would stand up for Jews across the world and deter future genocides, and even a degree of Jewish anti-Semitism in America – established and upwardly mobile Jews whose ancestors had arrived earlier from Europe did not want to see their social position undermined by a new wave of Jews from poverty-stricken regions of the Old World. The eastern seaboard of the Mediterranean offered a solution for all these reasons, not just because of American socialist Zionism.[47]

It would in fact be an error to make too sweeping a generalization about the left-wing nature of US foreign policy. Yes, there is a case for saying that the CIA had liberal/left inclinations. But it also contained diverse strands. Take James Angleton. He would become legendary as the CIA's chief of counter intelligence, and held the conservative (and almost certainly erroneous) view that the CIA harbored a Soviet mole or agent. Angleton fought against the implementation of Opening to the Left policies in Italy. Illustrating the complexity of international politics, this arch-conservative did work with the leftist Ben-Gurion and helped establish the Israeli secret service Mossad. As Angleton intended, Mossad would work for security and stability, not for left-wing or otherwise unsettling reforms.[48]

Outside Israel and the white-European world, the CIA resorted to less liberal and more ruthless methods of enforcing an anticommunist agenda. It played a part in the overthrow of elected left-wing governments in Iran (1953) and Guatemala (1954). This was a major feature of America's policy in the Cold War – but did it typify the US political climate?

There were contrary indications. Republican politicians kept the issue of socialism alive, the Civil Rights Congress made its mark, individual leftists prepared the way for an effective antimilitarist movement, the CIA pursued some left-wing goals, and this was not all. For under Eisenhower, the New Deal's welfare state received bipartisan approval. While American corporations worked to undermine and privatize the social insurance provisions of the 1930s, the basic structure remained. The majority of Republicans condemned New Deal socialism while accepting its outcomes. At the end of Eisenhower's first year in office, Senator Joe McCarthy famously used the phrase "twenty-one years of treason" to indicate that, after twenty years of Democrats surrendering to socialism, a Republican president had now committed the same sin.[49]

The irony was not lost on the Democrats. Two years after losing the 1952 election to General Eisenhower, Adlai Stevenson said that the Republicans had practiced a deception by denouncing the Democrats' "great program of domestic reform as 'creeping socialism' and then accepting the whole thing."[50] When a little later in the same year, 1954, President Eisenhower persuaded Congress to accept an extension of the Old Age and Survivors Insurance System to cover an additional 10.5 million people, the veteran fiscal conservative Senator Walter F. George (D-GA), passionately denounced the measure: "The marvelous thing is that the party dedicated to free enterprise, the party that is dreadfully afraid of creeping socialism, does this thing to a free America."[51]

Some final reflections. In order to defeat the Democrats in 1952, the Republicans had breathed life into the waning specter of American socialism. But because of anti-Red persecution, their re-invented bogeyman to a large degree became socialism without socialists. By crushing the organized left that had made the rhetoric credible, they stood in danger of having killed the goose that laid the golden political egg.

Moreover, the pendulum of public opinion turned against McCarthyism, and the Republicans had to moderate their anti-socialist rhetoric. They could not effectively indict Democratic presidential candidate John F. Kennedy in the election of 1960. Socialism was no longer the domestic menace it had once seemed, and anti-socialism was in any case unfashionable. In political discourse, the phrase "American socialism" was giving way to the phrase "American left", and "New left" lay just around the corner. The re-invented socialism orgy was, for the time being, over.

Chapter 8

THE NEW LEFT SHARES THE CREDIT

Not many movements have extricated a nation from war, but the American New Left claimed precisely that, and many of its critics agreed. What added luster to the asserted triumph was that the war in question was unwise and unjust. America had no vested interest in Vietnam, and there was no threat to national security. The Vietnamese communists the United States fought were undemocratic and barbaric, but the South Vietnamese regime America tried to defend was no better. Congress gave its approval to the war only after an outright deception, an assurance by the Johnson admin- istration that North Vietnamese ships has attacked US Navy destroyers on August 4, 1965.

In the period of its prominence, roughly 1960–73, the New Left could also lay claim to other achievements. For example, it propelled America to a more open form of government, and refined direct action as a weapon in the arsenal of the oppressed and powerless.

The New Left did not carry all before it. It had its failings, for example in the area of gender equality. Moreover, it did not monopolize the leftist agenda. This is evident in the cases of the new feminism, civil rights, and the campaign against poverty. Where these movements made advances, the New Left could not claim all the plaudits. It shared the credit with Old Left survivors and other radicals, and also with the administrations of both Lyndon Johnson and Richard Nixon.

Yet the New Left was unrivalled as a promoter of debate, and was the accelerator of change in its era. The Johnson and Nixon reforms were reactions to the demands of New Leftists and their fellow radicals. The story of the New Left forms a significant chapter in the history of the left's achievements.

To understand and measure the New Left's role, the first step must be to consider what it was. Its goals and composition were fluid. This was an empowering characteristic in two ways. First, it broadened its appeal to anarchic protesters who were in the vanguard of fighting for American liberties. Second, it made the New Left an elusive and moving target. For that reason, its opponents found it difficult to make a hit. Take the FBI. The bureau's old enemy, the communist party, had been an easy mark. But when it came to the radicals of the 1960s, the FBI was all at sea. There were no membership lists or organizational charts that could be stolen to help the plodding sleuth. The kaleidoscopic nature of the New Left did not shield it from criticism, but it did save it from destruction.

It can with confidence be said that New Leftists were prominent in university towns like Austin, Texas; Madison, Wisconsin; Ann Arbor, Michigan and on the East and West Coasts. It is plainly true that New Leftists mostly preferred the word "left" to the word "socialism." It is also safe to say that the New Left was never large in terms of declared adherents. According to a credible estimate by the historian Paul Buhle, while it may have had a "supportive milieu of millions," it never at a given time numbered more than 150,000 "steady participants."[1]

Some of the New Left's characteristics come into sharper focus when it is considered in an international context. The *Nation* noted in 1955 that the term *nouvelle gauche* or "new left" was gaining currency in France.[2] C. Wright Mills, soon to be a guru of the American New Left, spent time in England in 1957 savoring the new breezes and meeting British socialists. His "Letter to the New Left," a call for action in the United States, appeared in the British *New Left Review* prior to its publication in the US journal *Studies on the Left* and as a popular American pamphlet in 1961.[3]

However, there were limits to the American New Left's foreign inspiration. Learning tends to be more effective when it is mutual and, with the British left unwilling to concede that its US counterpart had anything to offer, the American New Left went its own way. It cut a distinctive path.

In its search for an engine for change, the American New Left switched vehicles. The "working class" or labor gave way to a youthful intelligentsia. It offered a practical critique of poverty. Its adoption of new methods of direct action made it cutting edge in the international context. It reflected and sponsored the intensifying struggle for civil rights in a way that made it an international inspiration to a degree that threatened to overwhelm the grudging attitudes of the European left. Lacking dogmatism, the American New Left spawned journals such as *Studies on the Left* with heterogeneous viewpoints. It contained significant religious elements – the Catholic

Ramparts was a leading New Left journal. And the American New Left developed an agnosticism about Marxism.

The New Left's demotion of Marx had an intellectual basis. The charismatic Mills was a Columbia University professor who raced around on a motorcycle, sported a leather jacket and spoke with the drawl of his native Texas. He offered an influential distinction between vulgar Marxists (the shouters of slogans), sophisticated Marxists (twisters of facts to suit the theory) and plain Marxists (who treated "Marx like any great nineteenth-century figure, in a scholarly way"). To Mills's good guy, the plain Marxist, Karl Marx was a source of ideas, but not the only source, and often wrong. Other gurus of the New Left, for example Herbert Marcuse in his *One Dimensional Man* (1964), similarly found fault with Marx and Marxists.[4]

Some factions in the New Left, for example the Weathermen group and a cabal in Students for a Democractic Society (SDS), continued to beat a Marxist drum. Anti-socialists and their compliant journalists tapped and amplified the same rhythm. But in general it was now evident to informed observers that Marxism was beating a retreat.

On the face of it, the critical attitude to Marxism was a new trend. It was consistent with the enrolment in the New Left cause of Christians and black Muslims who had little truck with the atheism espoused by Karl Marx. Yet it should be remembered that Marxism had not dominated the Old Left, either. The vital role of Christian socialists attests to that. Equally, it is worth recalling that many influential advocates and implementers of socialist-like reforms in the past had already stopped calling themselves socialists, let alone Marxists. Leading lights of the New Left no doubt avoided the socialist label with similar tactical considerations in mind. For example, Michael Harrington did not proclaim his socialist beliefs even though he had them.

The New Left's repudiation of Marxist doctrine and its abandonment of the idea that the working class was the most promising agency for social change made it more acceptable to public opinion and thus more effective. In a nation whose citizens overwhelmingly thought of themselves as middle class, reliance on working-class consciousness was not a great idea.

The new critique incorporated further insights. The labor movement, supposedly the tribune of America's workers, had for years been a disappointment to the left, and for the New Left this was irredeemably the case. The CIO unions formed in the 1930s had seemed more promising than the old craft unions affiliated to the AFL, but they, too, retreated into a defense of the ground they had already won. They left the great majority of

American workers outside their protective umbrella, delivering high wages and privileged health insurance packages to the fortunate minority. The CIO unions had joined in the anticommunist purges of the late 1940s and 1950s. The AFL-CIO merger of 1955 signified less the radicalization of the AFL than the calcification of the CIO.

The AFL-CIO stance on foreign policy was another reason for the New Left's repudiation of the mainstream labor movement. One of the New Left's targets was Jay Lovestone, a former communist who became an arch Cold Warrior. Lovestone had orchestrated foreign aid through such organizations as the Free Trade Union Committee. Even before the revelation that the money came from the CIA, there were objections that he was using US funds to undermine socialist unions in foreign countries. In a series of episodes far removed from the "Opening to the Left" policies on other occasions followed by the CIA, Lovestone worked to uphold conservative clones of the AFL-CIO.

Even more provocatively, the labor movement's anticommunism moved it to support the Vietnam War. AFL-CIO president George Meany recalled "We had some vocal opposition [to the war] at the local level, but at the top level we had no opposition at all." In its 1965 national convention, the AFL-CIO adopted a resolution pledging President Johnson its "unstinting support" for the war effort. National Security Affairs Advisor McGeorge Bundy gave Lovestone his "warm thanks" for sending him a copy of the resolution: "This thoughtful expression of support of the President's policy is indeed appreciated." Not until 1974, when America had officially withdrawn from the war, did Meany admit that his support had been a mistake all along.[5]

The New Left's split with organized labor theoretically meant the loss of an increasingly powerful ally – against a background of war-induced prosperity, union membership increased from 15.5 million to 21 million between 1960 and 1970.[6] But then, mainstream labor never had been a consistent ally of the left. Unlike social democrats in other countries, the American democratic left has had to get by without the support of organized labor.

The New Left thus made no sacrifice by investing in a new agency for change, the students of America. The students looked like a promising new political class. There were lots of them. In the decade when post-World War II baby boomers came of age, university expansion was rapid. By 1970, half of all high school graduates went on to higher education, compared with less than a fifth in 1940. College students numbered three million in the 1960s, rising to ten million in 1970. This was more than six-fold the rate of growth in union membership.[7]

Two years after its formation in 1960, Students for a Democratic Society adopted a defining manifesto at its national convention in Port Huron, Michigan. It inveighed against "power rooted in possession, privilege, or circumstance," as well as against imperialism, the Bomb, and racism. It still sought an alliance with labor, but looked to the campus as the real engine of change: professors should "import major public issues into the curriculum." There should be discussion of relevant issues like war and peace, and not "dull pedantic cant." Relevance was one of the SDS's most popular demands. So was participation. A 1969 poll indicated that 90 percent of college students wanted more say in determining their curriculum.[8]

Students protesting at the University of California, Berkeley, (1964) and the University of Michigan, Ann Arbor, (1965) gave unprecedented salience to the critique of universities. They called for more democracy on campus and for a replacement of materialist values by a renewed sense of community. They complained that the governance of America was in the hands of white old rich men (WORM) – where were the blacks, the young, the poor and women? They flocked to hear professors like Howard Zinn, Herbert Gutman and David Montgomery who looked past the roles of elites and tried to represent the outlook of the American masses who had viewed the history of the nation "from the bottom up."

Amongst the professors to whom the radical students looked for inspiration were scholars who re-interpreted foreign policy – examples are Norman Graebner, Walter LaFeber, Gabriel Kolko, and, at that old engine house of the left the University of Wisconsin, William Appleman Williams. These historians elaborated the story of America's "new imperialism", of control of foreign lands not through the exercise of brute force or through wholesale colonization, but by economic means designed to swell the profits of American corporations.

Students were the adrenalin behind the New Left accelerator. Their methods of protest, such as sit-ins, teach-ins, marches, demonstrations and "child stealing" (the indoctrination of the offspring of the nation's leaders), attracted publicity that was an aid to further recruitment. They were at their most potent in the mid 1960s, when the protest against the Vietnam War took off. As time wore on, there would be a higher profile for *in loco parentis* issues such as universities' right to regulate young people's amatory conduct. However, when the Southeast Asian conflict escalated and more students were drafted into the military they protested the war anew, if with less moral force because they seemed to be self-interested. Because of turnover – each year seniors graduate, freshmen arrive, mores change – the actions of student protestors were nigh on impossible to predict or control. And unfolding events gave them continuing impact.[9]

One of these events was the *Ramparts* affair. In March 1967, the West Coast magazine ran a story on the CIA's involvement in the affairs of the National Student Association (NSA).[10] The birth year of the NSA was the same as the CIA's, 1947. In the following years when the CIA was courting the moderate left, the association had seemed to be appropriately situated politically. To the right of SDS, it was nevertheless well to the left of Young Americans for Freedom, the conservative students' organization formed in 1960. At a time when Jim Crow still prevailed and not just in the South, the NSA's second president, James T. Harris Jr., had been a black man.

However, the NSA had pursued an anticommunist line in its numerous foreign ventures. Recognizing that the NSA was well placed to undermine efforts by the Soviets to influence worldwide student opinion, the CIA had secretly bankrolled the association's emissaries to foreign universities and conferences. It was not a matter of suborning the NSA's activists, but of empowering them to do what they wanted to do anyway. "Wittingly" or "unwittingly" (to use the CIA's own terminology), talented individuals ranging from Henry Kissinger to Gloria Steinem consequently helped the CIA with its propaganda activities.[11]

The 1967 exposure of the NSA's CIA connection reverberated through the press, which in a muckraking orgy unearthed all kinds of other stories about the CIA's deployment of voluntary organizations ranging from organized labor to newspaper syndicates. One reason why the reports caused a sensation was because the CIA's charter made it illegal for it to recruit domestic groups. Perhaps more profoundly, people with an innocent outlook on life found it scandalous that the CIA had engaged in nefarious activities that compromised the cream of American youth. But there was yet another reason why the conduct of the NSA's leadership shocked. Just when the SDS was demanding openness and honesty from those who presided over America's universities, it emerged that Washington was actively recruiting students for programs that were inherently deceptive. An age-old thirst began to consume the nation. It was a thirst for honesty and freedom of information, and in the mid 1970s it would culminate in a powerful stream of reform legislation.[12]

In the fall of 1958, the CIA looked for students it could help travel to a youth conference in Vienna, Austria, young folk it could rely on for their ability and soundness of opinion. One person it identified was Zbigniew Brzezinski, a future national security affairs adviser then fresh out of Harvard. Another was Michael Harrington – the young socialist was known for his anti-Stalinist opinions. But Harrington was suspicious about the origin of the money on offer, and said he would attack Stalin only on the understanding he could also attack capitalism. In a move illustrative of the limits to its Opening to the Left policy, the CIA blocked the funds allocated to Harrington's trip.[13]

Harrington went on to develop one of the major defining features of the New Left, its attack on poverty. What kind of person was he? The sole child of lace-curtain Irish professionals from St. Louis, he received a Jesuit high school education then graduated from Holy Cross College in Massachusetts. He came to social activism through the Catholic Worker movement of Dorothy Day, a former Wobbly who had since the early years of the New Deal turned her energies to developing hospitality houses for impoverished laborers down on their luck. Harrington was one of a number of Catholics associated with the New Left. Others included the *Ramparts* editors, the brothers Daniel and Philip Berrigan (pacifist priests who made it onto the FBI's Ten Most Wanted Fugitives list), and Port Huron manifesto author Tom Hayden. Indeed, Catholics fed significantly into the mainstream of religious protest against the war in which Protestant clergymen such as Yale University's chaplain, William Sloan Coffin, were also prominent.[14]

Harrington would go on to chair the Socialist Party (1968–73) – this was a successor to the SPA, the older party having disintegrated into factionalism. However, his main contribution to American politics was of an intellectual nature. He shared other New Left intellectuals' reservations about Marxism; he criticized Lenin for predicting class polarization in a way that ignored the steady rise in real wages for most workers in Western democracies. In a stance that alienated him from many of his fellows on the left, he refused to demand unconditional withdrawal from Vietnam on the ground that to do so would be to leave the Vietnamese to the distinctly untender mercies of the communist Viet Cong. By drawing attention to the survival of poverty in America, however, he gave the left a unifying cause and made his mark on social thought.[15]

Harrington took his inspiration at least partly from *The Affluent Society*. The author of this book published in 1958 was a Canadian-born Harvard professor who had a claim to being America's most distinguished economist. John Kenneth Galbraith argued that Big Government should be a "countervailing" force in society, helping to prevent excessive concentration of power in the hands of Big Business and Big Labor. Like the English economist John Maynard Keynes who had influenced his views, Galbraith's opinion of socialism teetered between rejection and reluctant tolerance – he did once write a pamphlet for the British Fabian Society, but only to praise the suggestion of neoconservative economist Milton Friedman that there should be a "negative income tax" to ensure minimum income. On the subject of poverty he was, however, uncompromising.[16]

In *The Affluent Society*, Galbraith argued that the 1930s assault on poverty had been so successful that it had lulled politicians into a false sense of security, and they had forgotten about the issue. The surge of post-war prosperity had shielded from the eyes of America the hidden problem of poverty amongst certain groups: workers in unorganized industry and in sweatshops, laborers in the South, members of minority groups, and older citizens. Arguing for a policy to ensure a minimum income to every family, he stated in a later edition, "A very large proportion of all black households (in the cities 37.5 percent in 1966 as compared with 15.3 percent of whites) fall below the poverty line." In mentioning the poverty line, Galbraith made no mention of Robert Hunter, the socialist who had introduced the idea to American discourse, or indeed to socialist tradition at all. On the contrary, he insured himself against salvoes from the right by inserting into the book a chapter denouncing the "Marxian Pall."[17]

Irony is a tricky weapon, and so it was with the title of *The Affluent Society*. Perhaps because so many people display a modish book on their coffee table without reading much beyond its title, Galbraith's attempt to focus attention on mass deprivation did not have mass impact. Penguin publishers did not help. In an example of catastrophic design, they placed an image of a champagne cork on the cover.

Then along came Michael Harrington's book, *The Other America* (1962). He opened with a chapter called "The Invisible Land" that reinforced Galbraith's "brilliant" but "widely misinterpreted" message about hidden poverty – Harrington noted that in popular parlance "the affluent society" was now a catch phrase that was being taken literally. Harrington had personally visited the homeless shelters and barrios of America. Correcting the popular error, he powerfully indicted suburban dwellers who were blind to the mean streets, and tourists who marveled at Appalachian splendor but never left the highway to see how poor the people were.[18]

Like Galbraith, Harrington referred to the poverty line. He noted that it was not just a problem of those below it. Millions had annual incomes only just above the benchmark of $3,000 for a family of four. The few extra dollars gave America its excuse to ignore them. Fifty million Americans struggled in poverty that was definable not just in terms of income, but in terms also of deprivation that amounted to lives free of hope, devoid of proper medical care, and embracing a culture of poverty. Like Galbraith, Harrington failed to credit Hunter. Nor did he mention the word socialism. His biographer Robert Gorman wrote: "Harrington never explained why, when he was intensely engaged with factions on the democratic left, he hid his full political agenda from the public." But it is not really surprising. Just as the socialists of an earlier era had dropped the word "socialism" to help them persuade America to adopt social security, so Harrington chose the most persuasive tactics in his effort to promote a campaign against poverty. In his key book, he erased socialism in order to make the poor visible.[19]

Harrington hoped *The Other America* would sell 2,500 copies. Within a year the figure was seventy thousand and Americans would go on to buy a million more. John F. Kennedy was reputedly an early reader, and was turning his mind to antipoverty legislation when an assassin's bullet ended his ambitions in November 1963. His successor President Johnson did take action, setting up a task force under Kennedy's brother-in-law, Sargent Shriver. Harrington joined Paul Jacobs, another left-winger, and the Labor Department aide Daniel P. Moynihan in writing a background paper for Shriver calling for massive public works New-Deal style, and a redistribution of income to those in need.

In a football-stadium address to University of Michigan students in May 1964, President Johnson now called for a Great Society. Congress approved the Equal Opportunity Act in time for the election campaign of that year. In an innovative move, funds would be concentrated on localities. Aid would encourage community action and autonomy. President Johnson finally allocated $963 million for a "War on Poverty" that ran until 1973. He also approved the Elementary and Secondary Schools Act of 1965. This dispensed aid to poorer school districts – the first federal intrusion into what had hitherto been a local domain.[20]

So was this a triumph for the American left? Certainly, there have been some acknowledgements of Harrington's input. In an editorial in 1987, the *Boston Globe* stated that Medicaid, Medicare, food stamps and extended social security benefits were "directly traceable" to *The Other America*. In the last year of the millennium, *Time* magazine included the book in its list of the ten most influential non-fiction titles of the twentieth century.[21]

However, an intellectual reaction set in. Moynihan began to argue that the culture of poverty had become, in consequence of leftist policies, a culture of dependency. Other former left-wingers joined in the critique, blaming everything from work aversion to single parent families on the welfare state. In the 1970s Harrington called them "neoconservatives", meaning it to be a term of opprobrium though those who wore the label took pride in it. Not only did the antipoverty program end in the Nixon presidency, but also the whole apparatus of the welfare state came under scrutiny then and in ensuing years on grounds of both expense and morality.[22]

It is true that the War on Poverty did not end the problems of the poor. It did not go far enough. Even on the basis of the administration's pared-down estimate of thirty-three million poor people in the US, the allocated $963 million was still only enough to eliminate about 9 percent of the poverty in America. Harrington told Shriver, "You've been given nickels and dimes for this program." With the escalation of the Vietnam War accounting for an additional military expenditure of over twenty billions annually and with inflation an increasing threat to the economy, there was little possibility that the poor would receive a meaningful increase in resources. The left may have stopped the war, but it not stop it in time to rescue the antipoverty program.[23]

Harrington's main contribution was that of a persuader, and the New Left in general had a similar role. That is not to say that it ignored the normal channels of electoral politics. The campus left supported the presidential primary campaign of Senator Eugene McCarthy (D-MN). There was then a measure of support for Robert F. Kennedy until his assassination in June 1968, when McCarthy once again became the main peace candidate. McCarthy lost to Hubert Humphrey at the Democratic convention. Four years later the New Left supported the presidential campaign of the Democrats' candidate, George McGovern. But the North Dakota senator suffered a heavy defeat at the hands of the incumbent, Richard Nixon.

In spite of such reverses, leftist involvement in politics was in some ways successful. It helped to elect certain candidates, some of whom were themselves of the left. One example was Bella Abzug (D-NY). As a "legal left" lawyer working in tandem with the Civil Rights Congress, Abzug had been lead counsel in the Willie McGee case of 1948–51, introducing the then-risky defense that sex between a black man and white woman need not be rape. She had also acted for fellow-victims at the Peekskill riot, in the course of which she had been injured.[24] Abzug was elected to Congress in 1970. Another successful left candidate was the Vietnam War veteran turned critic Ron Dellums. Elected to represent California's Eighth District

(San Francisco), Dellums entered the House with Abzug in 1971. The former marine was a socialist. In yet another example of how the left could be a hidden force, he ran on the Democratic ticket.

The New Left's impact on electoral politics was subject to a significant inhibition. Until the Twenty-Sixth Amendment of 1971, people under the age of twenty-one could not vote. This encouraged young radicals' interest in direct action.

Was that a delayed triumph for the IWW? Daniel Bell thought so. Bell was a distinguished sociologist, an authority on American Marxism, and a neoconservative whose book *The End of Ideology* (1960) Mills had savaged. Writing a revenge article in the CIA-subsidized British journal *Encounter*, Bell asserted: "Mills, basically, is an American anarcho-syndicalist, a 'Wobbly'."[25]

The Wobblies had stressed direct action for reasons similar to those that would motivate the New Left. For the tactic empowered those without the vote such as under-twenty-ones, blacks, migrants, women and recent immigrants. Even a half-century later, there was some evidence of the Wobblies' influence. Students for a Democratic Society militants wore "IWW" buttons obtainable from the Wobbly headquarters in Chicago. Student activist Carl Davidson issued a pamphlet on "student syndicalism." The first teach-in against the Vietnam War took place in Ann Arbor in 1965, and in that very year the University of Michigan Press launched an anthology of IWW songs.

Wobbly refrains and melodies resonated once again in the music of protesters' favorites Bob Dylan, Joan Baez and Pete Seeger. Ralph Chaplin's 1915 Wobbly anthem "Solidarity Forever" brought forth a rendering by Seeger, and was on the lips of New Left students who knew the words by heart; Baez revived the song "Joe Hill" at the Woodstock festival in 1969 and recorded it in the following year bringing the elegy to a wide audience. Students took inspiration from their professors, and vice versa. The 1960s peak in books devoted to Wobbly history attests to the revival in interest, with a spate of sympathetic works both on the history of the IWW and on the songs and trial of Joe Hill.[26]

The Wobbly impact should not be exaggerated. Some activists refrained from summoning up IWW memories, perhaps because the IWW's commitment to sabotage was too strong to stomach. Suggesting another possible reason, New Leftist historian David Montgomery pointed to the influence of a book of 1967 by James Weinstein that spoke of the Wobblies' anarchistic failure to take a united stand against World War I. The American left had in fact been much more tenacious in its opposition to the war than its European counterpart, but the book may have dampened Wobbly enthusiasm amongst the New Left, for whom opposition to war was a cardinal issue. Todd Gitlin, president of SDS 1963–4, recalled that while he and other New Left leaders read about the Wobblies and found them inspiring, they took less of an interest in IWW history than had the Old Left, which had been more bound by socialist traditions.[27]

Gitlin was one of those who placed greater weight on another factor – the influence of the civil rights movement. The struggle for African American equality helped to define both the New Left and its tactics, especially in its protest against the Vietnam War. With so many black citizens disenfranchised since the Jim Crow legislation of the 1890s, orthodox democratic methods had not been an option. Direct action was more promising. It included sit-ins at segregated facilities, boycotts of segregated bus services, marches and demonstrations. As the pre-eminent leader of the Southern Christian Leaders Conference (SCLC, established in 1957), the Rev. Dr. Martin Luther King developed a tactic of nonviolent resistance. The award to him of the Nobel Peace Prize in 1964 (he was the youngest-ever recipient) added authority to his message. As it was meant to, King's stress on nonviolence and the religious ethic began to win over white opinion.

The alternative waiting in the shadows further assisted King. Malcolm X led a separatist Black Muslim movement that pointedly refrained from condemning the ultimate form of direct action, violence. Black militarism continued after his assassination in February 1965, and the outbreak of serious rioting in the urban ghettoes, for example in Watts County, Los Angeles, in August 1965, reinforced the notion that drastic alternatives lurked in the wings. Seen against that backdrop, King became the messiah of choice for Americans who might otherwise have ignored the civil rights issue.

King continued to stage direct-action dramas well into the 1960s. He aimed to end the deregistration of the black voter. Because of determined work on the local level, black voter registration in the South had already risen from 3 percent in 1940 to 43 percent in 1964, but the job was incomplete. In Dallas County, Alabama, where whites were in the minority but had 99 percent of the vote, and where only 2 percent of the over-twenty-one black population was registered, King in March 1965 initiated a protest march. It headed out of Selma toward Montgomery and the police violence directed at it attracted major media attention. According to King's biographer David Garrow, the march contributed to the passage of the federal Voting Rights Act five months later.[28]

Having benefited substantially from the support of the Old Left, the civil rights movement was a bridge along which the insurrectionary torch passed to the New Left. Here, it is important to note the continuing socialist sympathies of some of the more charismatic black leaders. Amongst Black Muslims, there developed an antipathy in some quarters to any movement, socialism included, that white people led. But the proscription was not absolute. Eldridge Cleaver, a disciple of Malcolm X who became a senior editor and writer for *Ramparts*, served as information officer for the Black Panther Party. The Panthers acquired a reputation for violent shoot-outs with the police and for black militarism. But Cleaver advocated black and white worker solidarity in pursuit of a socialist revolution, and in 1968 ran for president on the ticket of the Peace and Freedom Party – a nod in the direction of democratic socialism.

Malcolm X himself was no admirer of the American business system: "Show me a capitalist and I'll show you a bloodsucker." He had been aware even in his dissolute youth that James W. Ford had run for vice president. He was dismissive of communism, but also of the anticommunists who belittled Ford. According to an FBI report, he praised the Russian Revolution and claimed that both Lenin and Stalin were non-white. If true, that may well have been mere provocation, one of black America's many attempts to shock white America out of its racism. But Malcolm X certainly reveled in the reception given to him when he visited Ghana, the first decolonized African state and a socialist one.[29]

Nor had the significance of Ghana been lost on W. E. B. Du Bois. Even at the age of ninety-three, this leading American intellectual was still a master of the art of shock. In October 1961, he joined the communist party. "Today," he wrote its chairman Gus Hall, "I have reached a firm conclusion. Capitalism cannot reform itself; it is doomed to self-destruction." Immediately thereafter, rather like a boxer landing combination punches, he quit the land of his birth for Africa. He had an invitation from President Kwame Nkrumah to travel to Ghana and edit his projected (sadly never completed in his lifetime) *Encyclopedia Africana*. The Kennedy administration refused to renew his passport when it ran out, and in 1963 the exiled Du Bois died in Ghana.[30]

This was not the end of Du Bois politically. In June 1964, a group of San Francisco radicals established the W. E. B. Du Bois Clubs of America to honor his name and to agitate for left causes. Aligned with what remained of the communist party, the Du Bois Clubs were an example of Old Left injections into the New Left agitation against the Vietnam War. They cooperated with a broad spectrum of New Left antiwar organizations. In 1966, they worked with the SDS and other groups in support of Robert Scheer's Democratic primary challenge to the local congressional incumbent, registering ten thousand new voters especially in black precincts. Scheer polled 45 percent of the vote and sent politicians a message about the potency of the antiwar movement. When San Francisco vigilante bombers attacked the peace organizations later that year, they devoted ten sticks of dynamite to the Du Bois Clubs headquarters before destroying the New Left's Vietnam Day Committee building, injuring four students. The Justice Department still launched a prosecution of the Du Bois Clubs; it took the Supreme Court to save them from extinction.[31]

The FBI suspected Martin Luther King of being a communist. They had information based on their surveillance of New York attorney Stanley Levison, who had helped the communist party manage its finances in the 1950s. Levison had ceased his work with the party when he became a close adviser and friend of King's. But because of his association with King, Levison came under intense scrutiny. The theory was that courtesy of Levison the civil rights movement's main leader may have been Moscow's pawn. When in his famous speech in Riverside Church, New York, in April 1967 King demanded American withdrawal from the Vietnam War he became, in the eyes of establishment figures from President Johnson down, a danger to the American Republic.[32]

King did advance a socialist critique of American policy. He regarded the Vietnam War as colonialism and as injurious to American society. He denounced it in his Riverside Speech as an "enemy of the poor." For although it had been initially a boost to prosperity, the war was sapping the social policy budget and the economic strength of the nation.

President Johnson agreed that the war was squeezing the nation's antipoverty programs, but was so deeply mired in the conflict he did not dare to extricate America. By comparison, King was free to act. He steered the SCLC away from its work in the South and toward opposition to the war. Then in October 1967, he launched the SCLC's Poor People's Campaign. There was to be direct action. A non-violent army would dramatize the issue of poverty by camping in Washington and disrupting the life of the capital. King was still addressing the issue when he was assassinated in April 1968.

Like so many on the American left, King was discreet about his socialism. Not long before his death he talked to one antipoverty group about his "democratic socialism", but first asked them to turn off the recording equipment. He told C. L. R. James he agreed with the Trinidadian's social-ist views but could not express them "from the pulpit." He explained to Levison that he could not use the word "socialism" in public because Americans "respond so emotionally and irrationally to it." For these reasons of discretion, his democratic socialism was, in the words of historian Adam Fairclough, "couched in the language of the Social Gospel."[33]

The civil rights movement as represented by King was an essential part of the antiwar movement. Those who shared King's outlook saw a racial dimension to America's war against a non-white Vietnamese adversary. King's SCLC articulated a logic that inspired the rest of the New Left in a way that the older civil rights organizations did not. NAACP and National Urban League leaders refused to oppose the war. They did not want to alienate opinion and risk losing recent gains for the African American population.[34] King and his SCLC gave a less fearful lead. So did two, more recently established organizations. Formed in 1942, the Congress of Racial Equality (CORE) organized "freedom rides" in the South – black and white volunteers would sit next to each other on buses in defiance of the segrega-tion laws. Formed in 1960 in Raleigh, North Carolina but having consider-able support in the North, the Student Nonviolent Coordination Committee (SNCC) also engaged in direct actions – freedom rides, sit-ins and the 1963 March on Washington.

Tom Hayden, who would be the most prominent campus opponent of the Vietnam War, was schooled in civil rights tactics. His first wife Casey was a SNCC activist from Austin, Texas. In 1961 Hayden found himself on a SNCC-organized freedom ride in Albany, Georgia. The local police arrested him and deposited him in a fetid prison where only the cock-roaches crawled between the white and black cells. For him, it was a "rite of passage." As in the case of "the early Christians, the jails were the places where a new faith was fortified." Back at the University of Michigan and editor of the students' *Michigan Daily*, Hayden rejected the NSA, drafted the SDS's Port Huron manifesto, and served as the new organization's first president, 1962–3.[35]

Thereafter, Hayden's radical and antiwar activities were manifold. And although he left Ann Arbor and the *Michigan Daily* lost its edge, his legacy remained there. In the spring of 1965, the students in one graduate class on industrial relations divided their time between challenging the professor, a defender of Selig Perlman's neoconservative interpretation of labor, and planning further freedom rides. Recent arrests reminded them of the murder of three civil rights workers in Mississippi and that preyed on their minds, as did the Ku Klux Klan's murder of Detroit activist Viola Liuzzo in the aftermath of the Selma march. But so did a new problem, the escalation of the war in Indochina. The first US combat troops arrived in Vietnam on March 8, 1965. The Ann Arbor students moved seamlessly into helping to plan the nation's first teach-against the Vietnam War. It took place on March 24 and teach-ins spread like wildfire across the nation.[36]

Between then and the cease-fire in January 1973, the New Left was involved in tens of thousands of protests against the war, the majority of them direct-action in character. To list some of the more prominent events, there were protests in Washington in August 1965 involving Du Bois Clubs, Women Strike for Peace, the Student Peace Union and the Mississippi Freedom Democratic Party; nation-wide protests in 1966 and 1967 focused on physically preventing troop movements, especially near points of embarkation on the West Coast, and in the latter year one hundred thousand marched on the Pentagon; the occupation at Columbia University took place in 1968; the Moratorium demonstrations of 1969 were the largest in American history; a quarter of a million protestors converged on Washington in the following year; eighty thousand demonstrated in Washington in 1970 to protest the killing of four students at Kent State University in Ohio who had been demonstrating against the extension of the war to Cambodia.[37]

Questions can be asked about the efficacy of the New Left and its tactics. There was a strong reaction in the press and in politics against radical tactics and against student rebels. Campaigning in 1966 for the governorship of California, Ronald Reagan denounced the Berkeley protesters: "The preservation of free speech does not justify letting beatniks, and advocates of sexual orgies, drug usage and filthy speech disrupt the academic community and interfere with our universities' purpose."[38]

Another problem was the heterogeneity of the New Left and its tendency to feud with the Old Left and sometimes with black militants. To be sure, young followers liked the freedom to do their own thing. And yes, the diversity made the movement difficult to repress. But the movement could appear formless and directionless. In his memoir of the march on the Pentagon Norman Mailer, whether in admiration or dismay it is hard to say, described the New Left as "revolution by theater and without a script."[39]

The New Left program's diversity gave it a broad appeal, but it was in danger of being all things to all men, and of lacking the strength that would have derived from single-issue focus. The *San Diego Free Press*, an underground biweekly devoted to challenging the "tubes and rags of the

Establishment", declared its goal as the restoration of power to the people, meaning "Black Power, Chicano Power, Student Power, Hippy Power, GI Power, Worker Power, Rock Power, Theater Power, and even white middle class power." As well as being too broad for precision, student aims could shift disconcertingly in focus. One survey of 232 campuses in 1969 concluded that the war was the main concern for 25 percent of students, but racial matters were now back as the foremost issue for 69 percent.[40]

Finally, it must be remembered that the New Left was a small minority and could not have ended the war alone. Pressures for withdrawal came also from many quarters having little to do with the New Left. They ranged from disenchanted soldiers to non-leftist religious organizations.

In spite of these qualifications, it can be concluded that the New Left was the chief inspiration of the movement that opposed the war, and that the movement succeeded. Both the Johnson and the Nixon administrations kept extensive files on the protest movement, worried about it constantly, and responded to it in significant ways. Johnson ended his escalation of the war and decided not to seek a second term as president. Nixon ended the draft as he "Vietnamized" the conflict, and finally withdrew from the war.

Historians sympathetic to the protest movement credit it with having been effective in these ways. More conservative historians agree with the analysis. They argue that the nation's leaders could have faced down the critics and defeated the Vietnamese communists, but instead capitulated to the New Left. The notion that America's withdrawal from the Vietnam War was attributable to the protest against it has also attracted some criticism from historians. However, in terms of public perception, the military withdrawal was a triumph for domestic opponents of the war – it is one of the most publicly acknowledged achievements of the American left. That perception has colored the politics of American foreign policy ever since.[41]

Effective though it may have been in its opposition to the Vietnam War, the New Left did not sweep all before it in the 1960s. Take the case of second-wave feminism, the movement that looked beyond voting and property rights and sought to extend women's liberties in terms of careers, family politics, sexuality, and reproductive rights. In 1963 Betty Friedan issued a famous challenge in *The Feminine Mystique*. In this book, she attacked "women's retreat to the home" and the commercial "perpetuation of housewifery." With the formation under her leadership of the National Organization for Women (NOW) in 1966, the new feminism was under way. The spread of oral contraception infused a new credibility into women's aspirations that would have cheered the socialist feminists of an earlier age. But did it have anything to do with the New Left?[42]

Friedan had an Old Left pedigree. After Smith College and a year at Berkeley, she went to work for The Federated Press, a news agency originally set up by SPA members in 1919. Then between 1946 and 1952 she was a journalist for *UE News*, a publication of the United Electrical, Radio, and Machine Workers of America (UE). In 1949 the CIO accused UE of being communist-dominated, and expelled it. However, Friedan found its left orientation to be congenial, and in particular liked its militant support for women's rights (the UE had a substantial number of women members). In 1952, she authored a union pamphlet showing how corporations hired women cheaply and how this hurt workers of both sexes, making it essential to fight for wage equality. Friedan wrote a similar demand for women's rights in the workplace into the NOW platform which, through her instrumentality, had a left-wing provenance.[43]

But the story of the writing of *The Feminine Mystique* evokes a familiar theme. As the work was going through its editorial process, Friedan decided to drop the original draft's references to her own radical past. The words "socialist" and "socialism" do not occur in the text. In his study of *The Feminine Mystique*, Daniel Horowitz notes that Friedan was indebted to Karl Marx and his feminist collaborator Friedrich Engels. She retained her sympathy for the left, and in the 1970s fought for the right of socialists to join NOW. But in *The Feminine Mystique* she "minimized her debt to Marx even as she relied on him," an action Horowitz thinks was a reaction to the Cold War. Another historian agrees "Friedan made a choice to be heard, not to be 'Red-baited'." The omission from *Mystique* of any reference to Marx or Engels partly reflects the breadth of Friedan's reading and her emphasis on psychological insights. At the same time, it is reasonable to conclude that her avoidance of left-wing terminology was tactical – she wanted to maximize the impact of her critique.[44]

Friedan's de-emphasis of Marxism was consistent with the approach of New Left intellectuals, but she was not one of them. There was a behavioral reason why Friedan and the new feminists steered away from the New Left. Women played a significant role in the antiwar movement and would have liked to do more, but they found that male chauvinism existed on the left just as elsewhere. Men insisted on chairing antiwar committee meetings. They expected women to prepare the food and wash the dishes. Tom Hayden habitually handed his dirty washing to the nearest woman. Even as SDS declared for women's liberation in 1967, its publication *New Left*

Notes published an infantilizing cartoon depicting a libber as a little girl in a fetching polka-dot minidress. There were complaints about an expectation that women could best serve the cause from a prone position; even the feisty Joan Baez posed with her sisters for an antidraft poster reading Girls Say Yes to Boys Who Say No.[45]

To place all that in context, the 1960s was a decade when women marched backwards even as they vowed to move forward. They regressed in the rest of society, not just in the New Left. Flying in the face of Betty Friedan's brave words, the number of women in Congress and the foreign service declined. The antiwar movement's shortage of New Men hardly set it apart from the rest of society and did not make it responsible for the nation's glass ceiling.

Furthermore, the New Left experience did contribute to feminist consciousness. The historian Sara Evans suggested that women's liberation activists learned how to be radical in the civil rights and New Left movements before striking out on their own in disgust at male chauvinism.[46]

Similar questions can be asked of another of the decade's great social movements, the struggle of the Mexican American farm worker. The seasonal fruit and vegetable pickers of California were largely from Mexico or the descendents of Mexicans. Though not the worst paid laborers in America, they were below the $3,000 poverty line, with vineyard workers receiving an estimated $2,000 to $2,300 a year. They needed help. The AFL-CIO unions took little interest in them. It was time for someone else to step in.

César Chávez knew all about poverty. Like his father and his Mexican immigrant grandfather he had harvested for small gains in sweltering heat. He had eight children to support. In 1962, Chávez organized the United Farm Workers (UFW). Not since the days of the IWW had there been such a serious effort to organize those who toiled on the land.[47]

In 1965, Filipino workers went on strike in the vineyards of Delano, California, a city known for its production of table grapes. The UFW stepped in to unify the Filipino and Hispanic pickers and to run the action, which continued for five years. It yielded ultimate victory, and reshaped collective bargaining in West Coast agriculture. Like the IWW and the antiwar movement, Chávez employed both work stoppages and other forms of direct action. Chávez went on a series of hunger strikes modeled on Gandhian passive resistance, and the UFW organized national grape and lettuce boycotts.

His enemies called him a Trotskyite and a communist, but Chávez was neither of these things. By seizing the initiative from the AFL-CIO, he implicitly shared the New Left's criticism of the organized labor establishment. There was a further New Left bond in that the grape boycott was militantly observed and publicized on campus. When UFW militants stood in the way of trucks and obstructed grape shipments to the GIs in Vietnam, that struck another chord with the student left. But the charismatic Chavez lived by his own rulebook. Stealing a march on the masculine-manqué New Left, he allowed the union's vice president Dolores Huerta a major negotiating role. Another difference: the movement he inspired was more nationalistic than anything in the New Left canon. A reflection of Mexican-American racial pride, in his day *Chicano* became a proud label instead of a term of abuse. Huerta's slogan *si se pueda* did pass into English language politics as "yes we can", but the story of *La Causa* forms a distinctively Hispanic-Catholic chapter in the history of the left.[48]

Turning to government policy, the New Left not only contributed to the ending of the Vietnam War and inspired the war on poverty, but also had cause to applaud other initiatives that were leftist in character. However, it did not in the main contribute to them directly. Indeed, a number of these initiatives ran on from a previous page in reform history, the New Deal, and from the page before that, the program of the SPA. Politicians did not acknowledge those socialist origins because it would have been impolitic to do so, and also because memories of the roots were fading. What reinforced the amnesia was the fact that the political right did not supply its usual vigorous reminder. Scare mongering was now distinctly out of fashion and frowned upon. The right was muted in its attack on what in other times it would have denounced as socialist policies.

Ventures in public ownership continued. The Communications Satellite Act of 1962 resulted in the formation of a publicly traded company, the COMSAT Corporation. It was run on the lines of a private company, but was controlled and partly owned by the government. It resulted in the launch of the first Early Bird communications satellite in 1965, the beginning of a major expansion in global communications.

Johnson's administration applied similar principles to the home mortgage industry. In 1968, the New Deal's Federal Home Mortgage Association, or Fannie Mae, became a private shareholder-owned corporation. However, the government kept its foot inside the mortgage business door. Wholly owned by the public, the National Mortgage Association (Ginnie Mae) in the same year undertook responsibility for guaranteeing mortgage loans for affordable housing. In 1970, the Nixon administration set up the Federal

Home Loan Mortgage Corporation (Freddie Mac) to compete with Fannie Mae. As ever, Washington politicians wanted to convey their support for competition and private enterprise; as usual, they found an element of public involvement was necessary to the delivery of social goals such as modestly priced housing.[49]

In 1965, Congress approved the addition of Medicare and Medicaid to the provisions of the 1935 Social Security Act. It was a victory against formidable opposition from those who worried about the costs, from southern segregationists who saw the welfare state as an interracial plot, and from the AMA. Medicare used additional Social Security taxes and diverted money from retirement payments to help the over-sixty-fives pay physicians' and hospital expenses. Medicaid rationalized existing insurance schemes and helped the less affluent with their medical expenses. In future years the schemes ran into opposition on ideological and financial grounds. For a while, though, they promised to realize a prime dream of the World War I era socialists – as well as, in this case, the aspirations of New Left apostle Michael Harrington.[50]

The Nixon administration proclaimed its devotion to a devolutionary "New Federalism", but in practice the president believed in federal power and enhanced it. As one token of this, between 1969 and 1972 the number of White House employees rose from 570 to six thousand. Nixon rolled out policy proposals that were consistent with the idea of a welfare state. His Family Assistance Plan was an attempt to provide a four-person family with a guaranteed minimum income; it would apply the negative income tax principle advocated by Milton Friedman and applauded by J. K. Galbraith. The president hoped to wind down the Vietnam War providing a peace dividend that would help finance the policy, but Daniel Moynihan (now advising the Republicans on antipoverty) warned that with many demands on the federal budget "the peace dividend tends to become evanescent like the morning clouds around San Clemente," Nixon's Western White House in California. The measure foundered in Congress in 1970.[51]

Nixon's National Health Insurance Partnership proposal endured a similar fate the following year, jointly speared by critics who thought it was too cautious, and the AMA, which thought it went too far. In his second term, the president came up with a new proposal. The Comprehensive Health Insurance Plan required all employers to provide health insurance coverage for their employees; the government would step in to help those not covered under the provision; the principles of private practice, patients' freedom to choose physicians, and competition (leading to lower costs) would be protected; Health Maintenance Organizations were to be the delivery vehicles for physician and hospital care. Such care would be based on pre-payment and would build on the experience of private insurance conglomerates Blue Cross (dating from 1929 and focusing on hospital services) and Blue Shield (1939, physicians' services).[52]

Congress refused to fund the project. According to Paul Starr's Pulitzer Prize winning study *The Social Transformation of American Medicine* (1982), this was because the AMA poured money into the opposition, and because of a Cold War fear of anything that smacked of communism. A Canadian-born reviewer of Starr's book argued that Nixon's scheme failed because the United States lacked the socialist tradition of the European countries that had achieved national health services. However, one needs to look beyond that routine argument. For in America, a powerful left tradition helped to make up for the lack of electable socialist parties.[53]

The Nixon blueprint failed for the reason Starr suggested, and there were other causes. One is that the president was losing authority on account of the Watergate scandal that would force his resignation in 1974. Another reason for Nixon's failure was lack of money. Just as World War I had stolen the funds needed to finance Meyer London's insurance proposal of 1916, so the Vietnam War had created budgetary and inflationary pressures that militated against reform. War expenditure compounded the effect of the insistence, by every administration not just Nixon's, that health care costs could only be kept down through competition. They dared not take the approach of keeping costs down by eliminating private profit.

In spite of legislative setbacks, social spending increased in the Nixon years. In 1972, his administration indexed social security payments, meaning they would rise with inflation. In 1970, federal spending on social welfare amounted to 40 percent of government outlay. By 1980, it was 53 percent.[54]

The Nixon administration responded to the environmentalist movement. An earlier Republican president with left-wing credentials, Theodore Roosevelt, had been the movement's political pioneer. In more recent times, the left typically pressed the cause. Renewed agitation was occurring. Linus Pauling, a scientist who had won Nobel Prizes in two different fields and had run foul of the FBI because of his socialist and antiwar beliefs, published a jeremiad in 1958 warning of the human and environmental effects of nuclear war. In 1962, Rachel Carson brought out her best-selling book *Silent Spring*, pointing to the effects of chemical fertilizers on songbirds and ultimately humans, and achieving a ban on the use of DDT.

Corporate America was coming under steady attack, with accusations of war profiteering, and with the publication in 1965 of Ralph Nader's *Unsafe at Any Speed*, an exposé of the poor safety record of the nation's automobile industry. The time was ripe for renewed attacks on profiteering despoilers of the wilderness and its wild life. Greenpeace came into existence in 1971 and its campaigns in defense of hunted species like whales and seals hit the headlines. Left wing, "radical environmentalism" took off in the 1970s.[55]

In 1970, the Nixon administration established the Environmental Protection Agency. In the same year the president signed into law the Clean Air Act, and endorsed the "Earth Day" environmental teach-in promoted by Senator Gaylord Nelson (D-WI). According to his critics, Nixon paid only lip service to the environmentalist cause. He did put jobs and profits first, and vetoed some attempts to enforce pure water regulations. He was heard to remark that going back to nature would mean living "like a bunch of damned animals . . . like when the Indians were here." But through his public endorsement of environmentalism, President Nixon did confer recognition and respectability on a left cause.[56]

So a number of left-style achievements occurred in the years 1960–73. The New Left could not claim all of the credit. However, the New Left did administer some sharp shocks to the system, such as its calls for direct action and open government. It helped to alert America to the inequality and poverty still in its midst, and won widespread credence for its claim to have stopped a war. By the time the United States withdrew from Vietnam, the war had so damaged the economy that America could not afford programs to end poverty and deliver racial equality. But the New Left had at least delivered a wake-up call on the deleterious consequences of ill-considered wars.

Chapter 9

THE NEWER LEFT

Gay Street has an attractive mix of Federal style and Greek Revival cornices. Constructed between 1826 and 1860, it originally housed the servants of the rich in nearby Washington Square. In a later age, its denizens were black musicians. Today, its bohemian ambience has succumbed to a reputation for money laundering.

Reach the end of the street going north and you arrive at the site of the Oscar Wilde Memorial Bookshop. Before it closed down in 2009, the store flew the rainbow flag of gay liberation – from 1967, its proprietors sold lesbian, gay, bisexual and transsexual (LGBT) literature. This is on Christopher Street, the oldest thoroughfare in West Greenwich Village. Turn left along Christopher, and after a few paces you arrive in Sheridan Square. At this spot, local residents rescued a number of freed slaves from potential lynching during the antidraft riots of 1863. The square relates to the Civil War in another way, too – it contains a larger-than-life bronze statue of Philip A. Sheridan, commanding general of a victorious Union engagement in the Shenandoah Valley in 1864. Tourist buses cruising down Seventh Avenue pause at its intersection with Christopher Street. Guides prompt, heads turn, and people gaze at Sheridan Square.

But the bus riders are not just thinking of long-ago events in West Virginia. Their attention focuses also on the square's four gay liberation statues, two men, two women, replicating a Palo Alto sculpture by George Segal – and on the story of a more recent eruption of violence in the early hours of June 28, 1969. It was the riot that marked the start of the modern phase of the LGBT revolution.

The riot centered on Stonewall Inn. Located on the north side of the square, this two-bar establishment was popular mainly with gay men. The Inn's Mob owner, Fat Tony, went in for dinginess and poor hygiene. But he served his purpose for he had hitherto escaped antigay persecution by paying off the police.

The trigger that set things off is uncertain. It may have been the man-handling of a lesbian in a patrol car following a rare swoop on the bar. It may have been the policeman who prodded Sylvia Rivera with his nightstick, provoking the transgender woman to throw a bottle in retaliation. According to one rather discredited "urban myth", the whole affair was an emotional response to news of the death of gay icon Judy Garland. Whatever the provocation, the events were dramatic, with the police barricading themselves inside the bar they had been trying to raid, and a firebomb thrown at the establishment.

Rioting broke out repeatedly over the next five days. According to Sherry Wolf, a surrealist painter engaged in lesbian and socialist campaigns, "organized leftists" took a hand in events. Crowds of up to two thousand chanted "Gay Power!" as they threw stones and bottles. Police raids on gay bars were commonplace, but the novel feature this time was the resistance to their incursion. So difficult was the situation that the New York Police Department (NYPD) sent in a unit originally trained to handle anti-Vietnam War riots. No less a figure than Deputy Inspector Seymour Pine, a hero of World War II's Battle of the Bulge, was in command. But even NYPD's elite found it impossible to establish control over the Christopher Street area.[1]

Stonewall did not turn America into an LGBT love-in overnight. Take, for example, the Nixon administration's attitude toward sexual diversity. In those days, conservatives of a certain type masked their objections to LGBT activities by leveling charges of obscenity and pornography. President Johnson had set up a commission to investigate the issue. The Nixon administration learned that this commission was about to recommend a more liberal approach. Nixon's staff looked into the matter. Pat Buchanan recommended sacking liberal members of the commission. However, Bud Krogh's recommendation prevailed. Let the commission submit its report, he said in a June 1970 memorandum, but hold up "its product at a distance with thumb and forefinger." The "left press" would create a fuss but "we have buried other commissions with no problem" and it would be an opportunity to "hammer home in strong moral tones." The idea was to reach out to a conjectural moral majority by beating the conformist drum.[2]

The stand at Stonewall nevertheless brought the gay rights issue to the attention of mainstream Americans for the first time. In the wake of the affair, the gender liberation movement gained momentum. People ranging from black lesbians to cross dressers found themselves in the grip of militancy. Gay scenes flourished all over America. Gay bars operated openly and offered a choice of scenarios. "Ramood", one of eighteen gay bars in Dallas, Texas, reminded potential customers that drag was legal in that city. In Fort Worth, drag was illegal. However, single-sex dancing was OK for both men and women and there was a choice of ambience – the "Rawhide" placed its accent on beer to the accompaniment of country and western music. In Oakland, California, the Women's Press Collective republished classics of lesbian literature, while in Minneapolis, Minnesota, Polly Kellogg worked on an anthology to help "teachers raise the lesbian and gay issue in all sorts of classroom settings." The genie was well and truly out of the bottle.[3]

Gay campaigners kept alive the direct action tradition of the American left. One example was the AIDS Coalition to Unleash Power (ACT UP) whose anticorporate logo was a fuchsia triangle bearing the slogan "Silence = Death." In 1987, ACT UP activists occupied the Wall Street Stock Exchange demanding a reduction in the price of anti-AIDS medication. They unfurled a banner urging "sell Wellcome", and the Wellcome firm did reduce the price of its AZT drug by 20 percent.

Political victories occurred. In 1977, Harvey Milk won election as city supervisor in San Francisco, the first explicitly gay candidate to win public office. His assassination soon thereafter by a defeated right-wing candidate made Milk a martyr figure in gay and left politics. Others followed his political lead, for example the redoubtable Barney Frank (D-MA), who came out publicly in 1987. First elected to the House in 1981, Frank became a notable left-wing legislator and was chairman of the Financial Services Committee at the time of President Obama's early reconstruction of the American economy. By the time Frank retired in 2013, six openly gay or bisexual colleagues had joined him as Representatives, while in the Senate Tammy Baldwin (D-WI) had declared herself a lesbian.[4]

Non-gay politicians began to get the message. The Democratic Party adopted a gay rights plank in 1980, and with the return of a Democrat to the White House in 1993, policy began to change. The FBI and CIA had always banned gays from employment on the ground that they could be blackmailed into being traitors, something that never actually happened. In 1993 Attorney General Janet Reno lifted the FBI ban. In 1995, President Clinton issued an executive order ending the CIA proscription, and soon a group of employees organized the Agency Network of Gay and Lesbian Employees (ANGLE). America was in the forefront in such matters. The

Stonewall protest culminated in liberation initiatives that would affect millions of people right across the world.

Two questions can be asked about the Stonewall revolution. The first is that old historical chestnut, how new was it – was it really a novel manifestation of assertive gaydom? Recent American history was dotted with well-known homosexual personalities. Aaron Copland, Tennessee Williams, F. O. Matthiessen and Countee Cullen were examples from the creative arena, and one critic has asserted "gay activists created much of modern American culture." Major cities had areas where homosexuals had long felt at home. The Castro area of San Francisco began its transformation from Irish working class to LGBT in World War II, and in the same period New York City experienced (a) hundreds of arrests for transgressions against various antihomosexual statutes and (b) a measure of restraint from its police, who were beginning to recognize informally a right to assert sexual identities that did not conform to the then conventional pattern.[5]

The second question is, was Stonewall a manifestation of leftism? Todd Gitlin, whose SDS is sometimes seen as synonymous with the New Left, sees the episode as New Left-inspired, and it was certainly a protest within the direct action tradition. The chanting of the word "Gay Power" was consistent with New Left chants like "Student Power" and "Black Power." However, the link between gay rights and left politics goes back earlier than this. And it contains an element of ambivalence.[6]

Modern political advocacy of the idea that homosexuality was not an unhealthy form of deviance but, rather, a variant of gender identity, went back to the Social Democratic Party (SDP) in Germany. In 1898 August Bebel, a socialist member of the Reichstag, proposed the decriminalization of homosexual acts. SDP leaders Karl Kautsky and Eduard Bernstein upheld the idea and from other countries Emile Zola, Leo Tolstoy and Sigmund Freud supported the campaign. There were stirrings of gay liberation in Russia before 1917, and the Bolsheviks at first supported liberalization. The Nazis' persecution and elimination of homosexuals further encouraged left-wingers in their homophile advocacy.

However, there is another side to the story. Under Stalin the Soviet Union changed its stance and a law of 1933 prescribed a sentence of five years' hard labor for the crime of homosexual sex. Back in America, the socialist W. E. B. Du Bois welcomed his daughter's marriage to Augustus Granville Dill and tolerated the fresh chrysanthemums ever present in his son-in-law's button hole – until he realized Dill was gay, whereupon he fired him from his post with the NAACP's *Crisis* magazine. The gender conservatism of the US communist party would be one more reason why people resigned from it after World War II.[7]

Yet it was a variable picture, and some American radicals associated with communism were militantly pro-gay. Emma Goldman was an early upholder of homosexual rights. The National Union of Marine Cooks and Stewards, expelled from the CIO in 1950 on the ground that it was communist dominated, had the reputation of being "one-half black, one-half gay, and one-half red." And in 1951, a group of Los Angeles former communists met in 1951 to form the pro-gay rights Mattachine Society.[8]

Two years later, some disaffected Mattachine members founded the magazine *ONE*. They resisted an obscenity prosecution and won their case in the Supreme Court in 1958. In some ways, however, the Mattachines subsided into respectability. They downplayed their communist origins in order to survive McCarthyism and, in the 1960s, the Washington, DC incarnation of the Society adopted conservative dress codes on the picket line. Like the feminist movement in the later nineteenth century, the respectability-seeking homophile movement sometimes wavered in its radicalism and in its cooperation with allies on the left. For its part, however, the democratic left remained steadfast in its support of the gender agenda. The largest socialist party, the Democratic Socialists of America, gave its support, as did left newspapers like the [US] *Guardian* and quarterlies like *Jump Cut*. Such support was a distinctive feature of gender politics until – in a triumph for gay rights and the left – the major parties began to steal the gay liberation plank.[9]

The LGBT movement can in some ways be related to the Old and New Lefts. However, it is more helpful to see it as a significant ingredient in what might be called the Newer Left. The Newer Left was a diversification beyond the goals of socialism, opposition to the Vietnam War, antipoverty and civil rights. Adherents of the Newer Left still supported most of the tenets of the older creeds, but with many Old Left reforms already in place as a result of past efforts, they were moving on.

The new, diversifying movement lacked a binding philosophy to guide its defense against the conservative tirade. However, it did have some discernible characteristics. For one thing, the Newer Left differed from the 1920s and 1930s left which had defined American society in a cohesively inclusive manner. The post-1945 right had usurped the nation-building approach of the pre-War left. Neoconservatives of the 1950s offered an image of one nation, undivided by class or race, and invincible in the face of communism. America the free nation was at the same time exceptional and a model for all to follow – nation building became an insistent ortho-doxy in American foreign policy.[10]

Meanwhile, the left had gone off the idea. The fascists and Nazis had shown only too graphically what nationalism could lead to. National iden-tity was an uncomfortably close cousin to nationalism and its excesses. Rejecting the underlying assumptions of conservative nation builders, socialists like Louis Adamic and contributors to his journal *Common Ground* from the early 1940s argued, instead, for a more tolerant cultural pluralism. Racial and ethnic diversity were to be cherished. The nation of immigrants was a salad bowl, not a melting pot.

The Newer Left went a step further and demanded respect not just for ethnic/racial identities but also for gender identities. Its "multiculturalism" was a step away from both nationalism and the Marxist idea that homoge-nous class consciousness should be the engine for change. Multiculturalism came to be associated with another catch phrase, political correctness. Those who, say, frowned on the spread of the Spanish language or on gay couples who wanted to adopt children were not "politically correct." Though often used ironically, the term and its popular abbreviation "PC" had their origins in the doctrinal intolerance of Mao Zedong and his Chinese communist party. It was literally a red rag to the right in American politics.[11]

By the 1970s, the time was propitious for the flowering of a "Newer Left." The Great Fear of the 1950s had helped to kill off the Old Left. Having delivered its sting, the McCarthyite bee died, facilitating the emer-gence of the New Left. This in turn lost its momentum when US withdrawal from Vietnam stripped it of its main mission. The way was thus open for further evolution.

One pointer to change had been the emergence of the "counterculture" of the late 1960s. Its adherents – insofar as one can adhere to an anar-chistic philosophy – rejected homogenizing social norms and in a variety of ways "dropped out." An estimated three million Americans rebelled through sex, drugs and rock 'n roll, by dressing and (non)grooming in a far-out manner, or by living out of rucksacks and traveling to Marrakech. Antiestablishmentarianism was rampant.[12]

In some of its manifestations, the counterculture was a liability to the left. For example, some of its adherents talked of "liberating" items belong-ing to those who possessed too much. It was an old idea. Back in 1840, the French anarchist Proudhon had announced, "property is theft." Roll forward to the late twentieth century when, in the frontispiece of a book furthering his brand name, the TV-fictional Bart Simpson quipped, "If you

. . . actually paid for this merchandise . . . . Welcome to Suckerville, man."
In practice, the purportedly antiproperty philosophy could degenerate into
flippant and conscienceless stealing not just from the rich, but also from
just about anyone right down to the humble hot dog vendor. Latter-day
Proudhonism could mirror the acquisitiveness it purportedly condemned.[13]

The Newer Left had more to offer and had arrived to stay, yet it was
frustratingly difficult to pin down. Indeed, some veterans of the left have
expressed concern about the lack of cohesiveness and communal spirit
in the multicultural movement. It came to be associated with defense
of science against Intelligent Design, opposition to compulsory school
prayers, agitation over the Abu Ghraib torture scandal and a host of other
issues that could be knit together only loosely, if at all. As with left-wing
movements in the past, there were significant fissures. For example, if the
right to abortion was a left-wing demand, there was also a Christian Left
that was pro-life. The Newer Left was more coherent than "liberalism" or
"progressivism", but still defied neat definition.[14]

The right attempted to impose its own brand of coherence on what it
depicted as a newly menacing left. Writing in the 1990s, the historian
Gertrude Himmelfarb saw a triumph of the left in the "culture wars."
She believed that her generation had lived through "a revolution in the
manners, morals, and mores of society." The new divisions in America had
little to do with the Old Left's social constructions: ". . . there is more in
common between two church-going families one of which is working class,
than between two working-class families only one of which is church-
going." As her observation indicates, the right was attempting to reclaim
Christianity as its own.[15]

The Newer Left neither destroyed the agendas of the Old Left nor
quashed the radicalism and commitment of New Left veterans, many of
whom continued to be active in radical causes. Still less did it signal the
disappearance of socialist-style government policies. An outline of developments until the millennium's end indicates, instead, that different types
of leftist activities continued side by side. The story is one of mixed strands,
and mixed fortunes.

The communist party underwent a slight revival in the 1970s, and,
although still constrained by ideological loyalties, its newspaper the *Daily
World* showed signs of vitality in the cultural commentaries that appeared
on its Page 8. Here as in few other places, one could learn that movie
director Francis Ford Coppola of *Godfather* fame was an avid supporter
of the Cuban revolution. Here, journalist Ronald Tyson revealed that the

all-white-cast musical-movie "Grease" starring John Travolta and Olivia Newton John was an example of "Blaxploitation" and an effort to "bring the politics of the 1950s back from the grave."[16]

Meanwhile radical environmentalism served as a reminder that the left had moved on. It gathered pace as the decade went by, with the Clamshell Alliance forming in 1976 to protest the plan to build one thousand more nuclear power stations by the century's end. A radioactive spillage from the Three Mile Island Generating Station near Harrisburg, Pennsylvania, in 1979 boosted support for the movement. Ralph Nader spoke to a protest meeting of two hundred thousand people in New York City, demonstrations continued into the next decade, and the nuclear industry was obliged to adopt more stringent safety measures. Membership in major environmental reform movements tripled to 6.5 million by 1990.[17]

The politics of identity spread into many corners of life in the 1970s. The GI journal *Your Military Left* demanded equality for women in the Army. Sexual liberation spawned a black lesbian movement. The American Indian Movement engaged in dramatic confrontations with the federal authorities. At the end of the decade, the Palestinian-American Columbia University professor Edward Said published his mold-shattering book, *Orientalism*, in which he argued that western perceptions of the Orient and the policies that stemmed from those perceptions were based on prejudice. Blinkered by the racial clichés inherent in their own culture, Said's Western "Orientalists" failed to understand Arab and Islamic identities. Through Said on this occasion, the left found itself in a position to offer yet another thoughtful and potentially influential critique of foreign policy just at a time when events in Israel, Iran and Afghanistan were becoming seriously problematic.[18]

Government actions in the 1970s were a mixed bag from the left point of view. One of the more promising developments was the move toward open government. First signed into law in 1966, the Freedom of Information Act acquired significance with amendments in the 1970s. The Government in the Sunshine Act of 1976 opened up the affairs of federal agencies to public scrutiny. In a process that dominated the politics of the mid-1970s, committees of inquiry in the House and the Senate investigated secret branches of government like the FBI and CIA.

These developments modified the Cold War tendency to tolerate an unusual degree of secrecy in the interest of national security. They sprang in part from popular disgust with President Nixon's attempt to cover up his administration's complicity in the Watergate affair. But the developments were also a response to the New Left's demands for greater openness, whether on campus or over foreign policy. The issue became more acute for the left when congressional inquiries showed how the FBI had in the 1960s spied on and harassed left wing and civil rights movements, how the CIA had tried to assassinate Cuba's communist-leaning leader Fidel Castro, and how the CIA had also conspired to overthrow democratically elected socialist governments in Iran, Guatemala, Guyana and Chile.

In vain did CIA leaders protest that they were open-minded and had in the past implemented an Opening to the Left policy. From now on, the agency would be an icon of the right at home, matching the common perception of it abroad. Conservative objections to the presence of Ron Dellums on the House investigating committee showed how the battle lines were drawn. When both the House and the Senate established permanent intelligence oversight committees, it was a victory for the left.[19]

Big Government may not be the left's most cherished goal, indeed the anarchist left regards it with abhorrence, but it offended the right and was on the march in the 1970s. The federal government spent 34 percent of GNP compared with 7 percent at the start of the century. The number of pages in the *Code of Federal Regulations* increased by eight thousand in the first three years of the decade – from 64,105 to 72,200. Presidents Gerry Ford, Jimmy Carter and Ronald Reagan all expressed concern and vowed to halt the expansion.[20]

By the end of the decade, federally created businesses occupied, in the words of one expert, "key spots in the US economy." In 1970, a railroad system established by the government, Amtrak, joined TVA, Fannie Mae and the rest. Modeled on the satellite communications facilitator COMSAT, Amtrak was an effort to introduce economic rationality to a crumbling nationwide system, and to end what one congressional committee described as the saga of "broken seats, broken beds, wet carpets, clogged toilets and leaks in sinks and ceilings." In 1974, Conrail followed, with the object of saving some bankrupt railroads on the northeast-midwest axis.[21]

Amtrak and Conrail were never fully funded but were nevertheless immediate and long-term successes. Unconvinced, conservatives portrayed them as challenges to the capitalist system. Signing an Amtrak/Conrail continuation bill in October 1975, President Ford said he did so only with reluctance. He and his team decreed that publicly owned enterprises would have to make profits so as not to undermine the private sector; they insistently rejected a foreign-style "nationalized system." Senator Frank Church (D-ID), a presidential aspirant who had chaired the Senate intelligence inquiry, complained that Amtrak was politically shackled from the beginning, denying America the truly national network it should have enjoyed.[22]

Conservatives radically disagreed with Senator Church's vision. In future years there would be vigorous and successful campaigns for the privatization of profitable sections of the railroad industry, partly to help individual private businesses, partly to sabotage a left-style triumph. It was a debate that would never die. In the presidential campaign of 2012, the Republican candidate Mitt Romney promised to cut Amtrak's federal subsidy. The *New York Times*'s editorial rejoinder, "That is no way to run a railroad", summed up the contrary view that there was a place for public enterprise in the life of the nation.[23]

The campaign for health reform in the Carter administration (1977–81) faltered. Congressman Dellums re-enacted the pioneering effort of his socialist forbear Meyer London when he introduced a Health Rights and Community Health Services bill. It went beyond national insurance and provided for a publicly owned and controlled health sector controlled by local communities. Medical journalist Peter Steinfels noted that this proposal had the effect of conferring respectability on a more modest bill being advanced by Senator Edward Kennedy (D-MA). There was popular support for such reform, and the outlook at first seemed bright. According to Carter's health adviser Peter Bourne, the AMA was less opposed to reform that in previous years, partly because physicians were making handsome incomes from the federal programs set up in the Johnson era.[24]

But in an address to medical students, the president noted, "we have failed so completely to control medical costs that only 38 percent of Medicare expenses are now being met." An inflation crisis prompted by oil shortages and in the case of drugs by the pharmaceutical industry's profiteering persuaded Carter to steer a cautious course. He aimed to conserve the value of Medicare and Medicaid by restricting costs. The limited nature of Carter's proposal was too much for the expansionists to bear. Kennedy and his supporters scuppered the Carter plan because it fell short of their ambitions. Health reform remained what Steinfels labeled "a brightly wrapped parcel marked, 'Do not open until next election – or the one after that'."[25]

The stuttering social reform performance of the Carter presidency heralded policies of retrenchment and reaction under his successor in the White House, Ronald Reagan. The Republican president's "New Federalism" called for a reduced role for federal government. In his second State of the Union address in 1982, he declared, "Those who still advocate far removed federal solutions are dinosaurs." After an initial surge in the federal budget caused by bigger military expenditure aimed at the communist adversary, Washington's expenditure as a percentage of GDP declined from a peak of 23.5 in 1983 to 18.2 by the century's end.[26]

The decade of the 1980s was mainly one of reverses for the American left. The poor got poorer. Men with four years of high school education or less suffered a fall in real income of 21 percent. Median white families at the start of the decade were already ten times wealthier than their non-white counterparts, and the gap doubled by 1990. The gulf between rich and poor reached its widest since 1929. The Reagan administration led an assault on food stamps, disability insurance and unemployment insurance.[27]

Though opposed to the growth of federal government at home, Reagan used his federal executive powers to the utmost to fight communism and democratic socialism abroad. Central America became a battleground where he hoped to reverse the Vietnam War's legacy of defeat. In Nicaragua, the left-dominated Sandinista movement had overthrown the Somoza dictatorship in 1979, and in neighboring El Salvador there was Catholic/left resistance to an oppressive regime. The Reagan administration declared that the Nicaraguan socialists were infiltrating El Salvador and threatening to roll a red carpet over Latin America. On this ground, it authorized the CIA to support the Contra movement whose aim was to overthrow the Sandinista government.

Circumventing congressional oversight committees and thus spurning the open government reforms of the 1970s, the Reagan administration helped by the Israeli government secretly supplied the Islamist regime in Iran with weapons to fight against its neighbor, Iraq, in return for an Iranian secret conduit of weaponry to the Contras. Compounding this error of judgment on the threats facing America, the US administration also armed Islamic fundamentalists who were engaged in overthrowing the communist regime in Afghanistan. In 1984, the CIA mined the harbors of Nicaragua, an action that distanced Reagan's America from the US tradition of respect for the rule of law in foreign relations – the international court in The Hague confirmed the illegality of the move. Reagan's America both shrank from the social democratic policies that had found favor in most other parts of the world, and embarked on an extra-legal unilateralist course in foreign policy.

Reagan's Central American policy failed, for the Sandinistas did not lose power until 1990, and then it was as a result of a general election, not undercover dirty tricks. Was this an achievement for the American left? Reagan's opponents did ensure that the Iran-Contra Affair became a national scandal, and perhaps inhibited more extreme measures against Nicaragua. These opponents included the Committee in Solidarity with the People of El Salvador (CISPES). *Human Events* described CISPES as a "client" of the "far-left." Reagan's unleashed FBI broke into a church in Cambridge, Massachusetts, and stole the membership list of a CISPES-associated Christian organization, Sanctuary for Central American Refugees. It spied on CISPES sympathizers in the United Automobile Workers and the Southern Christian Leadership Conference. The words of its critics and the actions of its persecutors marked out CISPES as an instrument of the left that had sufficient impact to worry the authorities, though it should be noted that it worked not just with socialists, but also with a broad spectrum of Christians, labor unions, peasants' organizations, and women's groups.[28]

As this suggests, it was not just left groups that inhibited Reagan's Central American policy. Disillusioned CIA officers exposed as fiction the claim that Nicaragua was trying to undermine the El Salvador government. Barry Goldwater (R-AZ), who chaired the Senate Intelligence Committee, offered a stinging conservative critique of the administration's disregard of democratic procedure. President Reagan later lamented that public opinion was against him on Nicaragua – people remembered the problems Vietnam had caused, and "few cared enough about the Communist penetration of the Americas." All this indicates that the domestic left was less a solitary sledgehammer aimed at foreign policy than a ginger group that played a part in the greater whole.[29]

The left was on the back foot in the 1980s, but it did display signs of continuing vitality. At the start of the decade, Warren Beattie won an Oscar for his direction of *Reds*. The movie was about the life of John Reed, an American socialist who had written a sympathetic eyewitness account of the Russian Revolution, and it showed nostalgic scenes of the IWW in action. Meantime Michael Harrington's Democratic Socialists of America publicized left-wing issues and held educational meetings attended by dozens of members of Congress – and by Jesse Jackson, a Baptist minister and civil rights activist who was an aspirant for the Democratic Party's presidential nomination in 1984 and 1988. Congressman Harold Washington was elected to be the first black mayor of Chicago (1984–7). Like his fellow African Americans Coleman Young and Gus Newport, mayors of Detroit and Berkeley respectively, Washington had longstanding connections with the communist party. He had attended Chicago's multi-racial Roosevelt University, and had there learned his economics in a department headed by the socialist Walter Weisskopf. One young politician who took inspiration from Washington was Barack Obama.[30]

For the gay liberation strand of the Newer Left, the outlook at first seemed unpromising. Reagan had arrived in the White House surfing on a wave of conservative moral expectations. In the past he had bent the knee to homophobic pressures, firing gay members of his gubernatorial staff in California. He had difficulties with his gay son, Ron. His administration left untouched a legislative framework that ignored gay rights and it did nothing to combat the AIDS epidemic sweeping the nation.[31]

But people kept coming out all over the place anyway. Public support for the legalization of homosexual sex between consenting adults rose from 43 percent in 1977 to 59 percent in 2007. Even the president was not immune to the currents of change. In 1984 there occurred the first known case of a gay couple spending the night together in the White House – the Reagans' interior decorator Ted Graber had brought along his partner to help celebrate Nancy Reagan's sixtieth birthday. One Washington journalist concluded that The Gipper was a "closet tolerant."[32]

The end of the Cold War in 1989 was another opportunity for the re-evaluation of old attitudes. The arms race ceased to be such a major factor in US-Russian relations, and communism collapsed behind Europe's Iron Curtain. According to one theory, the discrediting of collectivist regimes signaled the end of any sense of society. It favored the social fragmentation dressed up as individualism that had gathered pace in Reagan's America and Margaret Thatcher's Britain. One poll indicated that 75 percent of the American workforce now saw a "breakdown of community." In parallel vein, there was speculation that 1989 spelled a final defeat for socialism. The German-British scholar Ralf Dahrendorf declared, "Socialism is dead."

In his influential book *The End of History*, US philosopher Francis Fukuyama cast a wider net and predicted that left-right conflicts would be a thing of the past. He conceded there were still fights to be fought, for example over homophobia. But Fukuyama was confident that leftist agendas such as the fight for African American equality could now be consigned to history.[33]

None of this sounded good for the left. Yet there were contrary indications, too. The end of the arms race promised a peace dividend, with more money for social policies. The removal of the threat of communism from abroad weakened the rationale for anti-socialism at home. It seemed there was less of a need for the superstructure of a national security state. Reagan's rejection of open government on the ground that it threatened national security no longer appeared to be valid. Senator Pat Moynihan (D-NY) proposed and almost obtained the abolition of the CIA.

Scanning 1990s America for signs of life on the left, the scene is not barren. Nation of Islam leader Louis Farrakhan in 1995 inspired a Million Man March in Washington, DC, an event criticized for its exclusion of women but still declaring for left issues like welfare and Medicaid. The decade was the first in which three declared socialists sat in Congress, Bernie Sanders from Vermont, Major Owens from New York, and Ron Dellums from California. Once on President Nixon's "enemies list", Dellums had been a public supporter of Barney Frank when he had gay troubles. The former marine was a leading critic of South Africa's apartheid, the CIA, the Vietnam War, and other US interventions. He had called for the military budget to be cut in half – and found himself chairing the House Armed Services Committee between 1993 and 1995.[34]

None of this is to deny that the chill winds of antisocietal philosophy were blowing through America. The evidence was starkly evident. For example, Atlanta, Georgia, failed to provide any kind of adequate public transport system when it hosted the 1996 Olympic games.

The election as president of the Chicago socialist Janet Jagan should have asked questions of America. How did she manage to be elected the leader of Guyana (1997–9) yet no woman had ever got near the presidency of her native country? Why could an American socialist reach highest office in a foreign country but not at home? The questions were not even asked.[35]

Like the left itself, the left political agenda continued to experience mixed fortunes in the Bill Clinton administrations, 1993–2001. President Clinton mounted an attack on poverty, and with his wife Hillary attempted to achieve health reform. But it was a story of shortcomings and reversals. There were those who faulted Clinton for not pushing forward firmly enough, for aiming at the political center in a way that disappointed the left and alienated conservatives. It was arguably a question of could he? not would he. Revelations about the president's sexual indiscretions with White House intern Monika Lewinsky left him at the mercy of his right-wing critics. Though a twice-elected president, on vital issues he failed to carry public opinion and Congress. Enacting his program became impossible regardless of his determination or lack of it.[36]

In an attempt to combat poverty, Clinton in his first year of office secured an expansion of the Earned Income Tax Credit (EITC) system of refunding tax to low earners. A derivative of Republican policy in the Ford and Reagan administrations, EITC by 1998 provided income tax relief to sixteen million poor families. Critics pointed out, however, that the EITC system benefited employers as much as workers by allowing them to pay low wages; they argued that it was no substitute for proper living wages.[37]

The president entrusted his wife Hillary with the task of planning health reform, and the Senate majority leader George Mitchell (D-ME) introduced a bill to Congress in 1993 that aimed at universal coverage. Employers and employees would contribute, while the government would step in to help the poor and small businesses. "Sin" taxes, especially on tobacco, would help defray the additional costs.

In spite of Democratic majorities in Congress, the Mitchell bill generated bitter and debilitating debate, and went down to defeat in 1994. Parties to the American health system had a vested interest in past reforms that had enriched them, and equally in opposing future reforms that might dilute the pot of honey. Vested interests poured $60 million into negative TV advertising, helping to turn public opinion against the Clinton-Mitchell reform. Another strain of opposition came from a familiar quarter, conservatives who smelled socialism. These critics did not focus on the deficiencies of the legislation, but on the principle behind it. As one analyst put it, the "*actual* health care crisis" meant less to them than "the rhetorically constructed *virtual* crisis of big government."[38]

There was also more than a hint of ambivalence in the president's own attitude. One of the aims behind his proposal had been to rein in the burgeoning costs of Medicare and Medicaid, which had in 1991 consumed 21 percent of federal revenue, up from 9 percent in 1971. As Clinton put it, forty million people were uninsured in the USA whereas all other wealthy nations had universal coverage – yet at a lower cost to the economy than in America. In the end, his parsimony got to him. Doubts about cost-control persuaded the president that health reform might nullify his plan to balance the federal budget. Early in Bill Clinton's administration, the peace dividend had yet to materialize, the economy was in depression, and it seemed imprudent to push an expensive program. Later in his administration, he had the money but the political opportunity had gone. Even after the passage of eighty years, a salient element in the Wisconsin socialists' dream remained unfulfilled.[39]

In 1995, Newt Gingrich, Speaker of the House of Representatives, filed a document in the House setting forth the policy positions of the resurgent Republican Party. He advocated "replacing the Welfare State with an Opportunity Society." There followed a concerted attack on welfare payments. An act of 1996 renamed the Aid to Families with Dependent

Children program. Henceforth it would be called Temporary Assistance for Needy Families, and nobody in future could benefit for more than five years. There was a return to the nineteenth century doctrine that the poor were poor because they were indolent. There occurred a 50 percent reduction in the number of people on the welfare rolls. As prosperity picked up, some of those struck off found jobs, but many were left in penury. By 1997, 20 percent of female-headed families with children had suffered a $580 decline in annual income. Half of those forced off the welfare rolls ended in poverty.[40]

With $1.6 trillion in budget surpluses forecast for 1998–2008, the Republicans proposed $80 billion in tax cuts over the next five years. Clinton wanted to use the surplus to shore up Social Security's ailing finances, but he had timed his run too late. On his watch America recovered from the military spending of the 1980s and filled its coffers, but only with the result that military adventures could be launched by his successor in the White House. At the end of his presidency the welfare state did remain intact and the original socialist dream was not shattered, but its effectiveness was reduced.[41]

Globalization seemed to be another chapter in the left's tale of woe. True to its name, globalization was a worldwide phenomenon. On one side of the Atlantic, the European Union abolished trade barriers between member states and expanded to admit nations in Eastern Central Europe. On the other side, the United States combined with Canada and Mexico in 1994 to sign the North American Free Trade Agreement (NAFTA). The liberalization of trade promised to raise general levels of prosperity and to make nations more mutually dependent, reducing the likelihood of international conflict. But, as implemented on each side of the Atlantic, it weakened the power of government and labor while giving an opportunity to multinational corporations. Companies moved their operations to countries where labor was cheap and health and safety regulations weak, leaving parts of the USA deindustrialized. Though committed in principle to internationalism and to raising standards universally, the left (like the labor unions) found it had been outpaced. It fell into a defensive mode, opposed NAFTA, and ended on the losing side of a policy debate.[42]

On all sides of the political spectrum, post-Cold War commentators now spoke of the triumph of the market. But the picture needs to be modified in a number of ways. First, it was not really a free market. Big corporations have a tendency to monopoly in the interest of profit, and thus to restrict competition. The Reclaim the Streets movement of the 1990s took direct action to protest and remove symbols of international corporate greed. In *No Logo* (2000), a book that sold a million copies and translated into twenty languages, Naomi Klein attacked the multinationals' monopolistic oppression. Though two of her grandparents had been communists, Klein saw an essential role for consumer (not worker) protest in resisting the worldwide exploitative behavior of, for example, the Starbucks coffee shop chain. The abuses of market dominance she complained of were a problem because potentially countervailing governmental power was divided amongst different countries and thus relatively weak.[43]

Second, there was an international political reaction against the imperfect market capitalism that was on offer. In 1998, *Newsweek* ran a front-cover headline asking "Is the world growing weary of market capitalism?" Commenting on a business downturn that had sparked government interventions in Hong Kong and some less affluent countries, its business journalist Robert Samuelson thought that "global capitalism is now destabilizing the economies of poor countries." He argued that this was because "Third World" nations had deficient "cultural values" and didn't understand how capitalism was good for them and for democracy. He was not open to the argument that those nations did not want to be exploited by unfair cartel capitalism.[44]

The emergence of convergence theory was a third challenge to the notion of market hegemony. In response to changing times, British socialists had contemplated the virtues of a "mixed economy" (part socialist, part capitalist), and eastern European thinkers had promoted the idea of "market socialism", the exposure of publicly owned enterprises to the forces of supply and demand.[45] American analysts, though, saw elements of socialism in capitalism itself. Take one of socialism's traditional demands, workers' control of industry. It just so happened that, in America, workers owned significant swathes of business because their pension funds had to invest the money somewhere – and where better than in the enterprises run by the capitalists who employed them?

As business consultant Peter Drucker put it, "If socialism is defined, as Marx defined it, as ownership of the means of production by the employees, then the United States has become the most 'socialized' state around – while still being the most 'capitalist' one as well." The historian Martin Sklar pointed additionally to the anticompetitive character of large corporations, and to what he thought was their socialist-style acceptance of collective bargaining, collective democracy, community responsibility and responsiveness to consumer groups. Banker and economist Marc Chandler concluded in an article of 2000 that it was anachronistic to ask why social-ism had failed in America: "The real, significant argument, which goes unaddressed, is . . . that, far from failing, socialism is very much alive in the United States."[46]

Conservatives worried as usual about that, but the rallying cry that had them going in the 1990s was very different. It had to do with culture and morality. The cultural wars had been rumbling even before Stonewall sent out a general signal, but in the 1990s they were defined and fought in a particularly vivid manner.

James Davison Hunter's book *The Culture Wars* appeared at the start of the decade. It opened with a discussion of homosexuality, and then broadened to embrace other issues. The University of Virginia professor argued that the nation was in the midst of a cultural debate about "abortion, funding for the arts, affirmative action and quotas, gay rights, values in public education [and] multiculturalism." It was a left versus right matter, and he asserted that the middle had been eclipsed. The political exchanges became vituperative. At the 1992 Republican Party convention, conserva-tive presidential aspirant Pat Buchanan electrified his sympathizers with an attack on what he saw as the moral depravity condoned by his opponents. The right launched on a crusade against moral turpitude in the White House and against deviations from postulated American norms at every level of society.[47]

There are two ways of reading this. On the one hand, it was bad news for the Newer Left with its agenda of social and moral tolerance. Cultural war had been declared and would intensify. On the other hand, the con-servative cultural crusade was based on the premise that the left had already won. Punching back against the left view that corporations had too much influence on university education, conservatives complained that lefties dominated the teaching in higher education and imposed a stifling political correctness. Research based on a 1999 survey of 183 prestigious universities would fuel their concerns: whereas 39 percent of faculty had been left-leaning in 1984, the figure was now 75 percent (87 percent in elite universities), with 84 percent in favor of abortion rights, 67 percent tolerant of homosexuality and 88 percent willing to pay a higher price for environmental protection.

And there were fears that the contagion had spread beyond the universi-ties. A contributor to the *New York Review of Books* wrote that America's high schools relied on history textbooks written in a politically correct style designed to forestall objections from the "multicultural left." Conservative talk show hosts attacked the *New York Times* for what they alleged was its left-wing stance.[48]

From Sean Penn to the Dixie Chicks, too many icons of popular culture seemed to the right to be coming from the wrong end of the political spectrum. Gertrude Himmelfarb saw gospel rock as an antidote to gangsta rap, noted that feminism and affirmative action were in decline and rejoiced in the rise of private and religious education, but on the whole the moral right fought with the fierceness of people who had their backs to the wall.[49]

From the left point of view, the 1990s were a decade of policy reverses with the likelihood of more to come. But they continued to offer the prospect of cultural change and multiculturalism, and therefore dialog with and influence on the rest of the world.

Chapter 10

THE REPUBLICAN ROAD TO NATIONALIZATION

On the evidence of the George W. Bush administration of 2001–9, the American right was as anti-left as ever. Subliminally, however, the conservative-dominated Republicans remained aware of socialist-style approaches to politics. Even as they revived anti-socialist slogans in attacking presidential aspirant Barack Obama, they embraced the ogre of their nightmares, nationalization.

It was not the only indication of the survival of left values. Another was the election of Bernie Sanders to represent Vermont in the Senate in 2006. He was the first member of that body to profess unalloyed socialism. It is true that he ran as an Independent, and had cooperated mainly with Democrats in his time in the House – here, he nodded to the convention that the official socialist label could be damaging to one's career. Also, he eschewed overt socialist leadership. In 1991 he had founded and assumed leadership of the Congressional Progressive Caucus, at first a small group including fellow socialists Ron Dellums and Major Owens and eventually the largest caucus amongst Democrats with over eighty members. However, he accepted no formal role in the Democratic Socialists of America: "As a Senator, I work seventy hours a week, so leading and organizing a socialist party would just not be possible on top of that commitment." Yet both he and others frequently referred to his socialist views. A portrait of Eugene Debs hung in his Senate office. In Debsian style, he had voted against the Iraq war. He subscribed to the agendas of the Newer Left: "I do have a one hundred percent voting record on gay and women's issues." At the same time, he placed his "special emphasis" on economic issues to do with the welfare of working people.[1]

Now let's look at the Vermont factor. Are we looking at a strange state? Like mountain folk everywhere, Vermonters invited mockery because they were apt to look askance at outsiders. New Yorkers who decamped into the

161

Green Mountain State were "Chardonnay sippers" and "flatlanders." Yet in practice Vermonters put up with, even welcomed them. In fact, according to a Works Progress Administration guide of the 1930s, Vermonters were individualists who tolerated the eccentricities of others. The WPA's example of such an incomer was Massachusetts-born Henrietta Green, the "Witch of Wall Street" and the nation's richest woman. Reportedly, Mrs. Green never changed her undergarments until they had worn out. This paragon of the accumulative ethic settled in Bellows Falls without apparent mishap.[2]

Sanders also arrived as an outsider. He never lost his Brooklyn Jewish accent as he expounded on "yooge" (huge) issues, and is sometimes regarded as an eccentric who came to represent a state full of them. The suggestion here is that the presence of a socialist on the Senate was freakish, especially during the conservative George Bush administration of 2001–9. According to the let's-explain-it-away doctrine, Sanders won election only because Vermonters suffer from a lunatic tendency.[3]

Yet there is a case for looking at the first decade of the twenty-first century a bit more closely, and not just in the case of Vermont. More deliberate scrutiny confirms that there were plenty of stirrings on the left across the nation, so Sanders did not lack company and did not stand out like the proverbial sore thumb. Meantime, occurrences on the right made the left look distinctly sane. The Bush administration fared so badly in its attempts to boost capitalism and ended up by undermining the principles of private business. Was it incompetence or was the system at fault?

Whichever, Wall Street was in a state of collapse by 2008. When the President asked the taxpayer to fork out $700 billion to save the system, conservative lawmakers expressed their dismay. Their leader Jeb Hansarling wailed that his fellow Texan George Bush was putting Congress at twenty-four hours' notice to place America "on the road to socialism." Perhaps Bernie Sanders was not so far out, after all.[4]

Some may have dismissed Sanders and his socialism as a local eccentricity, but in contrast the right would renew its faith in the socialist threat and make it a prime issue on the 2008 presidential campaign. However, a brief consideration of the changing nature of neoconservatism is in order here.

The old neo-conservatives had included renegade socialists or communists. In the second half of the twentieth century they brought a well-informed anti-socialism to the American right. According to one theory, at least a few New Lefties may have undergone a similar transformation, their anarchism of the 1960s yielding to conservative individualism and respectability in subsequent decades. Prospectively the new neo-conserv- atives, like the old neo-cons, would evolve as a perverse achievement of the American left. Perhaps in this vein, former SDS leader Todd Gitlin repudiated direct action and demonstratively gave blood for Iraq War soldiers. However, the New Left-to-neocon transformation theory has limited credibility. Gitlin denied vehemently that he and other aging 1960s protestors were swelling the ranks of neoconservativism, and the Sixties generation of radicals showed a continuing commitment to left causes as the decades rolled by. Gitlin opposed the Iraq War even as he gave blood for its wounded.[5]

The New Left failed to replenish the ranks of US neoconservatism. It did not have the Old Left's history of moral disasters (notably Stalinism) productive of a host of apostates.

The newer generation of neo-conservatives drew their intellectual inspiration instead from other sources. There was a certain reliance on the philosophy of Leo Strauss. The German-Jewish professor died in 1973, but several of his disciples had an impact on the Bush administration. While the Straussians were anti-socialist, anti-socialism was not their main concern. Straussian "truth squads" at one time stalked the corridors of the University of Chicago aiming to purge the nation not of socialism but of political correctness. They and their acolytes were more relevant to the culture war against the Newer Left than to the now distant and faded Cold War. Conservative it may have been, but the Bush administration neglected anti- socialism in favor of anti-Islamism. It is quite possible that the resultant absence of the fear factor contributed to many young Americans declaring their sympathy for socialism by the end of the decade.[6]

The *neo*-neo conservatives broke with the time-honored tradition of diplomacy associated with Woodrow Wilson, a president who had offended the Republican canon by favoring the League of Nations. President Theodore Roosevelt was the new messiah. The neo-neos either ignored or were unaware of the fact that Roosevelt had offered a "square deal" to labor, called for a system of widows' pensions, and favored social security including federal health insurance. What appealed to them was the attitude of a man who, in a trademark escapade in the Cuban theatre of the War of 1898, captured San Juan Hill. He had done so astride his horse Little Texas and at the head of the "Rough Riders", cavalrymen recruited in the badlands of the southwest. The neo-neos admired Roosevelt's panache, his imperial- ist doctrine, and his belief as president in using the unilateralist "Big Stick" in foreign policy. Just as the similarly-revered President Reagan had defied international law, so the Bush administration sidelined the United Nations and resorted to frontier-style rough justice in foreign policy. Israel, once the darling of the left but now expansionist in defiance of world opinion, acted as the neo-neo policymakers' proxy Rough Rider in the Middle East.[7]

The twenty-first century neoconservative had new themes to pursue, yet anti-socialism once again became a theme in the 2008 election. This was because Senator Obama was perceived in a certain way, and because reversionary attitudes are easy to adopt when things go wrong – as they did in the Bush administration.

The Bush administration dug a number of holes for itself in a manner that not only imperiled the capitalist system, but also motivated a broad spectrum of the left. Following "9/11", the terrorist attack of 2001, it adopted draconian measures that threatened civil liberties. Its invasion of Iraq in 2003 caused outrage because it was justified on a false pretext (Iraq did not, as claimed, possess "weapons of mass destruction") and because it was undertaken without a clear legal or UN mandate.

The bellicosity of the administration sat uneasily with its commitment to tax cuts. Introduced in 2001 and 2003, these were meant to stimulate the economy, in this way paying for themselves by increasing the net revenue take. However, they contributed to a budget deficit. The expense of the Iraq war, and of subsequent hostilities in Afghanistan, compounded the problem – there were claims that the Iraq War alone had cost $1 trillion by 2008, and some estimates put the figure three times higher.[8] All this diverted funds from social programs at home to which the administration had an ideological objection anyway. At the same time a laisser-faire approach to economic policy led to irresponsibility in the market place, and to a repetition of the mistakes of the 1920s, which had resulted in a widening in the gap between rich and poor, leading to flaccid purchasing power and economic depression. The left looked on with despair, and knew that, in spite of the advances of the previous century, major challenges remained.

These were years of concerted assault on America's social democracy. People worried about the cost of the welfare state, and how to pay for it. A demographic development made the problem more acute. According to a Congressional briefing paper of 2005, within twenty years there would be a 69 percent increase in the number of people over sixty-five, meaning a bigger draw on Medicare and retirement benefits and potential exhaustion of the trust fund in 2041. By 2009, with constant warfare and the economic recession taking their toll and Social Security and Medicare costing $1 trillion annually (one-third of the federal budget), the bankruptcy date had been brought forward four years, to 2037.[9]

The approach of the Bush administration was to propose moving to a position where only the poor would get welfare benefits. This would save money and would be consistent with lower taxation levels. That, in turn, would generate prosperity and enable the more affluent to make private provision for retirement as well as health care. Furthermore, the social security system would be privatized, resulting, according to the proposal's proponents, in greater efficiency and an arrangement more closely aligned to the goals of a free society. The plan would essentially negate what the New Deal had put in place seventy years ago.

It was not to be, or at least not entirely. A wave of sympathy for those in need following the devastation of Hurricane Katrina in the fall of 2005 and reverses in the mid-term elections of 2006 prevented the Republicans from implementing the plan in full. Yet through sins of omission and commission (doing nothing and waging war), social welfare was allowed to atrophy. And in foreign policy, Bush and his colleagues worked against the spread of New Deal-style socialism – notably in Latin America.[10]

Although the Bush administration engaged in relatively little anti-left hysteria, in practice it undermined socialist facets of US society. According to the editor of *Harper's Magazine*, a government of the super rich was out to "privatize – i.e. appropriate or destroy – the public infrastructure" that gave the nation its sense of "public enterprise." His list of examples included schools, levees and even bird protection. Turning to another sphere, he pointed out that the administration had allowed private employers to pay less than the minimum wage on government contracts, and additionally lifted the affirmative action requirement.[11]

Already a problem in terms of social justice and potential economic implications, the gap between rich and poor widened further during the Bush administration. The poverty rate increased. Average household incomes unprecedently failed to rise during Bush's first term. Wages and salaries made up the lowest share of America's gross domestic product since records began in 1947. Meantime the income of the top quintile of earners was by 2004 up 63 percent on what they had been in 1979. In order to survive, colleges began once again to favor the offspring of the rich. The American rich did pay more into the national tax pot than their European counterparts, but this neither redressed the balance nor satisfied the critics. Even the non-radical press targeted the high earnings of individual transgressors, like the hedge-fund manager who took home $1.7 billion.[12]

The left criticized wealth polarization, and launched an attack on foreign policy. The war in Iraq was a clear-cut invitation for leftist rebellion. The protest that duly took place in some ways lacked the vigor of the protest against the Vietnam War, but appearances masked a hidden potency.

In a vain attempt to prevent the outbreak of military conflict, there took place on the eve of the US invasion of Iraq the largest peace demonstration since the Vietnam War. San Franciscans saw a quarter of a million gather. Elsewhere there were two hundred thousand in Sydney, six hundred thousand in Madrid, three-quarters of a million in London and an estimated three million on the streets of Rome.[13]

Then, as the doubters point out, the numbers declined. To be sure, three hundred thousand New Yorkers turned out on March 22, 2003, to protest the first falling of the bombs on Baghdad, and half a million congregated to pour scorn on the Republican National Convention when it met in the same city two years later. But other demonstrations were sparsely attended. The march on the Pentagon in the spring of 2007 was a shadow of its famous precursor of 1967 not just in numbers – fifty thousand instead of double that number – but in pugnacity, color and style. If you were in search of direct action IWW-style, you could still find it in the antiglobalization movement that disrupted life in cities around the world whenever international finance ministers met. In 1999 fifty thousand took to the streets of Seattle to disrupt a meeting of the World Trade Organization. But the campaign was not American-led, and follow-up demonstrations in the United States attracted small numbers and were, in the words of historian Michael Kazin, "a niche concern."[14]

A little scholarly industry has developed, devoted to explaining why the anti-Iraq War movement lacked the salience of anti-Vietnam War protest, and, by implication, why it was less effective. There is no shortage of theories. America used professional soldiers in Iraq, so there was no draft to inflame the passions. Because of Iraq's oil resources and the world shortage of oil, it was in the national interest to have a friendly regime in Baghdad (Saigon had offered no comparable advantages) – so regime change was desirable even if it had been justified with spurious arguments. Then there was the notion that Saddam Hussein could not be an icon for protestors as Ho Chi Minh had been. Okay, the Vietnamese communists were unsavory as became clear once they had won control of their nation and proceeded to persecute dissenters and to bully their neighbors. However, they did not compare in degree of iniquity with the Hussein regime in Iraq with its record of external aggression and internal genocide against the Kurds. The

Al Qaeda terrorist group that became active in Iraq after the US invasion had attacked the American homeland, which the Vietnamese communists never did. For all these reasons, the argument runs, the left and the rest of the antiwar movement generally were muted in the case of Iraq. It was a case of understandable and forgivable failure, and of inflated expectations of success created by memories of the anti-Vietnam War protest – in reality, the latter protest may in any case not have been "quite the wonder of democracy-in-the-streets-stopping-an-imperialist-war it is often made out to be." To advance such explanations and comparisons is to reinforce the impression of failure on the left.[15]

However, it would be wrong to underestimate the potency of the anti-Iraq War protests. Organized labor, so often berated in American history for ignoring social issues and supporting wars, turned a new page. From 2003, US Labor Against War (USLAW) campaigned for workers' rights in Iraq and for the withdrawal of US troops. By 2005 it had 110 affiliates and was a significant caucus in the labor movement. In that year, USLAW persuaded the AFL-CIO leadership to accept a conference resolution demanding "rapid withdrawal" of America's armed forces.[16]

The print media and conservative talk shows overlooked another new element in protest. Their oversight reflected not just ideological bias, but also a dated obsession with action drama and an equally dated and perhaps fearful inability to come to terms with new technology. Democracy was moving off the streets and onto the keyboard. Created in 1998 as an email group to urge that people "move on" from the obsession with impeaching President Clinton, MoveOn.Org was an online advocacy group and political action committee that raised millions of dollars for candidates on the left of the political spectrum. By 2004, it was a force to be reckoned with in the campaign against the war.

There were plenty of other online forums, too. Common Dreams News Center was an offshoot of Gitlin's activities developed by civil libertarian Craig Brown in the 1990s. Another 1990s group, AlterNet, focused on opposing the war and by 2010 boasted three million visitors a month. Huffington Post was named after its founder Arianna Huffington, who had time-traveled in reverse in her journey from the right to the left. There was even AntiWar.Com that drew on conservative libertarian principles to challenge war, imperialism – and the left's monopoly of protest. A leading historian of the Vietnam War commenting on the anti-Iraq protest movement has suggested, "No amount of Internet activity can compare with those heady days of the 1960s when telegenic and often thrilling 'demos' helped to spread the dovish message." Perhaps indeed it is easier and thus less of a commitment to send an email than it is to get out there on the street. However, each generation defines its own theater, and the web held center stage at the start of the new millennium. It is estimated that by 2008 there were fifty million bloggers for peace and withdrawal.[17]

The Newer Left had developed a Blogging Left tendency, but as ever there were elements of continuity, and these boosted the antiwar cause. As in the past, feminists were a source of dissent. In anticipation of that, the Bush administration stressed the issue of women's rights in Iraq and Afghanistan, hoping by this means to have "removed a left column." But his expatriation of the feminist plank did not deter female antiwar protest at home. Established in 2002, the group "Code Pink: Women For Peace" chose a color that might at first sight seem to imply a post-feminism that would have shocked Friedan and Beauvoir. But pink was actually a derisory take on Homeland Security's color-coded terrorism threat advisory scale running from green (low) to red (severe). Code Pink's adherents needed no tuition in militancy. They mounted a women's vigil in front of the White House, then a ten-thousand-person march. They heckled the president's second inaugural address in 2005, blocked the Golden Gate Bridge in 2006, and invaded the House of Representatives in 2007.[18]

As in the 1960s, there were innumerable local groups, such as the Dorchester (MA) People for Peace. There were coast-to-coast networks: ANSWER (Act Now to Stop War and End Racism) came together in the wake of 9/11 and drew on West Coast support though its headquarters were in Washington, DC. From 2002, United for Peace and Justice operated nationwide as a coalition of antiwar groups, and there were 1,400 of them by decade's end. Iraq Veterans Against the War recruited soldiers who had served since 2001 and advocated immediate withdrawal. In a throwback to the impeachment of President Nixon, the left-wing Representative Dennis Kucinich (D-OH) in 2007 filed impeachment proceedings against Dick Cheney. He charged that the vice president had deceived the American people into going to war, lied about the initial Al Qaeda presence in Iraq, and conspired to extend the war to Iran. In 2008 the radical International Longshore Union, whose predecessor had been quick off the mark in its protest against the Vietnam War, again made its voice heard. It struck the entire West Coast, and declared its solidarity with the longshoremen of Iraq.

Senator Sanders slammed the motives of the oil-enriched Bush administration in Iraq and stated, "The corporations own foreign policy." Asked how many senators would agree with that view, he replied "None." But in the nation at large, he was not alone. The initial action against Iraq had the backing of 69 percent of Americans, but support fell away when the first war gave way to a second, the counterinsurgency. By 2005, six in ten Americans opposed the war, according to a Gallup poll. Two years later, seven in ten believed the war was ruining the economy. The political scientist John Berg suggested that instead of taking to the street to protest, millions of Americans were now "waiting for Lefty," a political candidate who would, once elected, pull them out of the militaristic mire.[19]

Time and again America had gone to war on the basis of deception or with dubious aims – for example in 1898 against Spain, in 1917 against Germany, and in 1964 against the Vietnamese communists. The New Left and its successors, including the blogging generation of the 2000s, had re-educated America, and people were no longer prepared to follow a presidential lead with their eyes shut. As the historian Marilyn Young pointed out, post-1960s US leaders had been aware of this, and were now usually canny enough to limit the use of the Big Stick to small and brief encounters that did not involve the draft and deployed the regular armed forces sparingly: no troops went to Nicaragua, and they quickly exited Grenada in 1983 and Iraq following the Gulf War of 1991.[20]

As Young put it, the "Vietnam syndrome", the 1960s war and protest against it, had resulted in a "lack of blood-lust on the part of the public." Confronting the Rough Riding ambitions of the Bush administration, the protestors of the 2000s kept that sanity alive, in spite of the fact that (in contrast to Vietnam) the USA was not visibly going down to defeat. The left seized on atrocities and shackled the ability of the armed forces to commit further ones; it deterred the administration from launching a further war against Iran; it contributed to the Bush administration's promise in 2007 of incremental disengagement followed by a phased withdrawal; and the left prepared the way for President Obama's announcement of an exit strategy in February 2009.[21]

Just as a majority of Americans opposed the war, so a majority favored a federally guaranteed health insurance program that would embrace every citizen. In 2007 a poll suggested that 64 percent were in favor, with 60 percent willing to pay higher taxes to fund such an arrangement. There was a pressing need for the implementation of the last unenacted segment of the social security plan advanced so many years ago by Selig Perlman and his socialist colleagues. For forty-seven million Americans were uninsured, up 6.8 million since 2000.

Well-resourced citizens benefited from the unparalleled excellence of US hospitals and doctors. But the existence of the uninsured dragged the USA down to a state of shameful inferiority and inefficiency. According to World Health Organization figures, in 2006 America spent 15.3 percent of its Gross Domestic Product (GDP) on health, with 45.8 percent of that as private expenditure. In the UK with its National Health Service, only 8.2 percent of GDP went on health with a mere 12.7 percent private, but the UK had a substantially higher number of hospital beds in proportion to population, and a higher life expectancy – eighty, compared with America's seventy-eight. Other figures on hospital survival rates suggested that the USA was bumping along toward the bottom of the list of first world countries, and it had a higher infant mortality rate than any European nation.[22]

Grassroots support for universal health insurance had increasing support and strength on the national level. Hillary Clinton, a high-profile candidate for the 2008 Democratic presidential nomination, continued to work for that goal. Representative Charles B. Rangel (D-NY), a veteran of the Black Caucus that intersected in the House with the Progressive Caucus led by Sanders before his elevation to the Senate, became chair of the Ways and Means Committee that in the previous century had, in the sanguine words of a *New York Times* journalist, "created the modern welfare state." Before a series of ethics and tax investigations eroded his authority, Rangel was a potent force for reform. So, too, was the transformed American Medical Association. When the financially squeezed administration tried to reduce the pay of Medicare doctors by 10.6 percent, the association, for decades the scourge of "socialized medicine", signaled a sea change. It condemned the move and launched a barrage of radio and TV advertisements opposing the cut.[23]

As with social insurance in the 1920s, there were powerful campaigns on the local level. In 2006, Massachusetts adopted a plan, paid for through a mixture of worker, employer and negative tax contributions, that would insure an additional 515,000 citizens, about 95 percent of those uninsured. The state's governor, Mitt Romney, had contributed to the successful architecture of the scheme – an indication that left-wing causes can cross party lines. Another Republican, California's Governor Arnold Schwarzenegger, favored a similar solution. Schwarzenegger's fellow-Republicans in California did not share his view and fought his health plan, so Democratic San Francisco went its own way, issuing Healthy San Francisco cards that gave health coverage to everyone not covered by private insurance. Chris Lehane and other leading Democrats formed an action group to support health reform. In a nod to the left tradition that they continued, they called themselves the Lincoln Brigade.[24]

While local initiatives on health insurance showed the way, most ended in defeat. Nationally, the picture was even less rosy. President Bush stuck to a narrow path. He favored a strengthening of Medicare that deployed tax breaks to make drugs more affordable to seniors, tempering this approach with an insistence that service provision should be privatized and competitive – the "American Way." Pressure from the American Association of Retired Persons (speaking for a powerful segment of the electorate) helped him overcome conservative opposition and secure passage of the Medicare Modernization Act (2003). However, under-eighteens don't vote. Quietly, in a move reported on page 17 of the *New York Times*, Bush vetoed a 2007 bill that would have improved health insurance provision for children. Overall, the health position remained dire. One of the left's most venerable dreams remained unfulfilled.[25]

The documentary film *Sicko* (2007) excoriated the weaknesses of America's health system and made adverse comparisons with its publicly funded and run equivalents in Canada, the UK, France, and Cuba. *Sicko* was a box office success and won an Oscar. It was one of a string of left-wing documentaries by filmmaker Michael Moore. Moore was a Michigan Catholic who had famously attacked the Iraq War at the 2003 Oscar ceremonies. He would run for the presidency on the Socialist Party USA ticket in 2008 (this small party was further to the left than the Michael Harrington-Bernard Sanders organization, the Democratic Socialists of America). Though unusual in being so overtly socialist, Moore was part of a wider left trend in US movie making. Errol Morris's *Standard Operating Procedure* (2008) was an acclaimed exposure of the US abuse of prisoners at Abu Graib (Baghdad Central Prison). The Hollywood left included a string of personalities including Jodie Foster, Sharon Stone and George Clooney.

The left was having a cultural impact, and shaping opinion. Conservative radio hosts like Rush Limbaugh were influential, but so were late night TV shows like *The Colbert Report* and *The Daily Show*, with their satirical take on neoconservatism. Left-leaning black talk stars like Warren Ballantine had an impact. A 2007 poll revealed that young people were turning leftward. Organized labor could no longer be relied upon to support the established order. Nor could Christians. An English clergyman concluded after his tour of America that God in the United States had "turned to the left." As for the universities, it seemed that tenure erosion had failed, after all, to complete the task of intimidating the left. Various studies suggested that academia was operating in a left-wing groove. Clearly the right had not triumphed in the culture war.[26]

Not only this, but old-fashioned socialism was about to make a comeback, both in terms of rhetoric and as a policy. It happened because of an all too predictable event.

In 2007, one hundred years after the Bankers' Panic that marred Theodore Roosevelt's administration, capitalism began to slide into yet another of its periodic crises. Forever cyclical, the economy on this occasion suffered not just because of war and maldistributed wealth, but also because successive administrations had subscribed to the mantra of deregulation. In 1999, President Clinton signed a measure that repealed a section of the New Deal-era Glass-Steagall law, which separated commercial banking from investment banking. The repeal gave speculators the opportunity to gamble with other people's money. Then in 2004, the US Securities and Exchange Commission relaxed its net capital rule, allowing banks to lend far in excess of the amount guaranteed by their assets. Leveraged funds and a trade in derivatives led to risky loans especially in the house-mortgage sub-prime market, and boom gave way to bust.

In February 2007, Freddie Mac had to toughen its sub prime mortgage lending criteria. A deluge followed that can only be epitomized here. In the first three months of 2007, the capital value of the New Century Financial Corporation, a mortgage business, collapsed from $1.75 billion to $55 million. Fannie Mae and Freddie Mac, flagships of privatization and now harbingers of doom, went into meltdown. Lehmann Brothers, a mainstay of Wall Street with $600 billion in assets, went into liquidation in September, the largest bankruptcy in American history. Automobile manufacturing, the traditional bastion of the economy, was in serious trouble – both Chrysler and General Motors were heading for bankruptcy.[27]

The mighty had fallen, but plain folk suffered the consequences. The unemployment rate, 4.8 percent in February 2007, more than doubled to 10.1 percent by October 2009. The faltering economy and the squeeze on government finance meant that welfare safety nets eroded just when they were needed to take care of larger numbers of impoverished people. By early 2009, thirty-four states had reduced programs for vulnerable groups. Frail seniors in Arizona had to do without trips to the doctor. More children in Ohio had to go into foster care.[28]

The Bush administration took steps aimed at saving the system. In March 2008, the US Federal Reserve Bank provided emergency help in the case of Bear Stearns Companies, Inc., whose wealth had only weeks earlier been trumpeted in trillions, and which now had to be taken over by the J. P. Morgan Chase company with federal help and on punitive terms. In September, the government re-asserted public control over Fannie Mae and Freddie Mac at an estimated cost to the taxpayer of $25 billion. Ten days later, it took $85 billion to rescue – and virtually nationalize – the derivatives-dabbling American International Group, the nation's largest insurer.[29]

It was far from unusual for the government to intervene in this way. The tradition stretched back to Hamilton. Nor was it uncommon for champions of hands-off government and free enterprise to use federal power to fix and promote the economy when they needed to. As Barack Obama pointed out, the business-orientated Republican Party had historically endorsed public investment: "It was a Republican, Lincoln, who launched the Transcontinental Railroad . . . It was Eisenhower who launched the Interstate Highway system . . . . It was Richard Nixon who created the Environmental Protection Agency."[30]

It was almost as if capitalism's champions made continuous mental reservations – we'll privatize this and that, but we can always reverse it if there is a really rough ride. Yet the capitalist climb-down of 2008 was traumatic, and no doubt guilt was involved. The scarlet letter "S" for socialism, not Hawthorne's "A" for adultery, burned the Bushites as they acted. Conservative voters could see it plainly. They flooded their congressmen with emails: "We are turning into a socialist country."[31]

Chapter 11

OBAMA: A PRESIDENT FOR THE LEFT?

Some long held ambitions of the left came to fruition in the Barack Obama presidency. Notably, there was the achievement of near-universal health care. "Obamacare" rounded out the welfare state plans the Wisconsin socialists had formulated almost a century earlier.

The widespread use of the term "Obamacare" indicates how an individual personality came to be associated with the reform. It suggests the need, in this chapter, for a new approach. Most of the left's achievements have come through persuasion, not the orthodox political activity of political parties. But the US Constitution does provide for the election of one individual in a manner that can transcend party organization – the president. The current chapter departs from the methodologies of its predecessors and concentrates on Barack Obama. It asks, was Obama a man of the left, and what did he achieve for the left?

A similar approach might have been adopted for the presidency of Franklin D. Roosevelt, when unemployment insurance and old age pensions came into being. Conservatives denounced FDR as a socialist. But Roosevelt did not come to be so personally associated with any single reform in the New Deal era. Rather, he was a political pragmatist who endorsed leftist policies if he thought they would work, and especially if they would work politically.

Can one detect in Obama a contrasting vein of conviction? Or is his leftist reputation an unconvincing projection by his conservative critics? The argument in this chapter is that, on balance, Obama was a president both for and of the left.

Conservatives of different types were in agreement in labeling Obama a man of the left. By the same process, they characterized two presidential elections as stand-offs between the left and the right in American politics. The logic of their language is that the left won in both 2008 and 2012. Like their precursors on the right wing in US politics, modern conservatives have helped to confirm the existence of the left, and to give it potency.

Republicans identified their line of attack on Obama as soon as he started his run for the Democratic nomination. Speaking on a Fox News show in July 2007, former House Speaker Newt Gingrich commented on the senator's proposed meeting with Fidel Castro: meeting the Cuban leader "makes perfect sense if you come from the American left because the American left fears the US military. They fear the CIA . . . . They never fear our enemies."[1]

At the height of the presidential campaign, on October 11, 2008, an event occurred that for conservatives crystallized the issue of Obama-as-leftist. On that day, a plumber called Joe Wurzelbacher was playing football with his son in the front yard of his house in Holland, Ohio, when Senator Obama turned up with the usual media pack. The campaigner had recently been explaining his "Making Work Pay" proposal whereby he proposed to give a tax incentive to poorer wage earners to stay off welfare and in work. To pay for this, there would be a tax hike for singles earning more than $200,000 and for joint filers making over $250,000.

There was an equalization element here. The rich in America were getting richer, the poor poorer. Between 1996 and 2006, the poorest 20 percent of income tax filers suffered a 6 percent decline in income, while the income of the top 0.1 percent of filers almost doubled. Obama saw a problem for the whole of society in the polarization of income and wealth. As he continued to press for the $250,000 tax hike following his re-election in 2012, he would declare, "Our economic success has never come from the top down. It comes from the middle out; it comes from the bottom up."[2]

The rugged, strong-jawed Wurzelbacher was having none of this. He stepped forward, shook Obama's hand, and denounced the new tax idea. He said it would catch him just at the point when he wanted to buy the business he worked for, valued in the range of $250,000–$280,000. Obama responded that for small businessmen like Wurzelbacher his proposed changes would be tax neutral, while having the advantage of redistributing some of America's wealth. Fox News instantly broadcast Wurzelbacher's reply – the Democratic candidate had expressed a "kind of socialist viewpoint."[3]

The Republican candidate John McCain, his vice-presidential running mate Sarah Palin and the media made "Joe the Plumber" an eve-of-poll celebrity. "Senator Obama's economic goal is, as he told Joe, quote, spread the wealth around," McCain told a rally in Washington's Virginian suburbia. Supporters within the meeting bore placards declaring their identities as "Phil the Bricklayer" and "Rose the Teacher." Outside the venue, a man distributed parody bumper stickers: "Obama for Change" with a Soviet red star and the "g" in "change" depicted as a hammer and sickle. For McCain, Obama's socialism (as he saw it) was real. He was bitter about a Democratic campaign that promoted socialism on the sly: "At least in Europe, the socialist leaders who so admire my opponent are upfront about their objectives."[4]

A first great wave of anti-socialist rhetoric having accompanied the 2008 election campaign, a second wave thundered in to greet the newly installed Obama administration. Some of this renewed vilification might be categorized as stale paranoia. The bumper sticker bearing the words "Comrade Obama" under the letters "USSA" was the work of people whose phonographs had stuck in the Cold War groove. The Tea Party movement, a campaign financed by rich Obama haters that drew on populist-style grassroots support, raised newer but just as quirky questions as to whether the president was a "natural born" citizen of the United States.[5]

Lumping Obama with the words "socialist" and "left" did not stop him getting elected in 2008 and had mixed success in frustrating his domestic policies. Nevertheless, in a display of conviction in the veracity if not the effectiveness of what they were saying, Republicans continued to label the president a leftist/socialist when he ran for re-election in 2012. Obama noted that his critics were accusing him of "socialist overreach." But he asked if his supposedly far-left policies were any different from the federal initiatives of past administrations, including those of Republican presidents: "it was a Republican, Lincoln, who launched the Transcontinental Railroad."[6]

There were rebuttals of the idea that Obama was a man of the left. One type of rebuttal rested on denial. Thus Stephen J. Wayne, a Georgetown University scholar specializing in the presidency, drew attention to Obama's own expression of antipathy to "the pursuit of ideological purity."[7] It was a type of denial that had a familiar ring. It belonged to the genus of apologia that obscured the left's impact in American political history.

A second type of denial was more aggressive. There were those on the left who thought that Obama did not go nearly far enough. Their attack cast doubt on his left-wing credentials, and opened up a debate on the nature of his political beliefs and conduct. In the wake of Obama's 2008 election triumph, there emerged an "angry left" that took issue with his appointments and policies. Representative Barney Frank (D-MA) took issue with the president-elect for inviting the evangelical pastor Rick Warren, an opponent of same-sex marriage, to deliver the inauguration invocation. The *New York Post* remarked on the rarity of such a "left-wing" attack on Obama. But it was not to be unique.[8]

The *Washington Post* rolled out two socialists who queried Obama's leftism. Its own columnist Harold Meyerson was a vice chair of the Democratic Socialists of America's national committee. Taking issue with a *Newsweek* cover story called "We Are All Socialists Now," he complained that Obama's vision for America was not really socialist, for he had gone down the road of Germany's nineteenth-century social democrat Eduard Bernstein, who had merely tried to "humanize capitalism." Billy Wharton was the editor of the Socialist Party USA's *The Socialist*, a bimonthly with a circulation of three thousand. For him, Obama was "not one of us." His list of omissions included the president's failure to withdraw immediately from Afghanistan.[9]

Left wing attacks on Obama did not fade away. Two years into his presidency, the socialist Bernie Sanders rose in the US Senate to attack the president's taxation plans. The eight-hour duration of his speech made him a Twitter sensation. With the nation already turning its attention to the next presidential election, the *Washington Post* concluded in the summer of 2011 that "the left isn't as in love with Obama as it used to be."[10]

What people believed about Obama was important politically. If as a black man he could be seen as symbolizing a racial breakthrough, this was a game changer and a source of empowerment for black and other non-white people. A black man's breakthrough was a success for the left agenda, too, in that the left had campaigned for equality. At the same time, it is helpful to look behind the reputation and to ask what kind of political animal Obama really was. He may have been significant as a symbol, but was he a proactive force for change, as well? After all, "change" was one of his oft-repeated promises in the election campaign of 2008.

Conservatives argued that Obama's youthful associations and subsequent behavior marked him out as a man of the left. They pointed to the influence on him of William Ayers, who had been active in SDS and the Weathermen, of the black journalist Frank Marshall Davis (a supporter of the International Longshore and Warehouse Union of Harry Bridges fame), of leftist Chicago community organizer Saul Alinsky, and of his pastor at the Trinity United Church of Christ – the Rev. Jeremiah Wright was a black militant who embraced a left critique of American society and politics. They highlighted a voting record in the US Senate and before that in the Illinois senate that, they said, put him to the left of Bernie Sanders.[11]

Obama's youthful associations spelled a message for the right, but it is possible to place more than one construction on them. It would be plausible to argue that the youthful Obama was no more than a campus poseur who dressed up in leftist airs and graces to impress others, but never really held left-wing views. Another interpretation would be that he did hold those views, but grew out of them with maturity. Still another possibility is that he retained the views, but learned to hide them in the interest of advancing his political career and getting things done. That would put him within the ambit of a time-honored political tradition, and has the ring of at least partial truth.

There can be no doubt about the youthful Obama's leftist associations. We have his word for it. In 1979 at the age of eighteen, he arrived at the Los Angeles liberal arts school, Occidental College. There, two of his particular friends were socialists from Pakistan. He admitted a hint of poseurship here: "To avoid being mistaken as a sellout, I chose my friends carefully." The smoking and the leather jackets went along with that. In his memoir there are also indications of Obama's deep concern with racial matters – he sought the company of the "more politically active black students." His sophomore bragging agenda is indicative of leftist orientation. He and his circle discussed Frantz Fanon, the black Francophone revolutionary anti-colonialist and author of *The Wretched of the Earth* (1961). They reveled in ideas about neocolonialism, Eurocentrism, and patriarchy. They listened attentively to the ideas advanced by "Marxist professors."[12]

At Columbia University, where Obama gained his bachelor's degree in political science in 1983, and then as a community organizer in Chicago, he still hung out with "friends on the left" – even if he later claimed to have disapproved of their tendency to denounce only right wing dictator-ships and not the Soviet Union. He kept up with his acquaintances in the Democratic Socialists of America (DSA). Running for the Illinois State Senate in 1996, for example, he attended a meeting organized by the youth wing of the DSA in conjunction with the University of Chicago Democrats. At about the same time, he told Todd Gitlin how much he admired his writing on the culture wars. The future president saw no reason to avoid having socialist friends.[13]

Obama did not, however, think of himself as a socialist, and poked fun at those who tried to label him thus, saying on the eve of the 2008 poll that he expected to be called socialist because he had shared his toys in kinder-garten. A pragmatist, he did not want to be tied to what people regarded as a hopeless cause – in one reference to campus communists, he described them as "wedded to lost hopes." In an address to ninety thousand people at the football stadium of the University of Michigan in Ann Arbor, he criticized protestors outside the venue who were displaying cards denouncing him as a socialist. However, he knew better than to alienate those whom he continued to call his "friends on the left." He issued no panicky, age-of-McCarthy denials. Instead, he said that he disliked extreme terms because they precluded political compromise. He thus exuded an air of reasonableness that reassured his supporters and annoyed his opponents.[14]

Turning to Obama's policies as president, they were sometimes not left wing at all. Yet some of them, such as health reform and his plans for rail transportation, were textbook socialist measures. Other Obama policies were left wing in character, without being socialist. There is a need to remember here that while all socialist policies are left in character, many left reforms are non-socialist or post-socialist in nature. In the domestic policy arena, the indications are that Obama was a president of the left with a socialist tinge who enjoyed a moderate-to-good success rate in the implementation of his polices.

In a move reminiscent of President Kennedy who had appointed Big Business and Wall Street figures to his cabinet to calm conservative nerves, the newly-elected Obama gave posts to individuals uncongenial to the left. President Bush's Secretary of Defense, Robert M. Gates, stayed in post. General Raymond T. Odierno kept his job as ground commander in Iraq until September 2010. As National Security Adviser, the incoming president chose James L. Jones, who had served on the boards of the Boeing and Chevron corporations and was a former Marine general. These were significant nods in the direction of conservative continuity, and it was no temporary phenomenon. When Obama nominated his second-term national security team he showed himself to be still bound by tradition. In January 2013, the journalist Annie Lowrey voiced one concern when she noted that he planned an inner circle "dominated by men."[15]

Yet some of the early first-term appointments did balance the picture. Signalling an advance for left goals, Obama in his first term nominated women to 43 percent of available posts. He appointed women to key positions. Senator Hilary Clinton (D-NY) became secretary of state. When her husband Bill was president, she had campaigned for health reform. As secretary of state in Obama's first term, she pressed for improved women's rights worldwide.

To be ambassador to the United Nations, Obama chose Susan Rice, a committed internationalist with an interest in fighting poverty. In a sign of his commitment to the UN, he gave her full cabinet status. Then there was Carol M. Browner. When Browner became director of the White House Office of Energy and Climate Change Policy, the *Washington Star* complained she was a "global warming czar" who believed in world government and had connections to the Socialist International. Against the background of mixed messages, *Nation* ran an issue on a split theme: "Reinventing Capitalism" and "Reimagining Socialism."[16]

To opponents of "Big Government" Obama's policies seemed socialistic because they involved federal intervention. Early in his presidency, he signed a $787 billion stimulus bill – putting America further in the red but hoping to create more jobs, more wealth creation, and eventually a greater tax take to ease the problems of debt servicing and repayment. Within a year, the package saved or created around 1.7 million jobs. At the same time, the government continued to support the nation's stricken banks and other businesses under the terms of the Troubled Asset Relief Program (TARP) set up in October 2008 under the previous administration. Some of the TARP rescues promised to yield a profit for the taxpayer in due course, for example about one billion dollars in the case of the Bank of America. But the Congressional Budget Office estimated the overall TARP loss at $99 billion, and that excluded a further $376 billion (by 2020) if the cost of the Fannie Mae and Freddie Mac rescues were thrown in, with $700 billion authorized for TARP in all.

That did not include government support to the auto industry, with General Motors (GM) and its post-bankruptcy reincarnation receiving $50 billion. The policy was a success. By November 2010 jobs were returning, the taxpayer received $7.4 billion from GM in interest and dividends, and the company was starting a return to private ownership with a $23 billion part-flotation. In spite of the last move, Obama's policies caused a widespread expectation that the government was going to nationalize several enterprises. The stimulus package and even more so the prospect of nationalization encouraged the belief that America was moving in the supposedly unAmerican direction of European-style socialism.[17]

Obama's own approach becomes a little more understandable when one considers that he admired Alexander Hamilton. A founding father of the American republic who advocated and promoted capitalism, Hamilton nevertheless wanted the federal government to play a role. Obama recalled how Hamilton had "nationalized" America's revolutionary War debt, and how he had proposed public works such as roads and bridges that would stimulate the economy. He remarked on the subsequent continuation of national projects by both Republicans and Democrats, by Lincoln as well as by FDR. The nation had benefited from public programs ranging from TVA to the Human Genome Project promoted in the presidency of George Bush Sr. "Our free market system," Obama wrote, "is the result neither of natural law nor of divine providence." He preferred it to communism and socialism, but still advocated a governmental role in the improvement of the economy.[18]

Obama's regard for Hamilton signals his endorsement of a very American brand of capitalism, one by no means removed from the practices of the democratic left, and one that had in the past commended itself to socialists. The political outlook of Broadus Mitchell, the greatest authority on Hamilton, illustrates the point. In the mid-1930s Mitchell ran for the governorship of Maryland on a socialist platform. Later in the decade, he resigned his professorship at Johns Hopkins because the university refused to admit a black student, Edward Lewis (later head of the New York Urban League). Mitchell then accepted a post at Occidental College, where Obama would in due course enroll as a student. Mitchell saw Hamilton as a "patron of government guidance" and a progenitor of "the collectivist developments during the depression of the 1930s." He portrayed him as a believer in federally sponsored industrial infrastructure such as transportation and even as a forbear of the socialist presidential candidate Norman Thomas.[19]

Obama was happy to go beyond federal buy-ins born of desperation and to undertake positive public enterprises. Take the railroads. Years before he became president, he told a French audience "I am always jealous about European trains . . . why can't we have high-speed rail?" So the Obama stimulus package included $8 billion to help with the development of faster rail networks in ten inter-city corridors spaced across continental America. To the horror of Congressman Mica, now the ranking Republican on the House Transportation and Infrastructure Committee, there would be no provision for private sector participation. The president's plan was to reduce traffic congestion, to combat pollution and to steer the nation away from its dependence on oil, which was a finite resource and had to be imported from unstable parts of the world.[20]

The new high-speed rail investment was a turnabout for the nation. The Bush administration had been committed to an oil strategy and had all but eliminated the public assistance given to Amtrak. The country's fastest intercity train, Amtrak's electrically powered Acela, managed to average 83 mph over the 209 miles between New York and Washington, DC. In China, the Harmony Express covered the 660 miles between Wuhan and

Guangzhou at an average speed of 217 mph. Obama had looked abroad and had seen a future where public investment could improve both economies and the quality of life. By the summer of 2012, three-quarters of New York to Washington, DC commuters were choosing to train not plane.[21]

The British Petroleum (BP) oil spillage in the Gulf in 2010 with all the damage it inflicted underlined Obama's case for government intervention and cleaner energy. The president strong-armed BP into establishing a $20 billion escrow fund to help the victims of the spill. It was a response to the public's demand for action, but also signaled his green commitment and his determination to regulate irresponsible corporate behavior. To Fox News and to the Tea Party crusade on the Republican right, it was further proof that he was a "closet socialist."[22]

Obama's administration was prepared to favor the public over the private on a case-by-case, pragmatic basis. Consider the case of the Pell grants. Senator Claiborne Pell (D-RI) had in 1972 secured passage of a measure to help poor students go to college by providing them with federally guaranteed loans. In 2006 the Bush administration froze the level of funding so there were fewer loans than previously, and at a lower level. This was at a time of escalating college fees – and of lenders making handsome private profits at the expense of students. In April 2009, the Obama administration proposed de-privatization of the loan industry. After eleven months of legislative combat, its supporters in Congress pushed through a law that saved the taxpayer $61 billion over ten years, and delivered an additional $40 billion in support to underprivileged students.[23]

Another reform of the early Obama period was the Matthew Shepard/ Hate Crimes Prevention Act that received presidential approval on October 28, 2009. This had its roots in the Old Left's antilynching campaigns. But its title honored the name of a Wyoming student murdered eleven years earlier on account of his gay orientation. It addressed a problem identified in FBI crime figures for 1998–2007, an upward trend in offenses against non-heterosexual victims. The 1969 Federal Civil Rights Law had made it a crime racially to abuse someone engaged in federally protected activities such as schooling. The new law extended the same protection to lesbian, gay and transgender people.

Under Obama's watch, the government also ended the ban on openly gay men and women serving in the military, with Republicans joining Democrats to vote for the measure in the Senate in December 2010. The measure was a triumph for the newer, more diversified left.[24]

In a White House ceremony on March 23, 2010, the president appended his left-handed signature to the Patient Protection and Affordable Care Act. Together with the Health Care and Education Reconciliation Act that he endorsed a week later, it reformed the US health care system and would be his landmark reform.

"Obamacare" was not as revolutionary as some might have wished. There was a continuing reliance on the private insurance industry. The model was by no means uncongenial to business and indeed would deliver healthier and more efficient employees. In Massachusetts, the conservative, business-orientated Governor Mitt Romney had gone down a parallel private road to widen access to health care – his 2006 scheme halved the number of uninsured in the Bay State and left only 2.1 percent of children outside the system.[25]

However, the 2010 reform was more radical in significant ways. Romney had envisaged a state-by-state expansion of his scheme, whereas Obama took the plunge of introducing a federal program. Even if it relied on private resources, the outcome he envisaged was not far from Europe's socialist-backed models. The Republicans' term of opprobrium, "socialized medicine", would seem to be apt descriptively, if not judgmentally.

Implemented in stages and coming into full force by 2018, Obama's reform aimed to reduce the number of uninsured residents by thirty-two million. The percentage of insured having declined from 90 percent in the 1970s to 85 percent in 2010, it would now rise to 95 percent. The citizens who remained uninsured included people who refused to insure themselves, those who were eligible for treatment but exempt from having to pay on account of their extreme poverty, and – about one third of the twenty-three million residue – illegal immigrants.

There had been a bitter debate over the legislation and Obama, together with congressional allies such as the House Speaker Nancy Pelosi, had fought on at the risk of a politically debilitating defeat. Journalists Sheryl Stolberg and Jeff Zeleny rightly considered that the proposal had been the president's "highest legislative priority." For although his allies in Congress did much of the arm wrestling, Obama toured the nation to win the support of America's voters. On the stump, he put a human face on the complex health proposals. For example at Grand Junction, Colorado, he told about a six-year-old local, Thomas Wilkes. Thomas had hemophilia, and his medical expenses were approaching the one-million-dollar cap imposed by his family's private health insurance company. The new legislation would abolish the practice of imposing health care caps.[26]

The health legislation addressed not just the uninsured, but also the problems of the insured. Its provisions made it illegal to refuse insurance on account of pre-existing medical conditions. They furthermore advanced preventive medicine, for example by requiring restaurant chains to declare the caloric content of their food – an attack on the problems caused by rising levels of obesity.

The measures were designed to be prudent in the context of straightened times. Cost-saving arrangements would help to pay for the widening of medical provision. For example, to restrain the pharmaceutical industry's inflation of prices, the Food and Drug Administration would now be authorized to approve generic versions of drugs. As Joe the Plumber had feared, redistributive taxes on the more affluent would help pay the costs not met by increased efficiency. Americans making more than a million a year would, according to one estimate, pay an additional $46,000 in taxes by 2013. If approved in its original form by legislators, the Congressional Budget Office predicted the health scheme as a whole in its first decade of operation would reduce the federal deficit by $143 billion.[27]

In its concerns for economic efficiency and universality, the Obamacare law matched the ambitions of Selig Perlman and his collaborators in their federally sponsored health insurance reports of 1914. It fell short of these socialists' plans in failing to make health insurance compulsory. Also, there was disappointment over the "public option." Mooted by Berkeley political science professor Jacob Hacker in 2005, this would have been a federally supported alternative to private insurance that would provide choice and competition. There was fierce opposition and tirades about the danger of socialized medicine. The former Democratic vice-presidential candidate Senator Joe Lieberman (Independent-CT) withdrew his support from the public option making it impossible to deliver enough aye votes in the Senate. The proposal formally died in the Senate Finance Committee in September 2009 when Health and Human Services Secretary Kathleen Sebelius said that non-profit cooperative insurance schemes would be an acceptable alternative.

Yet in spite of such setbacks the Obama reform could still be said to have rounded out, in significant ways, the Wisconsin program for an American welfare state . In some ways, for example its withdrawal of support from branded medicines, Obamacare extended the Perlman program. In no other advanced industrial country did 33 percent of the population have to forego medical care for reasons of cost, and the Obama reform promised to end that tragedy.[28]

The defeat of the public option proposal still infuriated the left. The socialist Senator Sanders lamented that the compromise kept him awake at night, as "the insurance companies and the drug companies will be laughing all the way to the bank." His allies in the Democratic Party felt the same way, and one journalist wrote of "an uprising on the Democratic left." Other commentators belittled Obama's reform plan by comparing it with past efforts. They noted variously that President Nixon had once proposed the federal government should step in to pick up the tab for those without private insurance, and that the Clinton proposal of 1993 had been more radical than the 2010 statute. But there was, of course, another difference. The Obama measure passed into law.[29]

A more serious challenge to the health reform came from the right. There was an all-out attack on what Palin called Obama's "evil" proposals. Conservative groups charged that the UK's National Health Service was Obama's model, and they paid for attack ads defaming the British system. They echoed the earlier generation of conservatives who had denounced "creeping socialism" and "British Fabianism" in the 1940s.[30]

While the British admired the excellence of US medicine, they had long been aware of the deficiencies of the American health care system, and they hit back. The British Embassy corrected American conservative misrepresentations. On the day of the bill's passage, a Gallup poll indicated that a majority of US citizens supported the health reform or a stronger version of it.[31]

In June 2012, the US Supreme Court passed favorably on the Affordable Care Act. The battle was still not fully won. Conservatives hoped to obstruct implementation on the local level. In spite of the fact that Mitt Romney was the Republican candidate for the presidency in the 2012 election, they also promised federal repeal, should the Republicans win. In the event, Obama was the victor, a circumstance that *New York Times* reporter Abby Goodnough thought "all but guarantees that the historic legislation will survive."[32]

Turning to the character of Obama's foreign policy and his achievements, one can begin by posing the question, what would a left-wing foreign policy look like, now that the left has changed since its socialist days? It may be inferred from foreign policy debates that a left-inclining president would oppose the foreign exploitation of workers, women and minorities, would tolerate the election of left-wing candidates in foreign countries, and would defend the civil liberties of dissidents in right-wing as well as in communist and other autocracies. Such a president would favor peace and distance himself from militarism including the unilateral imposition of US military outcomes, favoring instead internationalist solutions through the UN and other means.

As a young man, Obama had been aware of the left's critique of US foreign policy, of its opposition, as he put it, "not only to the Vietnam War but also to the broader aims of American foreign policy." He took on board its objections to the CIA, to the military-industrial complex, to the World Bank, and to "manifestations of American arrogance, jingoism, racism, capitalism, and imperialism." He also recalled "arguments with some of my friends on the left" in the course of which he would defend "aspects of Reagan's worldview." Osama bin Laden, he pointed out, was "not Ho Chi Minh." If Obama was anti-imperialist, he also offered a critique of the anti-imperialism of the left, and favored "the ideals of free markets and liberal democracy." Yet none of this precluded a leftward drift. He used the phrase "my friends on the left" on occasions too frequent to be reliably counted, but rarely if ever referred to his "friends on the right." Obama pitched for the middle ground, but with a left curve.[33]

The political scientist Rob Singh suggests that in spite of the stereotyping of George Bush as right wing in his foreign policy and Obama as left wing, continuities and similarities exist. But he does see Obama as a president who is open to the idea that we may be living in a "post American" world, with US power in relative decline and a concomitant need for greater international cooperation. Recognition of this potential reality is less likely to come from the drum-beating "patriotic" wing of American politics.[34]

A sampling of Obama's policies in practice yields a mixed picture. We can begin with Iraq. Early in May 2010, the Obama administration agreed a deal to end the de-Ba'athification of Iraqi politics. The Bush administration had introduced and enforced de-Ba'athification, and the reversal of the policy does open up the possibility that Obama had shifted to the left.

Pan Arabist, secular and opposed to western imperialism, the Ba'ath Party had been the bedrock of Saddam Hussein's power in Iraq. This was one reason why, after the 2003 war, the American-led coalition excluded Ba'athists from the Iraqi armed forces and civil administration. There was justice in this, in that the Ba'athists had been responsible for atrocities, including genocide against their fellow citizens, the Kurds. However, the blanket disqualification stripped out the administrative experience that was necessary to a functioning society. In addition, the purge made it difficult to establish an Iraqi government that would command support. The restoration of Ba'athist rights meant a degree of recognition for a party that could be relied on to oppose Islamic extremism, and with other factors potentially helped to limit the operations of Al Qaeda. But the Ba'ath Party had also had a formal commitment to socialism and a history of implementing socialist policies while being opposed to communism – another reason for the Bush administrations' hostility, as it had wished to further the interests of private oil companies in Iraq. The Ba'athist restoration raised the possibility that an Obama foreign policy might prove to be congenial to the international left.[35]

There had been widespread hopes at home and abroad that president Obama would usher in a foreign policy based on the principles of peace and equality. In October 2002, he had explained to a peace group in Chicago that he regarded President Bush's plan for war against Iraq as a ploy to distract attention from inequality at home and from an impending economic depression. Once in the Senate, Obama refused to vote against funds for America's soldiers in the field, or in favor of quick withdrawal, but he maintained his antiwar stance. Expectations soared when he entered the White House.

Within days of taking the presidential oath in January 2009, Obama banned torture as an instrument of national security. He ordered the closure of the Guantanamo Bay facility where suspected terrorists kidnapped by US forces were incarcerated indefinitely and without trial. Implementation would be a problem – where could the Guantanamo detainees be safely sent? – but Obama seemed to promise new departures. Reacting to what they saw as real change, the American right spoke contemptuously of Obama's "apology tour."[36]

Within nine months of assuming office, Obama had won the Nobel Peace Prize for his "extraordinary efforts to strengthen international diplomacy and cooperation between peoples." The chairman of the awarding committee, Thorbjorn Jagland, was the son of a welder who had risen to be Prime Minister of Norway and a vice president of the Socialist International. An American journalist put the inevitable question to the former premier, "Here in the United States, 'socialism' is one of the words bandied about by Obama's critics. When people hear 'socialist', they worry you're going to take away their cars and make them ride bicycles." Jagland replied, "Look at the welfare state in Norway that the Labor Party Social Democrats built. Everyone has better cars than most of the Americans."[37]

There were, however, less sanguine feelings on the left, with suspicions that early expectations had been too high. There was a fear that Obama would not fully deliver the "change" he had promised as a candidate, and that the judgment of the Nobel Prize committee would prove to have been premature. Extrication of America from the quagmires of Iraq and Afghanistan proved to be a challenging task, and Obama decided against a sharp break with past practices. In a move that was unsympathetic to the left agenda, Congress in May 2010 approved his request for $60 billion to continue America's two wars. Inflation-adjusted figures showed the United States had by 2010 spent more money on Iraq and Afghanistan than on any other conflicts in its history, barring only World War II. Nothing could have been more invidious to the pioneers of left wing antimilitarism stretching back to Tom Paine via Norman Thomas, Eugene Debs and Henry Thoreau.[38]

The Obama administration furthermore used remote-control drone attacks to assassinate people in far away places whom it deemed, without benefit of trial and jury, to be enemies of the United States. It did not consult the governments of the target countries, and there were civilian casualties. Arguably the drone strikes, like clandestine CIA operations, were a substitute for war and an alternative to militarism. But they also continued the unilateralism of the preceding Bush administration that had introduced the drone in 2004, and the operations offended many foreigners, including the foreign left.

The 2011 Navy-CIA special forces operation against Bin Laden's compound in Abbottabad, Pakistan, that resulted in the terrorist leader's death may have caused rejoicing in America, but it was done without consulting the host country, just as in the case of the drone strikes that hit northwest Pakistan on many occasions. Rumors of unadmitted Pakistani complicity in some of America's operations did not erase the impression of Washington's high-handedness. Foreign policy unilateralism had clearly not ceased with George Bush. In fact, Obama had embraced the principle. In 2007, he had warned, "No president should ever hesitate to use force – unilaterally if necessary – to protect ourselves."[39]

Even as he accepted the Nobel Prize with Jagland likening him to Martin Luther King, President Obama was in the process of escalating the war in Afghanistan. Congress having opened the taxpayers' purse, he sent in an additional thirty thousand troops with the declared aim of starting a withdrawal from a position of strength in July 2011. In his Nobel acceptance speech the chief executive reassuringly invoked the concept of fighting only "just wars." However, the "push" was unmistakably military aggression. The left was unhappy about it. One historian of American socialism, Paul Buhle, suggested that the Obama foreign policy was a variant of the "Empire Liberalism" that US organized labor had traditionally favored

– rights for mainly white, male workers at home, and imperial subjugation everywhere else.[40]

Other grave problems that President Obama confronted were nuclear non-proliferation and Israel. The 2010 Review Conference for the 1970 Treaty on the Non-Proliferation of Nuclear Weapons (NPT) took place in New York under the auspices of the UN between 3 and 28 May. Obama had prepared the way by promising the USA would not use any of its 9,600 nuclear warheads against non-nuclear nations that were in compliance with the existing NPT, and that America would eschew the development of new nuclear weapons.

Nations like North Korea and Iran that were developing or thinking of developing nuclear weapons had hitherto been exploiting the American position, which appeared to be, "I've got one, but you can't have one because you are a rogue state – and by the way, I reserve the right to be a rogue state myself whenever I want to." By showing more restraint itself, Obama's America hoped to bring effective pressure to bear on countries like Iran.

Signed in Prague, the "New Start" treaty with Russia provided for a 50 percent reduction in nuclear missile launchers and for the resumption of inspection regimes. Risking his political credibility, the president pushed the measure in the teeth of Republican opposition in the Senate. He won, and the treaty came into effect. The left was not alone in agitating for such reductions – the Republicans' President Eisenhower had been a champion of nuclear restraint – but the reductions were certainly consistent with the left's antimilitarist tradition.[41]

Israel was an impediment to nuclear disarmament initiatives. Perhaps because they did not yet have nuclear weapons, its Arab neighbors wanted the Middle East to be a nuclear-free zone, an idea that appealed to America because it would embrace Iran. But although it was an open secret that Israel had a nuclear arsenal, that nation was not a signatory of the NPT, and refused to play ball unless its neighbors recognized its right to exist.

Obama was not pleased with Israel and was sympathetic to the Palestinian cause – his first international telephone call out of the White House was to Mahmoud Abbas, a biddable Palestinian leader. Obama and Israel's prime minister Benjamin Netanyahu had little love for each other. The president may well have intended to get tough with Israel, if not over nuclear weapons, then over its policy of expropriating and settling Palestinian territory on the West Bank – a policy widely regarding as destructive of the Middle East peace process. In the event, Israel continued to colonize the West Bank, blockaded and bombarded the Gaza strip in retaliation for missiles being fired into Israel, and used lethal armed force against international attempts to ship supplies to Gaza. The "Arab spring" of 2011 and then from 2012 the Libyan civil war destabilized the region. Against this background and to the annoyance of the left who by now regarded Israel as a bastion of the right, Obama remained silent over Tel Aviv's more aggressive actions.[42]

To gain a sense of perspective, it is appropriate to look at Jewish-American opinion. Attention often focused on the American Israel Public Affairs Committee (AIPAC). This lobby described itself as "Pro-Israel" but more accurately defended the hawks running Israeli foreign policy, a stance that endeared AIPAC to America's neoconservatives and Tea Party activists. However, to focus on AIPAC is to ignore a very real left tradition in the US Jewish community.

Nation-wide, an estimated 78 percent of the Jewish vote had gone to the candidate who was the best available antithesis to neoconservatism, Barack Obama. In April 2008, a group of American Jews formed the J Street lobby – so named because it offered an alternative to the established lobbying industry on Washington, DC's K Street. J Street offered criticisms of Israeli foreign policy.[43]

Such people could take their cue from the opposition in Israel, which was, after all, a democratic nation. Its leading daily newspaper, *Ha'aretz*, was critical of Gaza policy. In America, groups like Los Angeles Jews for Peace made parallel criticisms, for example of the Israeli navy's piratical actions. Significant numbers of American Jews could claim to be on the left of the president in regard to Middle Eastern policy. Obama's sympathies may have been with them, but they and others on the left could complain he did not deliver.[44]

The 2012 presidential victory empowered Obama to continue his programs. It was also a potent symbol of change in America, change of a type for which the left had long fought. When Obama articulated his policy, however, he observed another American tradition, the one that dictated that the left and its variants – liberalism, socialism, progressivism – should rest unacknowledged. As ever, the motive for the omission was the ambition to win.

In December 2011, Obama delivered a speech making his pitch for a second term as president. He chose as his location Osawatomie, Kansas. It was a community of just four thousand people. But it had symbolic significance. The abolitionist John Brown had made his base there in the 1850s. And it was the place where, in 1910, Theodore Roosevelt had delivered his famous "New Nationalism" speech in which he demanded government for "the welfare of the people", and a "graduated income tax" to counter the privilege of those of "swollen fortune."[45]

For articulating such a program, Obama said, the former Republican president "was called a radical, a socialist, even a communist." Obama offered this history lesson about an iconic figure for Republicans and neo-conservatives in the hope of winning bipartisan support. He was saying, without in any way admitting to his own radical tendencies, that great leaders are sometimes accused of leftism.[46]

In spite of his health care achievement in Massachusetts, Obama's Republican opponent Mitt Romney ran in the 2012 election as a conservative businessman with an appeal to the American right. He never quite escaped the image that he was the candidate of WORM, White Old Rich Men, whom the left had reviled ever since the days of the student-led New Left revolt against the Vietnam War. When he announced, "I'm not concerned about the very poor," he made himself a hostage to fortune. People overlooked his add-on, that he believed in a safety net for the poor.[47]

The Occupy movement was anti-Romney. Its adherents, largely young and successors tactically to the New Left students of the 1960s, had as their slogan "We are the 99%", a reference to the wealth held by 1 percent of Americans who paid less and less taxes. Beginning as Occupy Wall Street in Zuccotti Park in September 2011, their movement spread right across the USA. In one way, it rebuked Obama for doing too little. In a more important way, the spontaneous uprising it was a nail in the coffin of the affluent right who had financed the supposedly grassroots Tea Party. It prepared the way for the election result of 2012.

For by the start of 2012, people under thirty favored Obama over his likely rival Romney by an estimated twenty-four points. Although the eighteen to twenty-nine year-old age group suffered disproportionately from unemployment, a Harvard-commissioned survey calculated that its support for Obama held up as the election approached, and on election day exit polls indicated that the incumbent substantially outpolled his challenger amongst the young.

Obama also enjoyed more support than his opponent from women. There were women in his cabinet, far more Democrat than Republican women in the House, and some Republican candidates were gaffe-prone in the campaign, for example Missourian Senate candidate Todd Akin had to apologize for using the phrase "legitimate rape." Minorities voters completed the roster of those who boosted Obama to his 2.4 percent majority of the popular vote. Romney won the white vote by 59 percent to 39 percent, but America's changing demographics meant that was not enough. Voters of Asian and Hispanic descent plumped for Obama. An overwhelming 96 percent of the black vote went to a man the color of whose skin was a political statement in itself.[48]

In his pronouncements as well as in his persona, Obama illustrated how different phases in the history of the left can overlap. His achievement of universal health insurance may well have marked the end of the socialist phase in the left's history (because of ultimate victory, not defeat). He still acknowledged his support for Old Left issues. In his second inaugural address of January 2013 he declared, "Medicare and Medicaid and Social Security – these things do not sap our initiative; they strengthen us." But in that speech he also endorsed that touchstone campaign of the Newer Left, gay rights – the first time a president had been so bold on a major occasion.[49]

Obama was not entirely a man of the left, but he was influenced by it, and strove with considerable success to implement reforms from the left agenda. He was significant both as a symbol and for his policies, in both senses being a credible left-wing figure. Perhaps most conservatives would agree with that, but non-conservatives persisted in questioning the president's commitment and performance. That has been the story of the left since 1900, a story of numerous achievements but muted acknowledgments.

APPENDIX:
DEFINING THE LEFT AND ADJACENT TERMS

This appendix offers a definition of terms and an explanation why, in a book such as this that covers a long period, the term "left" is more useful than the currently fashionable label "progressive." Let's look, in turn, at the political meanings of the main words in contention – progressive, liberal and left.

Progressivism is rooted in the nineteenth-century idea that the world was becoming a better place. The America of 1900 was an improvement on the America of 1800 and the America of 2000 would be better still. So prevalent did this mode of thought become, that politicians began to call themselves "Progressives" with a capital "P", and in the 1912 presidential election an independent Progressive Party polled 27 percent of the votes cast, more than the Republicans (the Democrats, many of whom also claimed to be Progressives, won with 42 percent).

The Progressive Party's platform contained a commitment to social security and several other planks with which present-day progressives would be comfortable. However, progressivism is a problematic label from the historian's point of view. The Progressives of the early twentieth-century "Progressive Era" were a mixed bunch. They contained moralists, precursors of today's conservative Christians, with agendas such as the elimination of "vice" and drunkenness. They were furthermore associated with an assault on civil liberties in World War I and the ensuing Red Scare.

The Progressives of the Progressive Era contained enlightened citizens within their ranks, but also racists who thought that America was more progressive than, say, India or Italy, because it was "Anglo-Saxon." For decades, the belief would persist that the United States was an exemplary "modern" nation that should be a model for the rest of the world, especially "developing" nations. A heritage of the Progressive Era, "nation-building", the attempt to reform foreign nations to make them more like America, is today part of the conservative agenda.

Progressivism with a capital "P" survived into the 1920s, but by this time the idea of progress had taken a brutal hit. The horrors of World War I discredited the idea that modern Americans and North Europeans were in some way more enlightened than, say, the headhunters of Borneo. Today, progressives with their lower-case "p" do not really believe in the reactionary baggage of the idea of progress. They have become synonymous with those of liberal or left persuasion.

In its pure form, nineteenth century liberalism was a wonderful ideal. Free trade with other nations and a government hands-off approach to commerce at home would ensure rationality in the market place and prosperity for all. That prosperity would spread worldwide, and export-import ventures would foster mutual dependency ensuring that wars would no longer be in anybody's interest. Liberalism extended also to personal freedoms, such as those guaranteed by the first ten amendments of the US Constitution.

This liberal philosophy first ran into the imperfections of human nature, and then went into reverse. The imperfections were deviations from pure doctrine that had the effect of discrediting it. Businessmen who wanted a free market in labor to keep wages low and opposed labor unions nevertheless insisted on protective tariffs, on federally financed internal improvements like harbors and bridges, and on government assistance against strikers, including the use of military force. This perversion of traditional liberal principles provoked the call for a new approach.

By the second decade of the twentieth century, the people labeled then and since as liberals had swung around to support the idea of government regulation as a means of ensuring the public good. The new approach was quite the reverse of the nineteenth century idea, and became entrenched. As the decades rolled by, liberals came to see the federal government more and more in terms of a countervailing force protecting the public against Big Business, and also Big Labor.

It was already a strange journey and a cautionary tale for those who would use the word "liberal" as if it were a terminological constant. Then, a further terminological u-turn occurred. By the 1950s, some people calling themselves liberals had become fervent anticommunists. They saw liberalism as a classless, ideology-free creed that could unite the nation against the Cold War foe, the Soviet Union. They were unsympathetic to civil liberties, and moved via a stage known as neoliberalism to become neoconservatives.

Doesn't that seem strange today? For there has been yet another u-turn. Over the last twenty or thirty years, "liberal" has become a dirty word on the lips of a later generation of neoconservatives. The reason why? To their critics, a still-newer, post-1950s generation of liberals have become indistinguishable from leftists.

Like progressivism and liberalism, leftism has undergone change over the last hundred years, and any definition has to take account of that. However, the left has by and large changed in an incremental way, embracing more and more causes as time has passed. It has not undergone drastic changes in meaning, and for that reason has had a consistent impact that can be coherently described.

For our discussion here, we can note but set aside the fact that the political use of the term "left" goes back to when the supporters of the French Revolution sat on the left side of their national assembly. For the term did not come into general political use in America until the 1930s. Historians use the terminology to describe political tendencies from around 1900.[1]

In the Progressive Era, some prominent Progressives could be said to have been on the left. President Theodore Roosevelt is an example, at least in domestic politics. Much of the burgeoning labor movement was also on the left, even if the president of the American Federation of Labor, Samuel Gompers, opposed involvement in politics and rejected socialism. Prominent religious leaders additionally gave their support to leftist reforms.

But the entity that most methodically defined the left agenda in the first three decades of the twentieth century was the Socialist Party of America (SPA). From the time of its first platform in 1904, the SPA made an escalating series of demands – for income tax, universal free education, old age pensions, free medical services and drugs, the public ownership of various utilities, antilynching legislation, a minimum wage, respect for civil liberties, opposition to militarism, and independence for the Philippines. They defined the program of the early American left.[2]

People who describe themselves as socialists are still present in American life – Bernie Sanders sits in the US Senate representing the state of Vermont, for example, while Brian Moore makes radical movies. However, it is not too harsh to say that by the 1950s the SPA, and with it the whole idea of socialism as a force in American life, was a fading dream.

The term "left", too, closely associated as it was with socialism, seemed distinctly old-fashioned in the 1950s. However, this was to change. In the 1960s, the "left" morphed into the "New Left" and became fashionable once again. The New Left of the 1960s concentrated on one aim in particular, ending American involvement in the Vietnam War. In its opposition to a war, it was more effective than the Old Left, but was still fighting a traditional leftist cause, antimilitarism.

What we have called the "Newer Left" succeeded it. This was more diversified, broke new ground, and between the 1970s and the present century defined much of the agenda associated with the left of the Obama era. In defining this broader left, we lack a convenient guide such as the successive platforms of the SPA, or the carefully articulated Port Huron statement of the New Left (1962). In search of alternative guidance, it is useful to consider what conservatives said.

In 1991, the University of Virginia sociologist James Davison Hunter published his influential book, *Culture Wars: The Struggle to Define America*. He departed from the view of Harvard's Arthur M. Schlesinger Jr., who had argued in 1949 that the pragmatism of the "center" had rendered obsolete the old left-versus-right struggles in American politics. Hunter wrote of the "eclipse of the middle" and of a polarized left and right. But the polarization was no longer (in Hunter's view) about such issues as workers' rights or federal management of the economy. The "new lines of conflict" amounted to a political "culture war" addressing the issues of "abortion, child care, funding for the arts, affirmative action and quotas, gay rights, values in public education, or multiculturalism."[3]

Political and cultural clashes did indeed take place. The battles raged within six broadly definable categories of debate. One of these was religion, with the left inclining to an antitheocratic if often Christian-inspired viewpoint. There were debates over evolution and intelligent design, school prayers, permissiveness, abortion, euthanasia, stem cell research, and separation of church and state.

Race and ethnicity was another forum for public discourse, with the left favoring toleration and proactive measures to ensure equality. For example, the left was more ready to defend affirmative action programs than the right, supported multiculturalism, and lined up against attempts to show that certain non-white races were relatively unintelligent.

The left characteristically adopted a pro-civil liberties stance. This applied in race relations but also to other issues. The left defended free speech, opposed capital punishment, defended privacy and opposed surveillance programs. It campaigned against the judicial oppression of minorities and poor people.

A fourth category of debate had to do with violence and foreign policy.

The left favored gun control legislation and opposed militarism, notably in the wars in Vietnam, Nicaragua and Iraq. It also campaigned for the preservation of American values in times of emergency, for example questioning the Patriot Act of 2001 and attacking such practices as the torturing of prisoners at Abu Ghraib, the illegal rendition (kidnapping) of foreign nationals and the unconstitutional detention of terror suspects in Guantanamo Bay.

Fifth, the left continued to advocate the use of federal government power. This embraced the continuation of traditional socialist reform, notably the campaign for universal medical insurance and care. It also meant using government power to defend consumer rights, and to advance green agendas such as those on the restriction of toxic emissions.

Finally, there was the family. The left opposed the corporal punishment of children, upheld the feminist cause and contraception, defended gay and transgender rights, and favored sex education.

NOTES

NOTES TO CHAPTER 1

1. London to Houghton, Mifflin & Co., January 31, 1900, Box 1, folder 12, JL.
2. London to Edward Applegarth, June 22, 1897, Box 1, folder 1, JL.
3. Jack London, "The Question of the Maximum," in London, *War of the Classes* (New York: Grosset & Dunlap, 1908 [1905]), p. 194, note.
4. Gitlin, *World is Watching*, p. 2.
5. Brian Stelter, *New York Times*, January 21, 2011.
6. Frank Rich, "The Billionaires Bankrolling the Tea Party," *New York Times*, August 28, 2010; Cantor, *Free and Reduced*, p. 15.
7. Reporters sans frontiers, Annual Worldwide Press Freedom Index, 2008, available at <http://en.rsf.org/press-freedom-index-2008,33.html> (last accessed June 15, 2010). The USA rose to number 20 in 2009.
8. *New York Times*, June 20, August 7, 2012.
9. *New York Times*, October 9, 10, 1917, undated clipping from *New York World* in Box 258, RM; Beard, "The Hire Learning in America," *The Dial* (December 14, 1918), 555. On the "military-industrial-university complex," see Stanford chapter, SDS, "Stanford, the Trustees and Southeast Asia" (undated, typewritten pamphlet), RFD. See also Lens, *Military-Industrial Complex*, chapter 7, "Academia in Harness," pp. 123–38.
10. *Commentary* article quoted in Lockman, *Contending Visions*, p. 255; Schrecker, *Lost Soul*, p. 146, citing David Horowitz, *The Professors: The 101 Most Dangerous Academics in America* (Lanham, MD: Regnery, 2006).
11. Kazin, *American Dreamers*, p. 255.
12. Hedges, *Death*, pp. 6, 21; Hodge, *Mendacity*, pp. 1, 19. The reference is to Obama's *The Audacity of Hope: Thoughts on Reclaiming the American Dream* (2006).
13. Google Advanced Search *New York Times* domain accessed on November 1, 2010 for the period November 2, 2009, to November 1, 2010; "philandering" quotation from Dinesh D'Souza, "How Obama Thinks," Forbes.com,

September 27, 2010, available at <http://www.forbes.com/forbes/2010/0927/politics-socialism-capitalism-private-enterprises-obama-business-problem.html> (last accessed November 8, 2010).

14. Milton and Rose Friedman, *Free to Choose*, p. 334. The planks and evidences of their enactment are listed on pp. 360–61.

15. Archer, *Why is there no Labor Party*, pp. 113, 233, 237 and throughout on the US–Australia comparison; Sklar, "Capitalism and Socialism", p. 305.

16. Anatoly Liberman, "The Sinister Influence of the Left Hand", available at <http://blog.oup.com/2010/09/left-hand> (last accessed January 25, 2013).

17. Friedrich Engels to Frederick Sorge, December 2, 1893, in *Science and Society*, 2 (1937–8), 374–75; Bimba, *History American Working Class*, p. 353; Tawney, *American Labour Movement*, pp. 56–57; Laski, *American Democracy*, p. 200–201; Pelling, "A British View", 227–41; Pelling, *America and the British Left*, p. 6; Jeffreys-Jones, *Violence and Reform*, chapter 2, "The Anatomy of a Myth," pp. 8–30; Jeffreys-Jones, *In Spies We Trust*, chapter 8, "An American Gift: Government in the Sunshine," pp. 152–72. Individual American writers did have an impact on British socialists, for example Edgar Snow's *Red Star over China* (1937) influenced the youthful Raymond Williams: Raymond Williams, *Who Speaks for Wales? Nation, Culture and Identity*, ed. Daniel Williams (Cardiff: University of Wales Press, 2003), p. 55.

18. Perlman, *Theory of Labor Movement*, p. ix; Lipset and Marks, *It Didn't Happen Here*, pp. 9, 16–17; Hartz, *Liberal Tradition*, p. 6. For a further critique of failure of American socialism theories, see Kazin, *American Dreamers*, pp. 112–13, 293n6.

19. Kazin, *New York Jew*, p. 221; author's interview with Frances Piven, March 29, 2009.

20. Benn, *Why America Needs Democratic Socialism*, p. 6.

21. Adams, *Epic of America*, p. 411. See also Drucker, *Post-Capitalist Society*, p. 5; Sklar in Becker and Sklar, *Postimperialism*, p. 12; Chandler, "Creeping Socialism," 38; Jo Blanden, Paul Gregg and Stephen Machin, "Intergenerational Mobility in Europe and North America: A Report Supported by the Sutton Trust," April 2005, p. 7: available at <http://cep.lse.ac.uk/about/news/IntergenerationalMobility.pdf> (last accessed September 24, 2010). See also Corak, *Generational Income Mobility*, pp. 8–9; Erikson and Goldthorpe, "American Rates of Social Mobility Exceptionally High?" 20; Erikson and Goldthorpe, *Constant Flux*, p. 318, 320; Levine, *U.S. Income Distribution and Mobility*, p. 14.

22. Markowitz email to author, October 6, 2011.

23. Richard Wolff, "What's Left of the American Left?" *Guardian*, 13 March 2011; Adam Price (formerly a Plaid Cymru M.P.), *Guardian*, 13 February 2012; table, "Views of 'Capitalism' and 'Socialism'," indicating relative preference for socialism of 18–29-year-olds, in Pew Research Center report of

December 28, 2011, available at <http://www.people-press.org/2011/12/28/
little-change-in-publics-response-to-capitalism-socialism/?src=prc-headline>
(last accessed November 30, 2012).

24. Richard J. Oestreicher, "America Left Ephemera Collection: Overview"
(University of Pittsburg): available at <http://www.history.pitt.edu/initiatives/
index.php> (last accessed December 3, 2012).
25. Peter Dreier, "The Fifty Most Influential Progressives of the Twentieth
Century," *Nation* (October 4, 2010), 11.
26. Kazin, *American Dreamers*, pp. xiii–xv, xvii.
27. *Washington Post*, September 12, 2001.
28. See London, "Question of the Maximum", Du Bois, "African Roots of War",
Beard, *Devil Theory of War*, Williams, *Tragedy*, and Said, *Orientalism*. The
study of popular influence on foreign policy has accelerated since the 1940s –
see the essays and bibliography in Johnstone and Laville, eds., *U.S. Public and
American Foreign Policy*.
29. Eckhardt, *Wright*, p. 3.
30. Burns, "Without Due Process", 246.
31. *New York Times*, September 6, 2010. Scholars have shown that, at the end of
the twentieth century, the federal government was spending 34.3 percent of
gross domestic product, compared with 48.2 percent spent by governments in
Europe's euro zone. Ten years later at the end of the supposedly free-enterprise
Bush administration, the US figure was up to 39.9 percent, compared with 47.1
percent, the USA–Europe gap having narrowed from 14 percentile points to 8.
If the willingness to engage in general government expenditure is, as conservatives not unreasonably assume, a measure of leftist influence, there has been a
significant policy rapprochement. In fact, some election results in Europe and
the western hemisphere (Latin America as well as the USA) suggest that the
Old World is becoming more conservative just as the New World is cutting a
left/progressive path. See Borcherding, "Hundred Years of Spending," pp. 27,
30, and *Newsnight*, February 16, 2009. In the early twenty-first century, both
total government expenditure and government social expenditure were still
lower in the United States than in most European countries, but it was by no
means bottom of the list: Baldwin, *Narcissism of Minor Differences*, pp. 62,
71.
32. Whiting, *Labour Party and Taxation*, pp. 269, 273; Levine, *U.S. Income
Distribution and Mobility*, pp. i, 4, 9.

NOTES TO CHAPTER 2

1. Fine, *Without Blare of Trumpets*, pp. 94–97; Blum, *American Lightening*,
p. 47.
2. Fine, *Without Blare of Trumpets*, p. 93.

3. Simply translated from the French, "syndicalism" was really just another word for unionism, but it had acquired the further meaning of an anarchistic rejection of politics. The work of the main French exponent of revolutionary syndicalism, Georges Sorel, was not translated into English until 1914, and would in any case have been unlikely reading material for Haywood and his not very literary followers. E. T. Devine, "Industrial Dispute or Revolution?" *Survey*, 26 (1911), 835–37; Georges Sorel, *Reflections on Violence*, trans. T. E. Hulme and J. Roth (New York: B. W. Huebsch, 1914).

4. Roosevelt quoted in Chace, *1912*, p. 167.

5. Adams, *Age of Industrial Violence*, p. 216.

6. Anon., "Feeble-Mindedness as a Cause for Homelessness," n.d., Reel 3, pp. 0887–89, 0912–14, RD.

7. Witte to Leiserson, January 12, 1910, Ameringer to Leiserson, April 22, 1905, and stenographer's minutes, pp. 274, 329–30, 410, CIR meeting, Washington, DC, December 30, 1913, all WML.

8. Nelson, *Unemployment Insurance*, p. 5; quotations, emphasis in the original, from Notes of Selig Perlman, Meeting of the Unemployed Conference, February 27, 1914, Reel 16, pp. 0160, 0165, RD; Leiserson to Walsh, March 14, 1914, WML.

9. Leiserson, "Memorandum in re National System of Labor Exchanges," n.d., Reel 3, pp. 0414, 0418, 0419, RD.

10. Leiserson, "A Proposed Plan to Establish a National Bureau of Employment in the Department of labor," n.d., Reel 11, pp. 0342, 0367, RD.

11. Edwin E. Witte, "Legal and Legislative. Outline of Subjects to be Covered, and Work Already Done," 1914, Reel 1, p. 0581, RD; "Social Insurance", n.d., a table of contents, Reel 3, CIRW; Wilbur J. Cohen, "Edwin E. Witte (1887–1960): Father of Social Security," *Industrial and Labor Relations Review*, 14 (October 1960), 7–9. Berkowitz, *American Welfare State* places the origins of social security in the 1930s.

12. Perlman, "Memoir of Selig," 518; Dubofsky, *We Shall be All*, p. 257.

13. Perlman, "Second Preliminary Report on Welfare Work and Social Insurance," November 1, 1914, Reel 15, p. 0254, RD.

14. Ghent, *Benevolent Feudalism*, p. 191; Perlman, "Preliminary Report on Welfare Work and Social Insurance," September 1, 1914, Reel 6, p. 0622 and Perlman, "Digest of Mr. Perlman's Report on Welfare Work and Social Insurance," September 1, 1914, Reel 6, p. 0609, both in RD.

15. Perlman to Ida Tarbell, October 12, 1914, Reel 15, pp. 0245-46 at p. 0246, Perlman, "Tentative Constructive proposals on Old Age Pensions," n.d., Reel 15, pp. 0318, 0319, and Perlman, "Digest of Mr. Perlman's Report on Welfare Work and Social Insurance," September 1, 1914, Reel 6, pp. 0613–14, all in RD.

16. Warren and Sydenstricker, "Sickness Insurance," n.d., Reel 15, pp. 0353,

0354, and Warren, "Second Preliminary Report on Sickness Insurance," November 1, 1914, Reel 15, p. 0279, both in RD.

17. Perlman, annotated summary of article in *Survey* (August 8, 1914), September 9, 1914, Reel 15, pp. 0248, 0250.

18. Perlman, annotated summary of article in *Survey* (August 8, 1914), September 9, 1914, Reel 15, pp. 0248, Perlman, "Digest of Mr. Perlman's Report on Welfare Work and Social Insurance," September 1, 1914, Reel 6, p. 0610, and Perlman, "Memorandum to McCarthy," November 1, 1914, Reel 15, p. 0252, all in RD.

19. Warren and Perlman, "A Tentative Plan for State Sickness Insurance," October 16, 1914, Reel 15, pp. 0262, 0266, 0272, 0274.

20. Warren, "Sickness Insurance," July 1914, Reel 6, p. 0707 and Warren, "Second Preliminary Report on Sickness Insurance," November 1, 1914, Reel 15, p. 0277, both in RD.

21. Commons to Helen L. Sumner, March 17, May 11, 1915, JRC.

22. Luke Grant, *The National Erectors' Association and the International Association of Bridge and Structural Ironworkers* (Washington, DC: Barnard & Miller [Chicago] for the U.S. Commission on Industrial Relations, 1915); Schipper, "Introduction," *Guide to CIR*, p. xiii.

23. Anderson, "Health Insurance", 383; Wilson quoted in Wynn, *Progressivism*, p. 120.

24. Dorfman, *Economic Mind*, IV, 623; Rutherford, "Commons and his Students," 173; Altmeyer, *Formative Years of Social Security*, pp. vii–viii.

25. *New York Times*, August 10, 12, 2009.

26. Thomas H. Marshall, *Citizenship and Social Class* (Cambridge: Cambridge University Press, 1950); Kathryn K. Sklar, *Florence Kelley and the Nation's Work: The Rise of Women's Political Culture, 1830–1900* (New Haven: Yale University Press, 1995); Patrick Wilkinson, "The Selfless and the Helpless: Maternalist Origins of the Welfare State," *Feminist Studies*, 25 (Fall 1999), 575, 577, 580.

27. Fink, "Fink Responds," 429.

28. Thomas, *Unsafe for Democracy*, pp. 124–25.

29. Commons, "Social Insurance and the Medical Profession," address to the State Medical Society at Oshkosh, Wisconsin, October 7, 1914, p. 5, Reel 3, CIRW; Fink, "Responds," 429–30.

30. Perlman, *Theory*, pp. 4, 102.

NOTES TO CHAPTER 3

1. London, "The Question", pp. 153, 161, 176, 179, 187, 192. For a further expression of London's views on imperialism, see London, "The Shrinking of the Planet," written in 1900 and published in *Revolution*.

2. Kazin, *American Dreamers*, p. 110.
3. Dewey, *School and Society*, pp. 34, 158; Curti, *Social Ideas*, pp. 438–39, 503.
4. Dewey, *School and Society*, pp. 7, 13, 18.
5. Blumberg, *Kelley*, pp. 43–46
6. Message to both houses at the start of the 1st session, 57th Congress, December 3, 1901, *Addresses and Presidential Messages of Theodore Roosevelt, 1902–1904* (New York: G. P. Putnam's Sons, 1904), p. 292.
7. Peter d'A. Jones, "Introduction" to Hunter, *Poverty*, p. vii.
8. Roosevelt quoted in David Denby, "Uppie Reddux? Upton Sinclair's Losses and Triumphs," *New Yorker*, (August 28, 2006), available at <http://www.newyorker.com/archive/2006/08/28/060828crbo_books> (last accessed June 20, 2010).
9. Sinclair quoting himself in *Autobiography*, p. 135.
10. Reed, *Du Bois*, p. 83.
11. Lewis, *Du Bois*, p. 567.
12. Foner, *Socialism and Black Americans*, p. 95; Ginger, *Bending Cross*, pp. 259–61; Kipnis, *Socialist Movement*, pp. 130–31.
13. Du Bois, "From McKinley to Wallace: My Fifty Years as a Political Independent," *Masses and Mainstream*, I:6 (1948), 7.
14. Du Bois quoted in Lewis, *Du Bois*, p. 15.
15. Dylan quoted in Adler, *The Man Who Never Died*, p. 20.
16. Hill to Elizabeth Gurley Flynn, n.d., letter in envelope postmarked January 18, 1915, EGF.
17. Dreiser quoted in E. G. Flynn, "The Rebel Girl," *Masses and Mainstream*, 7/4 (April 1954), 30.
18. Hill to Flynn, September 30, 1915, EGF. *Songs of the Workers* (known as the "Little Red Song Book"), 28th ed. (Chicago: Industrial Workers of the World, 1945), mistakenly states that another socialist orator, Katie Phar, was Hill's Rebel Girl. Katie Phar was only ten in 1915, and in his own hand Hill dedicated the original musical score of "The Rebel Girl" to Flynn: Foner, *Case*, pp. 9, 14. But Flynn was not the only woman Hill had in mind. Earlier in the year, he had suggested the aim of the song was to "line up the women workers in the OBU [One Big Union]": Hill to Sam Murray, February 13, 1915, "Last Letters of Joe Hill," *Industrial Pioneer*, 1 (December 1923), 54, quoted in Kornbluh, ed., *Rebel Voices*, p. 145.
19. Adler, *The Man Who Never Died*, pp. 294–97; Hill to Flynn, n.d., letter in envelope postmarked August 18, 1915, EGF.
20. The foregoing texts are from "The Little Red Song Book," above, pp. 9, 46–47, and reprinted (and re-sung) widely.
21. For a discussion of Hill's longstanding impact, see Rosemont, *Hill*, generally and, on songs, pp. 150–53.

22. Goldman quoted in Gornick, *Goldman*, pp. 4, 77.
23. Leonard D. Abbott to Stokes, February 21, 1916 and Emma Goldman Defense Fund circular, May 3, 1916, both in folder 7, Box 2, reel 67, RPS.
24. *Milwaukee Leader*, circa May 5, 1916, clipping in folder 7, Box 2, reel 67, RPS.
25. H. P. Hough of Fort Monroe, VA, to Stokes, December 3, 1916, in folder 7, Box 2, reel 67, RPS.
26. Nichols, *Promise and Peril*, p. 223.
27. Debs quoted in Guy A. Aldred, *Convict 9653* (pamphlet: Glasgow: Strickland Press, n.d.), p. 6.
28. Press clippings and citations in Freeberg, *Democracy's Prisoner*, pp. 318, 362n41.
29. O'Brian to E. S. Wertz, US attorney, Cleveland, Ohio, June 20, 1918, text of Debs speech, and indictment filed by Wertz for the District Court of the United States, Eastern Division of the Northern District of Ohio, June 19, 1918, all in Folder 6, Box 288, DPM.
30. Kutulas, *American Civil Liberties Union*, pp. 17, 33–34.
31. Mowry, *Era of Roosevelt*, p. 271; Shannon, *Socialist Party*, p. 174. On Roosevelt as a neoconservative foreign policy icon, see Norton, *Strauss*, pp. 186–87.

NOTES TO CHAPTER 4

1. Doris Berger Welles, fragmentary draft of unpublished biography of Victor L. Berger, n.d. (henceforth "Welles, fragmentary"), "Chapter 4", p. 8, Reel 13, VB. Welles made several attempts at writing several chapters. The Wisconsin Historical Society's microfilm reflects the chaotic state of the original literary artifact.
2. Welles, fragmentary, untitled but possibly Chapter 1, pp. 3, 11 and transcription of Berger letter to his future wife dated August 13, 1895, both Reel 12, VB.
3. Welles, "Synopsis of the Biography of Victor L. Berger," p. 1 and Welles, fragmentary, untitled but possibly Chapter 1, p. 12C, both Reel 12, VB.
4. Quotation from Muzik, "Berger", p. 5; Miller, *Berger*, 17.
5. Miller, Berger, p. 28.
6. Available at <http://clerk.house.gov/art_history/> (last accessed September 3, 2009).
7. *Boston Globe*, November 3, 2006. Cf. William J. Frieburger's contention that Meyer London was "one of only two Socialists ever elected to the United States Congress": Frieburger, "Lone Socialist", abstract.
8. Meyer, *Marcantonio*, p. 54.
9. Michael Tremoglie, "Socialist Scholars," *Front Page Magazine*, May

28, 2002, available at <http://archive.frontpagemag.com/readArticle. aspx?ARTID=23962> (last accessed March 27, 2013).

10. Patterson speech of March 24, 1950, cited in Stephen E. Ambrose, *Ike's Spies: Eisenhower and the Espionage Establishment* (Garden City, NY: Doubleday, 1981), p. 222.

11. Zarnow, "Braving Jim Crow", 1012; Jeffreys-Jones, "Bella Abzug", in *Changing Differences*, pp. 131–54.

12. Douglas, *Coming of a New Party*, p. 207.

13. Freeberg, *Democracy's Prisoner*, p. 227.

14. Diggs article of 1892 in *Arena* quoted in Gene Clanton, "'Hayseed Socialism' On the Hill: Congressional Populism, 1891–1895," *Western Historical Quarterly*, 15 (April 1984), pp. 144–43n13; *New York Times*, December 19, 1892.

15. Quint, *Forging*, p. 222; Debs quoted in Salvatore, *Debs*, p. 147. For an example of neutral academic use of the phrase "prairie socialists", see John Laslett's review of Paul Buhl's *Marxism in the USA* (1987) in *Oral History Review*, 18 (Spring 1990), 158.

16. Destler, *American Radicalism*, pp. 162–74, 222–54.

17. European socialists were still, however, divided over the respective virtues of reform and revolution. See Berman, *Social Democratic Moment*, pp. 12, 210.

18. Miller, "Socialism," 1838–40. On the suggestion of the historian Ellen Schrecker, I have added to the list Congressmen John T. Bernard and E. Hugh De Lacy, both of whom worked with or aligned themselves with the communists in their single terms on the Hill in the New Deal and immediate post-New Deal years. De Lacy was the leader of the Washington Commonweath Federation which tried to swing the Democratic party to the left and later succumbed to direct communist party influence: John de Graaf, "Washington Commonwealth Federation," in Buhle, *Encyclopedia*, pp. 820–21.

19. *Daily Worker*, May 21, 1937 and report of January 17, 1938, both in "FBI file," Box 2, GB.

20. Frank nominated by historian Marilyn Young, Kucinich nominated by Michael Kazin, the author of *American Dreamers*, and Abercrombie nominated by Todd Gitlin, who also supplied the estimate of the DSA's following in Congress. Author's interviews in New York with Young, May 7, 2008, Gitlin, May 8, 2008 and Kazin, May 14, 2008.

21. Thomas, "History", p. 39; correspondence and data on pensions together with a copy of H.R. 11474 (70 Cong., 1 sess., February 28, 1928), Reel 20, VB.

22. Miller, *Berger*, pp. x, 77.

23. SPA executive committee manifesto of August 12, 1914, quoted in Rogoff, *East Side Epic*, p. 62.

24. Miller, *Berger*, p. 205.

25. Rogoff, *East Side Epic*, pp. 9, 31, 33, 58.

26. Morris Schuman deposition as an SPA poll watcher, November 5, 1912, and quotations from undated clipping from the *New York American*, both Box 2, ML.
27. London speech titled "Woman Suffrage", 65 Cong., 1 sess., September 24, 1917, in Box 4, ML.
28. Goldberg, "London and Insurance," 59, 61; Nelson, *Unemployment Insurance*, p. 20.
29. Isaak M. Rubinow, *Social Insurance* (New York: Holt, 1913); Nelson, *Unemployment Insurance*, p. 20; handwritten notes on Gompers, "Voluntary Insurance versus Compulsory: Shall the Toilers Surrender their Freedom for a few Crumbs?" *American Federationist*, 22 (May 1916), 333–57, as well as on an article in *Survey* (March 30, 1918) indicating that organized labor might support compulsory insurance after all – by implication, if the socialist label was dropped, both in Box 209, EEW.
30. Goldberg, "London and Insurance," pp. 60, 61, 68, 70; Rogoff, *East Side Epic*, p. 131; William M. Leiserson to London discussing the prospects for social insurance legislation, March 13, 1916, Box 2, ML.
31. Typescript of London speech in Box 2, ML; Rogoff, *East Side Epic*, p. 89–90; Frieburger, "Lone Socialist", p. 226.
32. All quotations from Rogoff, *East Side Epic*, pp. 71, 97–8; London's appeal to Kerensky, from 1917 but otherwise undated, Box 2, ML.
33. The late diplomatic historian Norman Graebner's recollections of Milwaukee conveyed to the author in the Spring of 1972, Charlottesville, VA; Pelling, *Socialism in Milwaukee*, pp. 100, 103; Schwantes, *Radical Heritage*, p. xi.
34. Judd, *Socialist Cities*, pp. 26, 159.
35. Hofstadter, *Age of Reform*, p. 98.

NOTES TO CHAPTER 5

1. Leiserson, "Dole or Insurance?" *Nation* (February 17, 1932), 194.
2. Douglas, *Terrible Honesty*, pp. 3–4; J. Martin Favor, *Authentic Blackness: The Folk in the New Negro Renaissance* (Durham, NC: Duke University Press, 1999). A. Robert Lee sees a "Second Black Renaissance" extending from the 1940s through the 1970s: Lee, *Black American Fiction*, pp. 5–11.
3. Avallone, "What American Renaissance?" 1103.
4. Locke, "New Negro" in Locke, ed., *New Negro*, p. 5.
5. Locke, "New Negro" in Locke, ed., *New Negro*, p. 14.
6. Perry, *Hubert Harrison*, pp. 5, 6, 109, 170.
7. Cruse, *Crisis*, p. 23; Douglas, *Terrible Honesty*, pp. 180, 290.
8. *Messenger*, March 1919, quoted in Cruse, *Crisis*, p. 41.
9. Bernard, *Van Vechten*, p. 27.
10. Osofsky, *Harlem*, p. 183.

11. Lewis, "Intellectual Luminaries," 68.
12. William J. Maxwell's discussion of the scholarship of Harold Cruse, Nathan Huggins and Henry Louis Gates: Maxwell, *New Negro, Old Left*, pp. 16–18.
13. Johnson paraphrasing himself in *Along This Way*, p. 327.
14. Du Bois quoted in Cruse, *Crisis*, p. 43.
15. Van Vechten paraphrased in Bernard, *Van Vechten*, p. 2.
16. Gregory Holmes Singleton discerned "a close resemblance" between the Harlem Renaissance and the "American Renaissance" as Matthiessen envisioned it, but perhaps it would be more accurate to compare the perceptions of culture by left blacks and the Harvard scholar: Singleton, "Birth", 31.
17. Matthiessen, *American Renaissance*, pp. (viii), 4, 239, 396.
18. Mead, *Character*, p. 164. *The American Character* is the title of the British edition of Mead's book that first came out in America in 1942 with the title *And Keep Your Powder Dry*.
19. Rideout, *Radical Novel*, p. 171.
20. Estimate in HUAC testimony of Ralph De Sola (formerly a communist official within the New York Federal Writers' Project) cited in Penkower, *Federal Writers' Project*, p. 196; Badger, *New Deal*, p. 225.
21. Darcy quoted in Cherny, "Prelude", 26.
22. Transcript of meeting of the Anglo-American Secretariat on the American Question, April 4, 1937, 495-20-521 and List of Members and Candidate Members of the US communist party Central Committee, January 31, 1938, 495-74-467, both in Records of the communist party of the United States, consulted in Moscow by Robert W. Cherny: Cherny, "Harry Bridges and the Communist Party," 3. See also Cherny, "Making of Bridges", 364n2, and Klehr and others, *Secret World*, p. 104n24.
23. Cherny, "Prelude", 21–22.
24. Olson's inaugural address, January 2, 1939, available at <http://www.californiagovernors.ca.gov/h/documents/inaugural_29.html> (last accessed November 3, 2009); Cherny, "Communist Party in California," 20, 23.
25. Bell, "Left Coast", 71.
26. Winston, *Holding Aloft*, pp. 1, 30, 123; Hall, "Long Civil Rights Movement," 1262.
27. Gilmore, *Defying Dixie*, p. 48; Mt. Kisco, N.Y., *Patent Trader*, January 13, 1957; obituary in *Daily Worker*, June 24, 1957; folder marked "Biographical", Box 1, JWF.
28. Quoted in Johanningsmeier, *Forging*, p. 262.
29. Gilmore, *Defying Dixie*, pp. 64, 186.
30. O'Reilly, *Racial Matters*, p. 18.
31. Diggins, *Rise and Fall*, p. 132.
32. Examples are Eldridge Cleaver (Peace and Freedom Party presidential candidate in 1964) and Angela Davis (communist party vice presidential candidate

in 1980 and 1984). The most successful pre-Obama black candidate was Lenora Fulani. The first woman and the first African American to achieve ballot access in every state of the union, she received 217,219 votes on the presidential ticket of the New Alliance Party in 1984. She had been an activist with the International Workers Party.

33. Temkin, *Sacco-Vanzetti Affair*, pp. 3, 47.
34. Record, *Negro and Communist Party*, p. 55; Baldwin, *Beyond the Color Line*, p. 1; Hughes, *Wonder*, p. 73.
35. Louise Thompson, "Toward a Brighter Dawn," *Woman Today* (April 1936), 14, 30; McDuffie, *Sojourning*, pp. 3, 9, 113. Louise Thompson married a fellow communist William L. Patterson in 1940 and is sometimes referred to as Louise Thompson Patterson.
36. Gilmore, *Defying Dixie*, pp. 161–66.
37. Carter, *Scottsboro*, pp. 18, 19, 161, 213, 221.
38. Hughes, *Fight for Freedom: The Story of the NAACP* (1962), quoted in Murray, "NAACP versus the communist party," 276.
39. F. Raymond Daniel's *New York Times* review quoted in Murray, "Changing America," 84.
40. Sitkoff quoted in Fairclough, *Better Day Coming*, p. 138.
41. Goluboff, *Lost Promise*, pp. 53–54; Nicola Pizzolato, "Peonage" (an outline of research in progress presented at the University of Edinburgh and kindly copied to the author in October 2009).
42. Goluboff, *Lost Promise*, p. 139.
43. Jeffreys-Jones, *FBI*, pp. 40, 94–99.
44. Gilmore, *Defying Dixie*, p. 4.
45. In his discussion of slave resistance, Peter Kolchin describes Aptheker's book as a "pioneering volume" marred by "exaggeration": Kolchin, *Slavery*, p. 276.
46. Sorel, *Reflections on Violence*, pp. 77, 112, 127, 186; Diggins, *Mussolini*, p. 112.
47. Jeffreys-Jones, "The Making of U.S. Revolutionary Theory," in *Violence and Reform*, pp. 31–39.
48. Author's interview with Parente, Boston, June 7, 1972; *Boston Nor' Easter*, 2 (December 1970), 1; Diggins, *Mussolini*, p. 113.
49. Diggins, *Mussolini*, pp. 117–18.
50. Quotations from Wesbord, "Black America," 230, 241; Gilmore, *Defying Dixie*, p. 308.
51. Plummer, *Rising Wind*, p. 58; Plummer, "Response to Haiti," 140.
52. Baldwin, *Beyond the Color Line*, p. 4; Duberman, *Robeson*, pp. 194, 208.
53. Ford, *The Communists and the Struggle for Negro Liberation*, p. 6; Plummer, *Rising Wind*, p. 50.
54. Plummer, *Rising Wind*, p. 37; Challenor, "Influence of Black Americans", p. 153

55. Collum, *African Americans*, pp. vii, 103, 119–22; Plummer, *Rising Wind*, p. 61.
56. Thomas, CBS radio broadcast reported in *The Socialist Call*, March 21, 1941; Thomas, Madison Square Gardens speech issued as a press release by the America First Committee, May 24, 1941, Box 27, DBRF.
57. *New York Times*, 23 January, March 9, 1941; Preston, "Religion and World Order," p. 82.
58. Ford speech to the Harlem Division of the communist party on the occasion of is twentieth anniversary, September 11, 1939, Box 1, JWF.
59. Wright, "Not My People's War," *New Masses*, 39 (June 17, 1941), 8.
60. Marcantonio speech, October 6, 1941, 77th Congress, in folder "Legislative Record of Marc," Box 41, VM.

NOTES TO CHAPTER 6

1. Schlesinger, *Coming*, p. 477; Wolfskill, *Revolt*, pp. 109, 159.
2. Divorce papers filed on October 3, 1913, in Box 1, GB.
3. *Wausau Daily Record-Republican*, August 6, 1930.
4. *Wausau, Wisconsin Magazine*, special issue, n.d., in Box 1, GB; Lorence, *Boileau*, pp. 166, 183; Robert Bendiner article in *New Masses* of February 9, 1937 cited in Lorence, *Boileau*, p. 168.
5. *Daily Worker*, May 21, 1937; FBI report of January 20, 1937, enclosing *New York Times* story of January 10, 1937, People's Congress for Democracy and Peace circular letter, November 18, 1937, FBI report of January 17, 1938, and FBI report with date redacted, all in Box 2, GB.
6. Thomas article in *The World Tomorrow*, January 18, 1934, reprinted in Morgan, *American Socialism*, p. 119; Thomas, *Human Exploitation in the United States* (New York: Frederick A. Stokes, 1934); Shannon, *Socialist Party*, pp. 231–33; "pills" quotation from Thomas speech of 1936 opposing the re-election of Roosevelt, reprinted in Zinn, *New Deal Thought*, p. 400.
7. Marcantonio report to his constituents quoted in Schaffer, "Caucus", p. 52; Kent to Marcantonio, July 13, 1940, and Marcantonio to Kent, July 20, 1940, Box 3, VM. Kent wanted permission to use the quotation, and Marcantonio gave him a corrected version of it.
8. Schlesinger, *Coming of New Deal*, pp. 455 ff; Wolfskill, *Revolt of the Conservatives*, pp. 108–10; Ransley's House address of May 1933 reproduced in Powell, *Compilation*, p. 456.
9. AMA *Journal*'s editorial quoted in Ernest K. Lindley, "Doctors and Dollars," *Today*, February 16, 1935; *Washington Post*, June 15, 1938; Badger, *New Deal*, p. 236.
10. The conservative view of Flynn, *Roosevelt Myth*; New left views of Conkin, *New Deal* and Bernstein, "New Deal"; disenchanted African American view

in Bunche, "Critique", 65; other historical interpretations in Hamby, "New Deal"; Brown quoted in *New York Times* editorial, September 21, 2008.

11. Nelson, *Unemployment Insurance*, p. 180.
12. Leiserson, "Dole or Insurance?" *Nation* (February 17, 1932), 194. Emphasis added.
13. Powell, *FDR's Folly*, pp. 2, 15; Schlaes, *Forgotten Man*, p. 7.
14. Graham, *Toward a Planned Society*, pp. xii–xiii, 14, 15.
15. Edwin E. Witte's handwritten notes on Alvin H. Hansen, *Fiscal Policy and Business Cycles* (New York: Norton, 1941) in folder "Economic Problems – Planning," Box 90, EEW.
16. Green in *New York Times*, December 17, 1934; Witte, annotated bibliography of works on planning, in folder "Economic Problems – Planning," Box 90, EEW.
17. Ickes in *New York Times*, October 14, 1934.
18. Salmond, "Civilian Conservation Corps and the Negro," pp. 383–85.
19. Leuchtenburg, *Franklin D. Roosevelt*, p. 125–26.
20. Goldwater, *Radical Periodicals*, p. 28
21. Edwin E. Witte's handwritten notes on the abolition of state planning boards, *National Municipal Review*, 28 (July 1939), 517, on Sachs's view on economic planning, *Social Research*, 6 (May 1939), 169 and on Alvin H. Hansen, *Fiscal Policy and Business Cycles* (New York: Norton, 1941), all in folder "Economic Problems – Planning," Box 90, EEW.
22. Witte's summaries of press reports and congressional debates dating from 1943, in folder "Economic Problems – Planning," Box 90, EEW; Graham, *Toward a Planned Society*, pp. 188–232.
23. Fine, *Laissez Faire and the General-Welfare State*, pp. 15–16.
24. Millward, "Industrial Organization," in Millward and Singleton, *Political Economy*, p. 3; Thorpe, *History Labour Party*, p. 38; 1928 SPA platform in Morgan, ed., *American Socialism*, p. 102.
25. Morgan, *Making of TVA*, p. 99.
26. *Fertilizer Review*, 7 (January–February–March 1932), 4–5; President Chamber of Commerce USA to members of House of Representatives, April 18, 1932, Box 80, TA; Priestley quoted in Schwartz, *New Dealers*, p. 206; Morgan, *Making of TVA*, p. 94.
27. Roosevelt's address of September 21, 1932 quoted in Rosen, *Hoover, Roosevelt*, p. 355.
28. Badger, *New Deal*, p. 175; Morgan, *Philosophy of Bellamy*; "Tennessee Valley Authority," *Hearings*, pp. 204, 206; *New York Times*, September 29, 1938; Lilienthal, *TVA*, p. 175.
29. Harrison, *Owen and Owenites in Britain and America*, p. 216.
30. Badger, *New Deal*, pp. 177–78; Wells, "Public Power", 2.
31. "Survey of the Great Lakes," Vol. I, p. 9.

32. "Savannah River," *House Document*, p. 4; *Message from the President . . . with a view to Internal Improvement*, p. 8.
33. "Establishment of 'The Port of New York Authority'," *Senate Report*, p. 1; "Development and Administration," *House Report*, p. 1; "Sale of Hoboken," *House Report*, p. 2; Doig, *Empire on the Hudson*, p. 490.
34. Pritchett, "Control Act", 495, 509; Musolf, *Uncle Sam's Corporations*, p. 6.
35. Wilbur J. Cohen, "Edwin E. Witte (1887–1960): Father of Social Security," *Industrial and Labor Relations Review*, 14 (October 1960).
36. Patterson, *Welfare State*, pp. 7, 9, 12; Galbraith, *Affluent Society*, p. 160.
37. Fausold, *Presidency of Hoover*, p. 17.
38. Blumenthal and Morone, *Heart of Power*, p. 32.
39. Myers, "Long-Range Trends," 13.
40. Summaries of polls reported in the *New York Times* and *Washington Post*, both June 15, 1938, and *Modern Medicine*, June 1938, in Box 90, EEW.
41. Sacramento *Union*, January 26, 1939; "Establishing a National Health Program," *Senate Report*, pp. 1, 5, 8; *New York Times*, 5 April, 1943.
42. Dies quoted in Leuchtenburg, *Franklin D. Roosevelt*, p. 263.
43. Miller, "Socialism," 1838–40; *Christian Science Monitor*, July 8, 1935; *Wall Street Journal*, January 25, 1939.
44. HR 8933, 72 Cong., 1 sess., February 5, 1932; *Planning for Abundance: A Positive Program for Industrial Expansion* (n.d., privately produced compilation of speeches by Allen, Voorhis, and Amlie), Box 77, TA.
45. House Joint Res. 637, 74 Cong., 2 sess., June 18, 1936.
46. Abraham Epstein, Executive Secretary of the American Association for Old Age Security to Amlie, January 14, 1932, Box 80, TA; House Joint Res. 637, 74 Cong., 2 sess., June 18, 1936.
47. Printed extension of Amlie's remarks in the House, *Congressional Record*, 74 Cong., 1 sess., August 26, 1935, pp. 1–5, Box 80, TA.
48. Lovin, "Agrarian Radicalism," 150, 153.
49. Lovin, "Amlie's Crusade,"105.
50. Bill Tidmarsh to "Uncle Charlie", March 10, 1940, VF.
51. Freeberg, *Democracy's Prisoner*, p. 116; Sweet quoted in *New York Times*, January 16, 1920; La Guardia quoted in *Brooklyn Times*, January 15, 1920.
52. La Guardia quoted in *New York Tribune*, February 19, 1920.
53. Galbraith, *Crash*, p. 146; Meyer, *Vito Marcantonio*, pp. 16–17; *The* [Daily] *Worker Magazine*, September 28, 1947.
54. Graham, *Encore for Reform*, Appendix; Goldberg, "Meyer London," 73 n. 30.
55. Roosevelt quoted in Perkins, *Roosevelt I Knew*, p. 333.
56. Berkowitz, *America's Welfare State*, p. xii.
57. Levine, *Poverty and Society*, p. 263; Commager, "Twelve Years of Roosevelt," pp. 20–21.

NOTES TO CHAPTER 7

1. Marjorie De Armand, "The Chaplin Trial," *New Masses*, 51 (April 18, 1944), 30.
2. Caute, *Great Fear*, p. 516.
3. Saunders, *Who Paid the Piper?*, p. 193.
4. Chaplin quoted in Anne Bauer, "An older Chaplin speaks," *National Guardian* (November 11, 1957), 10.
5. Mr. X, *The Roosevelt Death: A Super Mystery: Suicide? Assassination? Natural Death? Still Alive?* (St. Louis, MO: Christian Nationalist Crusade, copyrighted by G. L. K. Smith in 1947), Box 23, JFR, p. 3.
6. Rovere, *McCarthy*, pp. 124–25.
7. Schrecker, *Many are the Crimes*, pp. x, 86.
8. Freeland, *Truman Doctrine*, p. 5.
9. Caute, *Great Fear*, p. 349.
10. Heale, *American Anticommunism*, p. xiv and *McCarthy's Americans*.
11. Dewey quoted in Mason, *Republican Party*, p. 126.
12. *Newsweek* quoted in Schaffer, "Caucus in a Phone Booth," iii; Folder "Bills by Marc," Box 41 and folder "European Recovery Program," Box 51, both in VM; *Congressional Quarterly* January February March 1948, S 7-11; Kaner, "Towards a Minority of One," p. 229; Wallace, *Democracy Reborn*, pp. 186–88; 233, 241 and *Sixty Million Jobs*, p. 50; Culver and Hyde, *American Dreamer,* p. 472.
13. Bell, *Liberal State*, p. 224.
14. Dorothy Sabin Winslow to State of Mainer, circular letter: Elections, 1948/"Smear Charges", MCS; *Portland Press Herald*, May 23, 1948; Gellman, *The Contender*, p. 310; Bell, *Liberal State*, p. 202; Nixon for US Senator Campaign Committee, *Douglas-Marcantonio Voting Record* (the "Pink Sheet", 1950), HGD (supplied by kind courtesy of Todd J. Losmerick, Archivist of the Carl Albert Center, University of Oklahoma).
15. *Congressional Quarterly* January February March 1948, S 7-11.
16. Jensen, "All Pink Sisters"; Denton, *The Pink Lady*; Smith replies to form letters of protest against the Vietnam War, for example to Mrs. David Gallup, September 15, 1967: Vietnam War, MCS; Jeffreys-Jones, "Margaret Chase Smith and the Female Quest for Security," in *Changing Differences*, pp. 113, 115.
17. "Falling Out with FDR", Leuchtenberg's review of a 1967 re-issue of Moley's 1939 memoir, *After Seven Years*, in *Book Week*, January 22, 1967; Moley, Speech II, "Creeping Collectivism" (October 1940), folder 1, and Speech III, "Creeping Despotism" (undated but probably October or November 1940), folder 2, both in Box 218, RM; *New York Times*, October 23, 1943.
18. Flynn, *Road Ahead*, pp. 9, 75; Karl Schriftgiesser's review for the *New York Times*, October 2, 1949; Moser, *Right Turn*, pp. 7, 59, 177–78.

19. Taft quoted in *New York Times*, April 2, 1950.
20. Moley, *The Liberal Faith: Lost, Strayed and Stolen* (Commencement address, Whitman College, May 28, 1950), p. 8, in folder 18, Box 241, RM.
21. Lehman quoted in *New York Times*, October 24, 1950.
22. Davies, "'Mr. Republican'", 136; *New York Times*, May 15, 1951.
23. Moley quoted in *Chicago Tribune*, March 1, 1952; Lacosse in *St. Louis Globe-Democrat*, March 30 1952; folder 12, reviews and clippings, Box 241, RM.
24. Thomas letter, *New York Times*, November 1, 1952.
25. "Establishing a National Health Program" (Murray's preliminary report), p. 38; Starr, *Social Transformation*, p. 280.
26. Benson, "Report", 148, 149; *Abolishing Private Medical Practice or $3,048,000,000 of Political Medicine Yearly in the United States* (National Physicians' Committee for the Extension of Medical Service, 1943), p. 1, Box 218, GR.
27. "National Health Program," 1, 2, 8; AMA quoted in a *New York Times* article sympathetic to health reform by business correspondent David Leonhardt, January 20, 2010; Starr, "Socialized Medicine and the Cold War," in Starr, *Social Transformation*, pp. 280–86.
28. Taft and Murray quoted in Blumenthal and Morone, *Heart of Power*, p. 77.
29. Blumenthal and Morone, *Heart of Power*, pp. 111, 113.
30. Kutulas, *American Civil Liberties Union*, p. 165.
31. Kutulas, *American Civil Liberties Union*, p. 164; O'Brien, "Historical Essay," pp. 159–65; Scales obituary, *New York Times*, August 7, 2002.
32. Johanningsmeier, *Forging*, pp. 324, 328.
33. Editorial, *New York Times*, June 14, 1962.
34. O'Brien, *Color of the Law*, pp. 2–3.
35. Erik S. Gellman, "Civil rights Congress," in Arnesen, *Encyclopedia of Labor*, I, 253-54.
36. Duberman, *Robeson*, p. 365; eyewitness description of the event conveyed in 1991 by the author's former literary agent, Frances Goldin, who lay on top of her daughter to shield her from blows.
37. The evidence is circumstantial but is given credibility by FBI records showing Hill to have been an informant in 1962: Phelps, "Hill", 565.
38. Borstelman, *Cold War and Color Line*, pp. 5–6; Anderson, "Bleached Souls", p. 95.
39. Patterson to Foster, November 16, 1951, quoted in Anderson, "Bleached Souls", p. 95.
40. Dudziak, *Cold War Civil Rights*, p. 6.
41. DuBois, "Negroes and Socialism," *National Guardian*, April 29, 1957.
42. DeBenedetti, *American Ordeal*, pp. 31–32.
43. Prados, *Lost Crusader*, p. 57; Colby, *Honorable Men*, pp. 127–28.
44. Wilford, *CIA, British Left*, p. 297.

45. McCarthy paraphrased in Reeves, *Life and Times*, p. 502; Jeffreys-Jones, *CIA and American Democracy*, pp. 74–75.
46. Arieh Lobewitz, "Socialist Zionism," in Buhle and Georgakas, *Encyclopedia*, pp. 729–31.
47. Jacobs, "Anti-Zionist left," 158; Stevens, *American Zionism*, pp. 71–72.
48. Smith, *Shadow Warriors*, p. 331; Jeffreys-Jones, *CIA and American Democracy*, p. 33; Holzman, *Angleton*, p. 153.
49. Klein, *For All These rights*, p. 13; McCarthy quoted in Fried, *McCarthyism*, p. 179.
50. Stevenson quoted in *New York Times*, April 3, 1954.
51. George quoted in *New York Times*, August 21, 1954.

NOTES TO CHAPTER 8

1. Paul Buhle, "New Left", in Buhle, *Encyclopedia*, p. 517. For examples of attempts to define the New Left and testimony to the taxing nature of the task, see Sargent, *New Left Thought*, pp. 1–4, Levy, *New Left and Labor*, pp. 5–6, and Gorman, *Harrington*, p. 185.
2. J. A. del Vayo, "France's 'New Left': What It Is and What It Needs," *Nation*, March 19, 1955.
3. Geary, "Becoming International," 710, 711, 715.
4. Mills, *Marxists*, p. 97; Marcuse, *One Dimensional Man*, pp. 24–25, 29.
5. Transcript, George Meany oral history interview, August 4, 1969, by Paige E. Mulhollan, pp. 16–17, LBJ; AFL-CIO Vietnam Resolution, December 1965, in Hall, *Vietnam War Era*, p. 208; Bundy to Lovestone, November 1, 1965, Box 359, JLov; Meany interview with Dick Cavett (ABC-TV, December 19, 1974) reported in *Dispatcher*, January 10, 1975.
6. Table, "Union Membership: Overall (1948–2004)", in US Bureau of Labor Statistics, Union Sourcebook 1947–1983, available at <http://www.work inglife.org/wiki/Union+Membership:+Overall+(1948-2004)> (last accessed February 3, 2010).
7. Anderson, *Movement*, p. 95.
8. Port Huron Statement, 1962, in Hall, *Vietnam War Era*, pp. 203–205; Hoefferle, "Students and Political Activism," p. 195.
9. Jeffreys-Jones, "Students," in *Peace Now!*, pp. 42–92.
10. Sol Stern, "NSA and the CIA," *Ramparts*, 5 (March 1967).
11. Wilford, *Mighty Wurlitzer*, pp. 3, 130, 144.
12. Jeffreys-Jones, *CIA and American Democracy*, p. 153.
13. Wilford, *Mighty Wurlitzer*, p. 144.
14. Hall, *Because of Their Faith*, pp. 1, 171.
15. Rossinow, *Politics of Authenticity*, p. 135; Harrington, *Accidental Journey*, pp. 121–22.

16. Galbraith, *The Great Crash, 1929* (Boston, Houghton Mifflin, 1955), *American Capitalism: The Concept of Countervailing Power* (London: Hamish Hamilton, 1952) and *The American Left*, p. 6; John Maynard Keynes, *A Treatise on Money*, 2 vols., II, *The Applied Theory of Money* (London: Macmillan, 1950 [1930]), 386.
17. Galbraith, *Affluent Society*, 2nd ed., pp. 80–90, 262, 264.
18. Harrington, *Other America*, p. 9.
19. Harrington, *Other America*, p. 178; Gorman, *Harrington*, p. 52.
20. Bernstein, *Guns or Butter*, p. 102.
21. Gorman, *Harrington*, p. 53; Maurice Isserman article in *New York Times*, June 21, 2009.
22. Isserman, *Other American*, pp. 305–306, 421n5.
23. Harrington quoted in Bernstein, *Guns or Butter*, p. 102.
24. Zarnow, "Braving Jim Crow", 1012, 1017.
25. Daniel Bell, "Vulgar Sociology," *Encounter* (December 1960), 56, in CWM.
26. Email, Paul Buhle to the author, May 24, 2007, (an authority on the American left, Buhle was active in the SDS at the University of Illinois in the 1960s); author's interview with Michael Kazin, Washington, DC, May 14, 2008, (the historian Kazin was briefly a member of the Weathermen); Carl Davidson, *The New Radicals in the Multiversity and Other SDS Writings on Student Syndicalism (1966–67)* (Chicago: C. H. Kerr, 1990); Kornbluh, *Rebel Voices*; Tyler, *Rebels of the Woods*; Renshaw, *Wobblies*; Conlin, *Bread and Roses*; Dubofsky, *We Shall Be All*. Another work from the 1960s was the compilation edited by Philip S. Foner, an "Old Left" figure by virtue of his membership in the communist party: *The Letters of Joe Hill* (New York: Oak Publications, 1965). Fired from City College of New York for his communism in 1941, Foner could not exchange views with students as he remained blacklisted from university employment at the time when his book appeared: conversation with author at Foner's office at the headquarters of the communists' International Publishers in New York, summer of 1965. But Foner did join the faculty at Lincoln University, Pennsylvania, in 1967. Also in 1965, Foner brought out *The Case of Joe Hill*, and in 1969 Gibbs M. Smith published his biography *Joe Hill* (Salt Lake City; University of Utah Press).
27. Email, Melvyn Dubofsky to author, June 2, 2008; author's interview with Todd Gitlin, New York, May 8, 2008; email, David Montgomery to author, September 25, 2008; Weinstein, *Decline of Socialism*; author's interview with Frances Piven, New York, March 27, 2009. Frances Piven was a go-between during the 1968 student occupation of the Columbia University administration building and wrote extensively on poor people and direct action. See, for example, her *Challenging Authority*.
28. Garrow, *Protest at Selma*, pp. 2, 7, 19, 76.
29. Malcolm X quoted in Payne, "Debating the Civil Rights Movement," p. 149;

Malcolm X, *Autobiography*, pp. 162, 467–76; partly redacted FBI report of May 17, 1961, in Carson, *Malcolm X*, p. 161.

30. Du Bois letter to Hall, October 1, 1961, quoted in Lewis, *Du Bois*, p. 567. There was a later fulfillment of Du Bois's project: *Africana: The Encyclopedia of the African and African American Experience*, eds. Kwame Anthony Appiah and Henry Louis Gates Jr. (New York: Basic, 2005, reissued in updated format by Oxford University Press in 2010).

31. DeBenedetti, *American Ordeal*, pp. 97, 152, 435n58; Rorabaugh, *Berkeley at War*, pp. 88, 99–103.

32. Garrow, *FBI and King*, p. 43; Jeffreys-Jones, *Peace Now!*, pp. 114, 123–24.

33. King's talk to a meeting of the SCLC's Operation Breadbasket as recalled by a member of the audience and remarks to James both quoted in Garrow, *Bearing the Cross*, pp. 591, 717n19; other quotations from Fairclough, *King*, p. 115.

34. Jeffreys-Jones, *Peace Now!*, pp. 116–17.

35. Hayden, *Reunion*, p. 70.

36. Eyewitnessed by the author, who audited the class during his graduate-school year at the University of Michigan, 1964–5.

37. Jeffreys-Jones, *Peace Now!*, p. 62; "Chronology," in Hall, *Vietnam War Era*, pp. xxv–xxxi.

38. Reagan quoted in Reagan for Governor press release, April 10, 1966, RRGC.

39. Mailer, *Armies of the Night*, p. 223.

40. *San Diego Free Press*, Nov. 1–14, 1968; results of Urban Research Corporation survey published in *New York Times*, January 14, 1970.

41. On the efficacy of protest from differing perspectives, see Small, *Johnson, Nixon, and the Doves*, pp. 225–34, and Lewy, *America in Vietnam*, p. 434. Though originally a New Left historian and activist, Marilyn Young cautions against over-estimation of the success of the antiwar movement: Young, "Reflections," 67. Priest notes that the Left and Right agreed on the success of the opposition forces, but thinks they were both wrong: Priest, "Power", p. 41. Ralph B. Levering expressed further doubt in his July 5, 2010, H-DIPLO online review of a special issue of *Diplomatic History* devoted to the subject: available at <http://www.hnet.org/~diplo/reviews/PDF/AR265f.pdf> (last accessed on July 23, 2010).

42. Friedan, *Feminine Mystique*, p. 181.

43. Oliver, *Betty Friedan*, pp. 35, 41–43.

44. Horowitz, *Betty Friedan and Feminine Mystique*, pp. 201, 206, 212, 247; Rosen, *World Split Open*, p. 6.

45. Jeffreys-Jones, *Peace Now!*, pp. 153–54; Rosen, *World Split Open*, p. 127; Evans, *Personal Politics*, pp. 117, 118, 160.

46. Jeffreys-Jones, *Peace Now!*, pp. 144; Evans, *Personal Politics*, p. 232.

47. Meister, *"La Huelga"*, pp. 262, 265.
48. Shaw, *Beyond the Fields*, pp. 28, 92.
49. Musolf, *Uncle Sam's Private*, pp. 33–34.
50. Conkin, *Big Daddy*, pp. 228–30; Blumenthal and Morone, *Heart of Power*, pp. 193, 195.
51. Heale, *Twentieth-Century America*, p. 259; Moynihan quoted in Mason, *Nixon*, p. 59.
52. Blumenthal and Morone, *Heart of Power*, pp. 238–46.
53. Starr, *Social Transformation*, p. 287; review of Starr's book by Cecil G. Sheps in the *Journal of Public Health Policy*, 5 (September 1984), 436. Trained as a Canadian military doctor, Starr became a Harvard professor of medicine and a US hospital administrator.
54. Murray and others, *Liberty*, p. 1015.
55. Linus Pauling, *No More War!* (New York: Dodd, Mead, 1958); Olmsted, "Linus Pauling", pp. 272–74; Rachel Carson, *Silent Spring* (Boston: Houghton Mifflin, 1962); Ralph Nader, *Unsafe at Any Speed: The Designed-In Dangers of the American Automobile* (New York: Grossman, 1965); Franklin Rosemont, "Radical Environmentalism" in Buhle, *Encyclopedia*, pp. 623–30.
56. Nixon quoted in Hoff, *Nixon Reconsidered*, p. 24.

NOTES TO CHAPTER 9

1. Wolf, *Sexuality and Socialism*, pp. 121–25.
2. Memo, Bud Krogh for John Erlichman, June 10, 1970, in folder "Obscenity and Pornography 1969–70," Box 16, WHSF: SMOF, Egil Krogh files, RN. Document supplied by kind courtesy of Douglas M. Charles. For further context on this episode see Charles, *FBI's Obscene File*, pp. 78–79.
3. *Pointblank Times* (Houston, TX), I (December 1975), 6; fliers, undated but probably 1976, on gay bars in Dallas and Fort Worth; Polly Kellogg letter to Frieda Lindfield, September 16, 1980. All in "Gay and Lesbian Community," folders 2 and 3, Box 3W72, FLW.
4. *New York Times*, January 25, 2013.
5. Quotation from Sherry, *Gay Artists*, p. 1; Chauncey, *Gay New York*, pp. 2, 265.
6. Isserman, *If I had a Hammer*, p. 202; Author's interview with Todd Gitlin, New York, May 8, 2008.
7. Meyer, "Gay/Lesbian", pp. 257, 261–62; Karlinsky, "Russia's Gay Literature," pp. 348, 361; Chauncey, *Gay New York*, p. 198. On resignations from the communist party because of its conservatism, author's conversation in New York on August 7, 1991, with Frances Goldin, literary agent and former party member.
8. Karlinsky, "Russia's Gay Literature," p. 358; quotation supplied via email

by Robert Cherny, July 20, 2010. The Mattachine Society was named after a French satirical group, the *mattachines*.

9. Charles, "From Subversion to Obscenity," 264, 285–86; Johnson, *Lavender Scare*, p. 201; Meyer, "Gay/Lesbian", p. 263.
10. Hartz, *Liberal Tradition*, p. 39; Boorstin, *Americans*, pp. 177–78.
11. Denning, *Cultural Front*, pp. 447–48; Degler, *Out of Our Past*, pp. 321–22. See also Stefan Berger, "History and National Identity: Why They Should Remain Divorced," *History and Policy* (November 2007), available at <http://www.historyandpolicy.org/papers/policy-paper-66.htmlcheck> (last accessed March 22, 2010). On the semantic history of the acronym PC, see Hughes, *Political Correctness*, pp. 62–65.
12. Estimate in Anderson, *Movement*, p. 242.
13. Groening, *Simpson's Guide to Life*, p. iv.
14. Author's conversation with Marilyn Young, May 7, 2008, and interview with Todd Gitlin, May 8, 2008; Swartz, *Moral Minority,* pp. 2–3.
15. Himmelfarb, *One Nation*, pp. x, 116.
16. Coppola interview with Anita Stacey for Radio Havana Cuba in *Daily World*, November 11, 1975; Ronald Tyson, "The Politics of 'Grease'," *Daily World*, June 29, 1978.
17. Putnam, *Bowling Alone*, p. 155.
18. *Your Military Left*, 1/9 (March 1972), 2 in Box 165, BN; Said, *Orientalism*, p. 40.
19. Francis J. McNamara, "Dellums and [Michael] Harrington [D – MA] Dangerous Choices for CIA Panel," *Human Events*, 35 (March 29, 1975), 8. *Human Events* was a conservative journal that opposed left tendencies such as socialism, feminism and sexual liberation.
20. Borcherding, "One Hundred Years of Public Spending," in Borcherding, *Budgets*, p. 26; "Government Intervention", *Business Week*, April 4, 1977, 47.
21. Musolf, *Uncle Sam's Private*, p. 1; 1974 report by House Commerce Special Investigative Subcommittee quoted in *Congressional Quarterly Almanac*, 30 (1974), 680.
22. *Congressional Quarterly Almanac*, 31 (1975), 659, 662; Statement of Frank Church, "Amtrak Improvement Act of 1976" *Hearings*, p. 63.
23. Editorial, *New York Times*, August 26, 2012.
24. Peter Steinfels, "National Health Insurance: Its Politics and Problems," *Dissent*, 24 (Winter 1977), reproduced in "How Can the Health Care?," p. 52; undated Bourne interview with David Craik, reproduced in Craik, "U.S. Presidents," and kindly supplied by the interviewer.
25. Carter, *Address to the Student National Medical Association* (Washington, DC, April 16, 1976, reference courtesy of David Craik); Morris, *Carter*, p. 280; Steinfels, "National Health Insurance," p. 42.

26. Reagan quoted in *Daily Telegraph*, January 28, 1982; Heale, *Twentieth-Century America*, p. 214.
27. Wolff, *Top Heavy*, pp. 1–2; Stricker, *Why America Lost the War on Poverty*, p. 188.
28. *Human Events*, February 13, 1988; "CISPES and FBI," pp. 119, 169.
29. Reagan, *American Life*, p. 479.
30. Obama, *Audacity of Hope*, p. 261.
31. Wills, *Reagan's America*, p. 359.
32. Wolf, *Sexuality and Socialism*, p. 128; quotation from Robert Kaiser, *Washington Post*, March 18, 1984.
33. 1992 poll quoted in Putnam, *Bowling Alone*, p. 25; Dahrendorf, *Reflections*, p. 42; Fukuyama, *End of History*, pp. 106, 237, 294.
34. Alterman, "Dellums", 36, 42.
35. *Guardian*, July 22, 1996; "Women Prime Ministers and Presidents, 1960–1994," table in Jeffreys-Jones, *Changing Differences*, p. 156.
36. Burns and Sorenson, *Dead Center*, pp. 130–35, 327.
37. Heale, *Twentieth-Century America*, p. 302; Bernstein, "Two Cheers", 66.
38. Heale, *Twentieth-Century America*, p. 303; quotation, emphases in the original, from Shelton, *Talk of Power*, p.106.
39. Heale, *Twentieth-Century America*, p. 302; Clinton, *My Life*, pp. 482–83; Blumenthal and Morone, *Heart of Power*, p. 365.
40. Gingrich, "Where We Go From Here," extension of remarks filed and reproduced in the *Congressional Record*, 104 Cong., 1 sess., April 7, 1995, accessed in 2008 through LexisNexis; Stricker, *Why America Lost the War on Poverty*, pp. 217–19.
41. *Washington Post*, September 13, 1998.
42. Author's interview with Senator Bernie Sanders, May 15, 2008.
43. Klein, *No Logo*, pp. 239–41, 243, 422; Kazin, *American Dreamers*, pp. 261–62.
44. Robert J. Samuelson, "Global Capitalism, R.I.P.?" *Newsweek* (September 14, 1998), 20–22.
45. Pierson, *Socialism after Communism*, pp. 80–81.
46. Drucker, *Post-Capitalist Society*, p. 5; Sklar in Becker and Sklar, *Postimperialism*, p. 12; Chandler, "Creeping Socialism," 38.
47. Hunter, *Culture Wars*, pp. 3ff, 34, 42, 156, 160.
48. Results of a Carnegie Foundation study of 1984 and of collaborative research based on 1999 data reported in the *Washington Post*, March 29, 2005; Klehr, Haynes and Firsov, *Secret World*, p. 17; Washburn, *University, Inc.*, p. ix; Stille, "Betrayal of History," 15. Assistant Managing Editor Craig R. Whitney defended the *New York Times* against charges of leftism in the issue of October 13, 2009.
49. Himmelfarb, *One Nation*, pp. 117, 128, 130.

NOTES TO CHAPTER 10

1. Author's interview with Bernard Sanders, Washington, DC, May 15, 2008.
2. Author's interview with John Peterson (Vermonter and political scientist), Edinburgh, February 11, 2008; WPA guide cited in *New York Times*, August 8, 2008.
3. Mark Leibovich, "Socialist Senator," *New York Times Magazine*, January 21, 2007.
4. Hensarling (Rep., TX: leader of a one-hundred-strong group of conservative lawmakers) quoted in *New York Times*, September 27, 2008.
5. Young, "Reflections", pp. 6–7, the pagination corresponding to typescript kindly supplied by Professor Young; Whalen and Flacks, *Beyond the Barricades*, pp. 4, 383; author's interview with Gitlin, May 8, 2008.
6. Norton, *Leo Strauss*, pp. 7, 9, 45, 77; Rasmussen Reports, April 9, 2009.
7. Norton, *Leo Strauss*, pp. 186–89; Klein, *For All These Rights*, p. 20. Edwin Witte noted Roosevelt's support for health insurance in a set of notes he took on Anderson, "Health Insurance," though Anderson's article itself contains no such information: Folder, "History of Health Security," Box 209, EEW.
8. Steve Schifferes (BBC News economics reporter), "The Iraq War: Counting the Cost," broadcast on March 19, 2008, available at <http://news.bbc.co.uk/1/hi/7304300.stm> (last accessed May 11, 2010). For a more conservative estimate of $715 billion between 2003 and 2010, see Daggett, *Costs*, p. 2.
9. Nuschler, *Social Security Reform*, p. 3; *New York Times*, May 13, 2009.
10. *New York Times*, April 30, May 1, 9, 2005; *Washington Post*, February 8, 2006; George Scialabba, "The Work Cut Out for us," *The Nation* (January 29, 2007), 23.
11. Lewis H. Lapham, "The Simple Life," *Harper's* (December 2005), 9.
12. Census Bureau figures cited in *New York Times*, August 31, 2005; Congressional Budget Office figures cited in *New York Times*, June 10, 2007; *New York Times*, August 28, 2006, March 31, 2009. The richest 10 percent in America accounted for 45 percent of the US tax intake, a higher percentage than the top tenth paid in any one of fifteen comparable European countries: Baldwin, *Narcissism of Minor Differences*, p. 36.
13. BBC News February 17, 2003, available at <http://news.bbc.co.uk/1/hi/world/europe/2765215.stm> (last accessed May 12, 2010).
14. Berg, "Waiting for Lefty," 83; Kazin, *American Dreamers*, p. 263.
15. Quotation from Young, "Reflections", p. 1; Berg, "Waiting for Lefty", 78–79.
16. USLAW, "Labor Rights in Iraq", available at <http://uslaboragainstwar.org/section.php?id=8> (last accessed November 15, 2010); Sears, "Peace Work", 715, 717–18.

17. Quotation from Small, "Bring the Boys Home," 543–44; Young, "Reflections", p. 13.
18. Quotation from Young: author's conversation with Marilyn Young, May 7, 2008.
19. Sanders interview, available at <http://edition.cnn.com/2005/POLITICS/06/20/poll/index.html> and at <http://edition.cnn.com/2008/POLITICS/03/18/poll.iraq.economy/index.html> (last accessed May 12, 2010); Berg, "Waiting for Lefty," 79, 96.
20. Young, "Reflections", p. 71.
21. Young, "Reflections", p. 70.
22. New York Times/CBS News poll reported in *New York Times*, March 2, 2007; WHO World Health Statistics reported in *Guardian*, *G2* (August 19, 2009), 6; Commonwealth Fund figures for 2002–3 reported in *Daily Telegraph*, March 10, 2010; Baldwin, *Narcissism of Minor Differences*, p. 45
23. Quotation from Robin Toner, *New York Times*, January 8, 2007; *New York Times*, September 16, 2007, July 7, 2008.
24. *New York Times*, April 6, 2006, January 9, September 14, December 25, 2007; *San Francisco Chronicle*, October 7, 2007.
25. Blumenthal and Morone, *Heart of Power*, pp. 401–405; *New York Times*, October 4, 2007, A17.
26. *New York Times*, June 27, 2007, July 27, 2008; Battista, *Revival of Labor Liberalism*, pp. 122, 139; Rev. Giles Fraser, "God Moves to the left," *Guardian*, February 8, 2008; Kelly-Woessner and Woessner, "My Professor is a Partisan Hack," 495.
27. Federal Reserve Bank's detailed time-line of the financial collapse available at <http://timeline.stlouisfed.org/index.cfm?p=timeline> (last accessed May 18, 2010).
28. Figures on unemployment as a percentage of the labor force from Bureau of Labor Statistics, available at <http://www.tradingeconomics.com/Economics/Unemployment-rate.aspx?Symbol=USD> (last accessed May 19, 2010); *New York Times*, April 12, May 10, 2009.
29. *New York Times*, September 8, 18, 2008.
30. Obama quoted in *New York Times*, April 3, 2012.
31. Message to the office of Senator Pete V. Domenici, (R-NM), quoted in *New York Times*, September 25, 2008.

NOTES TO CHAPTER 11

1. Gingrich on Fox News, "Hannity and Colmes" show, July 27, 2007 (Lexis).
2. Hungerford, *Changes in the Distribution of Income*, p. i, Obama quoted in *New York Times*, December 10, 2012.

3. *Washington Post*, October 16, 2008; *Washington Times*, October 22, 2008; *Los Angeles Times*, October 24, 2008.
4. *Washington Times*, October 19, 2008; *Washington Post*, October 22, 2008; McCain radio address quoted in *Dallas Morning News*, October 19, 2008.
5. *New York Times*, March 1, 2009; Richard Kim, "The Mad Tea Party", *Nation* (April 12, 2010); Norman J. Ornstein, "Obama: A Pragmatic Moderate Faces the 'Socialist' Smear", *Washington Post*, April 14, 2010; Foreman, "Ambition", 247.
6. Obama speech to The Associated Press, *New York Times*, April 3, 2012.
7. Wayne quoting Obama's *The Audacity of Hope* in his book *Personality and Politics*, p. 44.
8. Jacobs, "Obama and the Angry Left", p. 181; *New York Post* editorial, n.d., reproduced in the *Washington Times*, January 2, 2009.
9. Jon Meacham, "We Are All Socialists Now," *Newsweek*, February 7, 2009; Meyerson in *Washington Post*, March 4, 2009; Wharton in *Washington Post*, March 15, 2009.
10. *New York Times*, December 11, 2010; *Washington Post*, June 20, 2011.
11. Manchester, NH, *Union Leader* (editorial), October 10, 2008; Corsi, *Obama Nation*, pp. xi, 221; Mark Hyman special to the *Washington Times*, March 1, 2009.
12. Quotations from Obama, *Dreams from My Father*, p. 100; Remnick, *Bridge*, p. 104.
13. Quotation from Obama, *Audacity of Hope*, p. 289; Niven, *Barack Obama*, pp. 12–13; Bob Roman, "A Town Meeting on Economic Insecurity," *New Ground* 45 (March–April, 1996), available at <http://www.chicagodsa.org/ngarchive/ng45.html> (last accessed February 25, 2010); Gitlin email to author, May 31, 2010.
14. *Toronto Globe and Mail*, October 31, 2008; "wedded" quotation from Obama, *Dreams from My Father*, p. xv; "friends" quotation from *New York Times*, July 9, 2008; *New York Times*, May 1, 2010.
15. Annie Lowrey in *New York Times*, January 8, 2013.
16. *Washington Times*, January 12, 2009; *Nation* (March 23, 2009), front cover.
17. *New York Times*, February 20, November 17, 2010; Webel and Labonte, *Government Interventions*, pp. 5, 8, 14; Princeton economist Alan S. Binder in *New York Times*, March 8, 2009; *Boston Globe*, March 11, 2009. The UCLA historian Peter Baldwin has collated statistical data to show that there are wide social-policy differences between European nations, and that the gap between Europe and the USA has been exaggerated: Baldwin, *Narcissism of Minor Differences*, pp. 6, 36, 70.
18. Obama, *Audacity of Hope*, pp. 151–53.
19. Obituary of Broadus Mitchell, *New York Times*, April 30, 1988; Oral History

Interview with Broadus Mitchell by Mary Frederickson, August 14 and 15, 1977, Interview B-0024, Southern Oral History Collection, available at <http://docsouth.unc.edu/sohp/B-0024/excerpts/excerpt_3993.html> (last accessed June 4, 2010); Mitchell, *Hamilton*, I, xiii; Mitchell, *Heritage*, pp. 37, 59.

20. Obama quoted in the *Guardian*, August 2, 2009; Mica press release, January 28, 2009, available at <http://republicans.transportation.house.gov/news/PRArticle.aspx?NewsID=774> (last accessed June 4, 2010); *New York Times*, October 4, 2010.

21. *Guardian*, August 2, 2009; *Daily Telegraph*, February 13, 2010; *New York Times*, August 26, 2012.

22. The quotation is a paraphrase by Frank Rich in "Why Has He Fallen Short?" *The New York Review of Books*, August 19, 2010.

23. *New York Times*, April 13, 2009, March 21, 25, 2010; *Washington Post*, October 8, 2009.

24. *New York Times*, October 9, 2009, December 18, 2010.

25. Starr, *Remedy and Reaction*, pp. 166–75.

26. *New York Times*, August 16, 2009.

27. Estimate by Washington DC's Tax Policy Center reported in David Leonhardt, "In Health Care Bill, Obama Attacks Wealth Inequality," *New York Times*, March 23, 2010; Douglas W. Elmendorf, Director, Congressional Budget Office, to Nancy Pelosi, March 20, 2010, p. 2, available at <http://www.cbo.gov/ftpdocs/113xx/doc11379/AmendReconProp.pdf> (last accessed June 8, 2010).

28. Perlman, "Memorandum to McCarthy," November 1, 1914, Reel 15, p. 0252, RD; *New York Times*, August 17, 2009; Alter, *Promise*, p. 258; Foreman, "Ambition", p. 255; Jacob S. Hacker, *The Case for Public Plan Choice in National Health Reform* (Berkeley Law, ca. December 2008), available at <http://institute.ourfuture.org/files/Jacob_Hacker_Public_Plan_Choice.pdf> (last accessed August 19, 2010); Commonwealth Fund news release, "11-Country Survey: U.S. Adults Most Likely to Forgo Care Due to Cost," November 18, 2010, available at <http://www.commonwealthfund.org/~/media/Files/News/News%20Releases/2010/Nov/Int%20Survey/IHP%20release%20FINAL%20111610.pdf> (last accessed November 22, 2010).

29. Quotations by the journalist Sheryl Stolberg and by Sanders in *New York Times*, December 18, 2009; Blumenthal and Morone, *Heart of Power*, p. 18; economics correspondent David Leonhardt in *New York Times*, January 20, 2010.

30. Obama and Palin quoted in the *Guardian*, August 12, 2009.

31. Douglas, *A Cure For Living*, pp. 22, 42; *Guardian* August 12 and (citing World Health Organization comparisons) 19, 2009. For a later assessment favorable to the UK, see Ingleby, "How the NHS Measures Up", 25–27. A Gallup poll

showed that 49 percent approved of the Obamacare bill on the day it passed, and some of the 31 percent who disapproved may have thought it did not go far enough, available at <http://www.usatoday.com/news/washington/2010-03-23-health-poll-favorable_N.htm> (last accessed June 8, 2010).

32. *New York Times*, November 8, 2012.
33. Obama, *Audacity of Hope*, pp. 287–88, 304, 315; New York Times Advanced digital index search (Obama's "friends"; accessed June 10, 2010).
34. Singh, *Obama's Post-American Foreign Policy*, pp. 57, 201.
35. *New York Times*, May 11, 2010.
36. Pedersen, *Obama's America*, p. 152; Giroux, *First Year*, p. 6.
37. Nobel citation from Giroux, *First Year*, p. 31; Journalist Deborah Solomon and Jagland quoted in *New York Times*, October 25, 2009; Singh, *Obama's Post-American Foreign Policy*, p. 57.
38. *New York Times*, March 24, May 27, 2010; Daggett, *Costs*, p. 5. Figures in the latter source indicate that war expenditure as an annual percentage of GDP was not exceptionally high in the period 2001–10 compared with the world wars and other foreign clashes. However, the length of the post-9/11 conflicts made the dollar drain seem endless.
39. Obama quoted in Lynch and Singh, *After Bush*, p. 43.
40. *Guardian*, December 10, 2009; Buhle email to author, February 23, 2010.
41. *New York Times*, April 5, December 20, 2010.
42. Singh, *Obama's Post-American Foreign Policy*, pp. 112–17.
43. Available at <http://www.aipac.org> (last accessed June 10, 2010); Chris McGreal, "Who Speaks for US Jews?", special report to the *Guardian*, October 24, 2009.
44. *Nation* (June 21, 2010), 3, 5, 9.
45. Roosevelt, "New Nationalism", pp. 30, 38.
46. Obama speech in *Washington Post*, December 6, 2011.
47. Romney quoted in *New York Times*, February 1, 2012: "I'm not concerned about the very poor. We have a safety net there. If it needs a repair, I'll fix it. I'm not concerned about the very rich, they're doing just fine." See also Rhodri Jeffreys-Jones, "The WORM [White Old Rich Men] and the Vietnam War," Society for Historians of American Foreign Relations *Newsletter*, 32 (March 2001), pp. 30–36, available at <http://www.shafr.org/passport/2001/mar/worm.htm> (last accessed March 28, 2013).
48. Akin quotation and apology available at <http://fox2now.com/2012/08/19/the-jaco-report-august-19-2012> (last accessed January 7, 2013); *Observer*, January 1, 2012; *New York Times*, October 17, November 7, 2012; *Economist*, November 10–16, 2012, 43.
49. Obama quoted in *New York Times* online, January 21, 2013.

NOTES TO APPENDIX

1. For example, see Diggins, *Rise and Fall*, p. 39 and throughout.
2. Texts of the 1904, 1912 and 1928 platforms in Morgan, ed., *American Socialism*, pp. 47–50, 55–60, 102–106.
3. Schlesinger, *Vital Center*, p. 36; Hunter, *Culture Wars*, pp. 42, 155–56, 160–61.

ABBREVIATIONS USED IN THE NOTES

Locations

BCUT	Briscoe Center for American History, University of Texas at Austin
CAC	Carl Albert Center, University of Oklahoma at Norman
DUL	Durham University Library
HI	Hoover Institution Library, Stanford, California
LBJ	Lyndon Baines Johnson Library, Austin, Texas
MCS	Margaret Chase Smith Library, Skowhegan, Maine
MLC	Manuscript Collections, Library of Congress
NA	National Archives, Washington, DC
NLS	National Library of Scotland, Edinburgh
NYPL	New York Public Library
PSC	Pacific Studies Center, East Palo Alto, California
RBMC	Rare Book and Manuscript Library, Columbia University, New York, New York
RN	Richard Nixon Presidential Library, Yorba Linda, California
SU	Stanford University Libraries, Special Collections
TL	Tamiment Library, New York University
UM	University of Michigan Libraries, Ann Arbor
WHS	Wisconsin Historical Society, Madison

Collections

BN	Boxed Newspapers, TL
CIR	Materials relating to the Division of Research and Investigation of the US Commission on Industrial Relations, NA
CIRW	US Commission on Industrial Relations, 1912–1915: Unpublished Records of the Division of Research and

226

	Investigation: Reports, Staff Studies, and Background Research Materials, WHS. These microfilmed records are separate from and supplementary to RD, below
CM	Charles McCarthy papers, WHS
CPUSA	Communist Party of the United States Collection, TL
CWM	C. Wright Mills papers, BCUT
DBRF	Daniel Bell Research Files, TL
DPM	Daniel P. Moynihan Papers, MLC
EEW	Edwin E. Witte papers, WHS
EGF	Elizabeth Gurley Flynn papers, Joe Hill Case, CPUSA, TL
EK	Egil Krogh files, RN
ET	Elizabeth Thomas papers, WHS
EVD	Papers of Eugene V. Debs, 1834–1945 (Sanford, NC: Microfilming Corporation of America, 1982), NLS
FLW	Papers of Frieda Lindfield Werden, BCUT
GB	Gerald J. Boileau papers, WHS
GR	Group Research collection, RBMC
HGD	Helen Gahagan Douglas Papers, CAC
JFR	John F. Russell Collection, HI
JL	Jack London papers, SU
JLov	Jay Lovestone Papers, HI
JRC	John R. Commons Papers, WHS
JWF	James W. Ford Papers, TI
LC	Joseph Labadie Collection, UM
ML	Meyer London papers, TL
RD	US Commission on Industrial Relations, 1912–1915: Unpublished Records of the Division of Research and Investigation: Reports, Staff Studies, and Background Research Materials (Frederick, MD: University Microfilms of America, 1985), DUL
RFD	Research files (domestic), PSC
RM	Raymond Moley papers, HI
RPS	Rose Pastor Stokes papers, TL
RRGC	Ronald Reagan Gubernatorial Collection, HI
TA	Thomas Ryum Amlie Papers, WHS
VB	Victor L. Berger papers, WHS
VF	Voorhis Family Papers, WHS
VM	Vito Marcantonio Papers, NYPL
WML	William M. Leiserson papers, WHS

BIBLIOGRAPHY

Adamic, Louis. *Dynamite: The Story of Class Violence in America.* Gloucester, MA: Peter Smith, 1963 [1931].

Adams, Graham, Jr. *Age of Industrial Violence, 1910–1915.* New York: Columbia University Press, 1966.

Adams, James T. *The Epic of America.* Boston: Little, Brown, 1931.

Adler, William M. *The Man Who Never Died: The Life, Times and Legacy of Joe Hill, American Labor Icon.* New York: Bloomsbury, 2011.

Alter, Jonathan. *The Promise: President Obama, Year One.* London: Simon & Schuster, 2010.

Alterman, Eric. "Ron Dellums: Radical Insider." *World Policy Journal* 10 (Winter 1993/94): 35–46.

Altmeyer, Arthur J. *The Formative Years of Social Security: A Chronicle of Social Security Legislation and Administration, 1934–1954.* Madison: University of Wisconsin Press, 1968.

"Amtrak Improvement Act of 1976." *Hearings before the Subcommittee on Transportation and Commerce of the Committee on Interstate and Foreign Commerce.* House, 94 Cong., 2 sess., March 9 and 11, 1976.

Anderson, Carol. "Bleached Souls and Red Negroes: The NAACP and Black Communists in the Early Cold War, 1948–1952." In *Window on Freedom: Race, Civil Rights and Foreign Affairs, 1945–1988.* Edited by Brenda Gayle Plummer. Chapel Hill: University of North Carolina Press, 2003. Pp. 93–113.

Anderson, Odin W. "Health Insurance in the United States, 1910–1920." *Journal of the History of Medicine and Allied Sciences* 5 (Autumn 1950): 363–96.

Anderson, Terry H. *The Movement and the Sixties.* New York: Oxford University Press, 1995.

Aptheker, Herbert. *American Negro Slave Revolts.* New York: Columbia University Press, 1943.

Archer, Robin. *Why is there no Labor Party in the United States?* Princeton, NJ: Princeton University Press, 2007.

228

Arnesen, Eric, ed. *Encyclopedia of U.S. Labor and Working-Class History*. 3 vols. New York: Routledge, 2007.

Avallone, Charlene. "What American Renaissance? The Gendered Genealogy of a Critical Discourse." *PMLA*, 12 (October 1997): 1101–20.

Badger, Anthony J. *The New Deal: The Depression Years, 1933–1940*. New York: Noonday Press, 1989.

Baldwin, Kate A. *Beyond the Color Line and the Iron Curtain: Reading Encounters Between Black and Red, 1922–1963*. Durham, NC: Duke University Press, 2002.

Baldwin, Peter. *The Narcissism of Minor Differences: How America and Europe are Alike: An Essay in Numbers*. Oxford: Oxford University Press, 2009.

Battista, Andrew. *The Revival of Labor Liberalism*. Urbana: University of Illinois Press, 2008.

Beard, Charles A. *The Devil Theory of War: An Inquiry into the Nature of History and the Possibility of Keeping Out of War*. New York: Vanguard, 1936.

Becker, David and Richard Sklar, eds. *Postimperialism and World Politics*. Westport, CT: Praeger, 1999.

Bell, Jonathan. "Building a West Coast: The Legacy of the California Popular Front and the Challenge to Cold War Liberalism in the Post-World War II Era." *Journal of American Studies* 46 (February 2012): 51–71.

——. *The Liberal State on Trial: The Cold War and American Politics in the Truman Years*. New York: Columbia University Press, 2004.

Bellamy, Edward. *Looking Backward, 2000–1887*. Oxford: Oxford University Press, 2007 [1887].

Benn, Tony. *Why America Needs Democratic Socialism*. Nottingham: Spokesman Books, 1978.

Benson, Robert L. "Report on the Work of the National Physicians' Committee for the Extension of Medical Service." *Bulletin of the Medical Librarians' Association* 29 (March 1941): 147–49.

Berg, John C. "Waiting for Lefty: The State of the Peace Movement in the United States." *Tamkang Journal of International Affairs* 12 (April 2009): 77–101.

Berkowitz, Edward D. *America's Welfare State: From Roosevelt to Reagan*. Baltimore, MD: Johns Hopkins University Press, 1991.

Berman, Sheri. *The Social Democratic Moment: Ideas and Politics in the Making of Interwar Europe*. Cambridge, MA: Harvard University Press, 1998.

Bernard, Emily. *Carl Van Vechten and the Harlem Renaissance: A Portrait in Black and White*. London: Yale University Press, 2012.

Bernstein, Barton J. "The New Deal: The Conservative Achievements of Liberal Reform." In *Towards a New Past: Dissenting Essays in American History*. Edited by Barton J. Bernstein. New York: Pantheon, 1968.

Bernstein, Irving. *Guns or Butter: The Presidency of Lyndon Johnson*. New York: Oxford University Press, 1996.

Bernstein, Jared. "Two Cheers for the EITC." *American Prospect* 11 (June 19–July 3, 2000): 64–67.

Berube, Maurice R. *Radical Reformers: The Influence of the Left in American Education.* Greenwich, CT: Information Age Publishers, 2004.

Bérubé, Michael. *The Left at War.* New York: New York University Press, 2009.

Blum, Howard. *American Lightening: Terror, Mystery, the Birth of Hollywood, and the Crime of the Century.* New York: Crown, 2008.

Blumberg, Dorothy Rose. *Florence Kelley: The Making of a Social Pioneer.* New York: A. M. Kelley, 1966.

Blumenthal, David and James A. Morone. *The Heart of Power: Health and Politics in the Oval Office.* Berkeley: University of California Press, 2009.

Bolt, Christine. *Sisterhood Questioned? Race, Class and Internationalism in the American and British Women's Movements, c. 1880s–1970s.* London: Routledge, 2004.

Boorstin, Daniel J. *The Americans: The Colonial Experience.* Harmondsworth: Penguin, 1965 [1958].

Borcherding, Thomas E. "One Hundred Years of Public Spending." In *Budgets and Bureaucrats: The Sources of Government Growth.* Edited by Thomas E. Borcherding. Durham, NC: Duke University Press, 1977.

Borstelmann, Thomas. *The Cold War and the Color Line: American Race Relations in the Global Era.* Cambridge, MA: Harvard University Press, 2001.

Brown, E. H. Phelps. *A Century of Pay: The Course of Pay and Production in France, Germany, Sweden, the United Kingdom, and the United States of America, 1860–1960.* London: Macmillan, 1968.

Buhle, Mari Jo, Paul Buhle, and Dan Georgakas, eds. *Encyclopedia of the American Left.* Urbana: University of Illinois Press, 1992.

Buhle, Mari Jo. *Women and American Socialism, 1870–1920.* Urbana: University of Illinois Press, 1983.

Bunche, Ralph J. "A Critique of New Deal Social Planning as it Affects Negroes." *Journal of Negro Education* 5 (January 1936): 59–65.

Burns, Adam. "Without Due Process: Albert E. Pillsbury and the Hoar Anti-Lynching Bill." *American Nineteenth Century History* 11 (June 2010): 233–52.

Burns, Dave. "The Soul of Socialism: Christianity, Civilization, and Citizenship in the Thought of Eugene Debs." *Labor: Studies in Working-Class History of the Americas* 5 (Summer 2008): 83–116.

Burns, James MacGregor and Georgia J. Sorenson. *Dead Center: Clinton-Gore Leadership and the Perils of Moderation.* New York: Scribner, 1999.

Cantor, Joseph E. and others. *Free and Reduced-rate Television Time for Political Candidates.* Washington, DC: Congressional Research Service, 1997.

Carew, Anthony. "The American Labor Movement in Fizzland: The Free Trade Union Committee and the CIA." *Labor History* 39 (February 1998): 25–42.

Carnegie, Andrew. *The Gospel of Wealth and Other Timely Essays.* Edited by

Edward C. Kirkland. Cambridge, MA: Belknap Press of Harvard University Press, 1962 [1900].

Carroll, Peter N. *The Odyssey of the Lincoln Brigade: Americans in the Spanish Civil War.* Stanford, CA: Stanford University Press, 1994.

Carson, Clayborne. *Malcolm X: The FBI File.* New York: Ballantine, 1995.

Carter, Dan T. *Scottsboro: A Tragedy of the American South.* Baton Rouge: Louisiana State University Press, 1969.

Caute, David. *The Great Fear: The Anti-Communist Purge under Truman and Eisenhower.* London: Secker & Warburg, 1978.

Chace, James. *1912: Wilson, Roosevelt, Taft and Debs: The Election that Changed the Country.* New York: Simon & Schuster, 2004.

Challenor, H. H. "The Influence of Black Americans on U.S. Policy Toward Africa." In *Ethnicity and U.S. Foreign Policy.* Edited by Abdul A. Said. New York: Praeger, 1977. Pp. 139–74.

Chandler, Marc. "Creeping Socialism?" *Nation* (September 4/11, 2000): 38, 40, 42.

Charles, Douglas M. "From Subversion to Obscenity: The FBI's Investigations of the Early Homophile Movement in the United States, 1953–1958." *Journal of the History of Sexuality*, 19 (May 2010): 262–87.

———. *The FBI's Obscene File: J. Edgar Hoover and the Bureau's Crusade against Smut.* Lawrence: University Press of Kansas, 2012.

Chauncey, George. *Gay New York: Gender, Urban Culture, and the Makings of the Gay Male World, 1890–1940.* New York: Basic, 1994.

Cherny, Robert W. "Harry Bridges and the Communist Party: New Evidence, Old Questions; Old Evidence, New Questions." Paper read at the annual meeting of the Organization of American Historians, 1998.

———. "Prelude to the Popular Front: The Communist Party in California, 1931–35." *American Communist History* 1/1 (2002): 5–42.

———. "The Communist Party in California, 1935–1940: From the Political Margins to the Mainstream and Back." *American Communist History* 9/1 (2010): 3–33.

———. "The Making of a Labor Radical: Harry Bridges, 1901–1934." *Pacific Historical Review* 64 (1995): 363–88.

"CISPES and FBI Counterterrorism Investigations." *Hearings before the Subcommittee on Civil and Constitutional Rights of the Committee on the Judiciary.* House, 100 Cong., 2 sess, June 13 and September 16, 1988.

Clanton, Gene. "'Hayseed Socialism' on the Hill: Congressional Populism, 1891–1895." *Western Historical Quarterly* 15 (April 1984): 139–62.

Colby, William. *Honorable Men: My Life in the CIA.* London: Hutchinson, 1978.

Collum, Danny D. *African Americans in the Spanish Civil War: "This Ain't Ethiopia, But It'll Do".* New York: G. K. Hall, 1992.

Commager, Henry Steele. "Twelve Years of Roosevelt." In *The New Deal:*

Revolution or Evolution? Edited by Edwin C. Rozwenc. Boston: D. C. Heath, 1949. Pp. 20–28.

Commons, John R. *Labor and Administration.* New York: Macmillan, 1913.

——.*Myself: The Autobiography of John R. Commons.* Madison: University of Wisconsin Press, 1964.

Conkin, Paul K. *Big Daddy from the Padernales: Lyndon Baines Johnson.* Boston: Twayne, 1986.

——.*The New Deal.* New York: Crowell, 1967.

Conlin, Joseph R. *Bread and Roses, Too: Studies of the Wobblies.* Westport, CT: Greenwood, 1969.

Constantine, J. Robert, ed. *The Papers of Eugene V. Debs, 1834–1935: A Guide to the Microfilm Edition.* Sanford, NC: Microfilming Corporation of America, 1982.

Corak, Miles, ed. *Generational Income Mobility in North America and Europe.* Cambridge: Cambridge University Press, 2004.

Corsi, Jerome R. *The Obama Nation: Leftist Politics and the Cult of Personality.* New York: Pocket Star/Simon & Schuster, 2008.

Craik, David. "U.S. Presidents and Public Opinion: The Carter Presidency." University of Keele PhD, 2005.

Cronin, Bernard C. *Father Yorke and the Labor Movement in San Francisco, 1900–1910.* Washington, DC: Catholic University of America Press, 1943.

Cruse, Harold. *The Crisis of the Negro Intellectual.* New York: William Morrow, 1967.

Cullen, Jim. *The American Dream: A Short History of an Idea that Shaped a Nation.* Oxford: Oxford University Press, 2003.

Culver, John C. and John Hyde. *American Dreamer: A Life of Henry A. Wallace.* New York: Norton, 2000.

Curti, Merle. *The Social Ideas of American Educators.* Totowa, NJ: Littlefield, Adams, 1959 [1935].

Daggett, Stephen. *Costs of Major U.S. Wars.* Washington, DC: Congressional Research Service, June 21, 2010.

Dahrendorf, Ralf. *Reflections on the Revolution in Europe.* London: Chatto & Windus, 1990.

Davies, Richard O. "'Mr. Republican' Turns 'SOCIALIST'." *Ohio History* 73 (1998): 135–43.

DeBenedetti, Charles, with Charles Chatfield. *An American Ordeal: The Antiwar Movement of the Vietnam Era.* Syracuse: Syracuse University Press, 1990.

Degler, Carl N. *Out of Our Past.* 2nd ed. New York: Harper and Row, 1970.

Denning, Michael. *The Cultural Front: The Laboring of American Culture in the Twentieth Century.* London: Verso, 1996.

Denton, Sally. *The Pink Lady: The Many Lives of Helen Gahagan Douglas.* New York: Bloomsbury Press, 2009.

Desai, Ashok V. *Real Wages in Germany 1971–1913.* Oxford: Clarendon Press, 1968.

Destler, Chester D. *American Radicalism 1865–1901.* Chicago: Quadrangle, 1946.

"Development and Administration of the Port of New York." *House Report.* 1039, 67 Cong., 2 sess., May 1922.

Dewey, John. *The School and Society.* Rev. ed. Chicago: University of Chicago Press, 1915 [1899].

Diggins, John P. *Mussolini and Fascism: The View from America.* Princeton, NJ: Princeton University Press, 1972.

——. *The Rise and Fall of the American Left.* New York: Norton, 1992.

Doig, Jameson W. *Empire on the Hudson: Entrepreneurial Vision and Political Power at the Port of New York Authority.* New York: Columbia University Press, 2001.

Dorfman, Joseph. *The Economic Mind in American Civilization.* 5 vols. New York: Viking, 1918–49.

Douglas, Ann. *Terrible Honesty: Mongrel Manhattan in the 1920s.* London: Picador, 1996.

Douglas, Colin (pseud. Colin Currie). *A Cure for Living.* London: Hutchinson, 1983.

Douglas, Paul H. *The Coming of a New Party.* New York: McGraw-Hill, 1932.

Dreier, Peter. "The Fifty Most Influential Progressives of the Twentieth Century." *Nation* 291/14 (October 4, 2010). Pp. 11–21.

Drucker, Peter F. *Post-capitalist Society.* Oxford: Butterworth Heinemann, 1993.

Du Bois, W. E. B. "The African Roots of War." *Atlantic Monthly* 115 (May 1915): 707–714.

——. *The Souls of Black Folk.* London: Longman, Green, 1965 [1903].

Duberman, Martin B. *Paul Robeson.* London: Bodley Head, 1989.

Dubofsky, Melvyn. *We Shall Be All: A History of the Industrial Workers of the World.* Chicago: Quadrangle, 1969.

Dudziak, Mary L. *Cold War Civil Rights: Race and the Image of American Democracy.* Princeton: Princeton University Press, 2000.

Eckhardt, Celia M. *Fanny Wright: Rebel in America.* Cambridge, MA: Harvard University Press, 1984.

Erikson, Robert and John H. Goldthorpe. "Are American Rates of Social Mobility Exceptionally High? New Evidence on an Old Issue." *European Sociological Review* 1 (May 1985): 1–22.

——. *The Constant Flux: A Study of Class Mobility in Industrial Societies.* Oxford: at the Clarendon Press, 1992.

"Establishing a National Health Program." *Senate Report.* 1139, 76 Cong., 1 sess., August 1939.

"Establishment of 'The Port of New York Authority'." *Senate Report.* 161, 67 Cong., 1 sess., June 1921.

Evans, Sara M. *Personal Politics: The Roots of Women's Liberation in the Civil Rights Movement and the New Left.* New York: Vintage Books, 1980.

Fairclough, Adam. *Better Day Coming: Blacks and Equality, 1890–2000.* New York: Penguin, 2001.

——.*Martin Luther King.* London: Cardinal, 1991.

Fausold, Martin L. *The Presidency of Herbert Hoover.* Lawrence: University Press of Kansas, 1984.

Final Report of the Commission on Industrial Relations. Washington, DC: GPO, 1915.

Fine, Sidney. *Laissez Faire and the General Welfare State.* Ann Arbor: University of Michigan Press, 1956.

——.*Without Blare of Trumpets: Walter Drew, the National Erectors' Association, and the Open Shop Movement.* Ann Arbor: University of Michigan Press, 1995.

Fink, Leon. "Leon Fink Responds." *American Historical Review* 96 (April 1991): 429–31.

Flynn, John T. *The Road Ahead: America's Creeping Revolution.* (New York: Devin-Adair, 1949).

——.*The Roosevelt Myth.* New York: Devin-Adair, 1948.

Foner, Eric. "Why is There No Socialism in the United States?" *History Workshop* 17 (Spring 1984): 57–80.

Foner, Philip S. *American Socialism and Black Americans: From the Age of Jackson to World War II.* Westport, CT: Greenwood Press, 1977.

——.*The Case of Joe Hill.* New York: International Publishers, 1965.

——.*Women and the American Labor Movement: From the First Trade Unions to the Present.* New York: Free Press, 1982.

Ford, James W. *The Communists and the Struggle for Negro Liberation: Their Position on Problems of Africa, of the West Indies, of the War of Ethiopian Independence, of the Struggle for Peace.* New York: Harlem Division of the Communist Party, n.d.

Foreman, Christopher H., Jr. "Ambition, Necessity, and Polarization in the Obama Domestic Agenda." In *The Obama Presidency: Appraisals and Prospects.* Edited by Bert A. Rockman and others. Los Angeles: Sage/CQ Press, 2012. Pp. 244–67.

Frank, Thomas. *Pity the Billionaire: The Hard-Times Swindle and the Unlikely Comeback of the Right.* London: Harvill Secker, 2012.

Freeberg, Ernest. *Democracy's Prisoner: Eugene V. Debs, the Great War, and the Right to Dissent.* Cambridge, MA: Harvard University Press, 2008.

Freeland, Richard M. *The Truman Doctrine and the Origins of McCarthyism: Foreign Policy, Domestic Politics, and internal Security, 1946–1948.* New York: Schocken, 1974 [1971].

Frieburger, William J. "The Lone Socialist Vote: A Political Study of Meyer London." University of Cincinnati PhD, 1980.

Fried, Albert, ed. *McCarthyism: The Great American Red Scare: A Documentary History.* New York: Oxford University Press, 1996.

Friedan, Betty. *The Feminine Mystique.* Harmondsworth: Penguin, 1965 [1963].

Friedman, Milton and Rose Friedman. *Free to Choose: A Personal Statement.* Harmondsworth: Penguin, 1980.

Fukuyama, Francis. *The End of History and the Last Man.* London: Hamish Hamilton, 1992.

Galbraith, John K. *The Affluent Society.* Boston: Houghton Mifflin, 1958.

———. *The Affluent Society.* 2nd ed., revised Harmondsworth: Penguin, 1975 [1958].

———. *The American Left and Some British Comparisons.* London: Fabian Society, 1971.

———. *The Great Crash 1929.* Harmondsworth: Penguin, 1961 [1954].

Garrow, David J. *Bearing the Cross: Martin Luther King Jr., and the Southern Christian Leadership Conference.* New York: Vintage, 1988.

———. *Protest at Selma: Martin Luther King Jr., and the Voting Rights Act of 1965.* New Haven: Yale University Press, 1978.

———. *The FBI and Martin Luther King Jr.* New York: Penguin, 1983.

Geary, Daniel. "'Becoming International Again': C. Wright Mills and the Emergence of the Global New Left, 1956–1962." *Journal of American History* 95 (December 2008): 710–36.

Gellman, Irwin F. *The Contender: Richard Nixon, the Congress Years, 1946–1952.* New York: The Free Press, 1999.

Ghent, William J. *Our Benevolent Feudalism.* New York: Macmillan, 1902.

Gilmore, Glenda E. *Defying Dixie: The Radical Roots of Civil Rights, 1919–1950.* New York: Norton, 2008.

Ginger, Ray. *The Bending Cross: A Biography of Eugene Victor Debs.* New Brunswick, NJ: Rutgers University Press, 1949.

Giroux, Gregory. *The First Year: Obama in the Oval Office.* Washington, DC: CQ Press, 2010.

Gitlin, Todd. *The Twilight of Common Dreams: Why America is Wracked by Culture Wars.* New York: Metropolitan Books, 1995.

———. *The Whole World is Watching: Mass Media in the Making and Unmaking of the New Left.* Berkeley: University of California Press, 1980.

Goldberg, Gordon J. "Meyer London and the National Social Insurance Movement, 1914–1922." *American Jewish Quarterly* 65 (September 1975): 59–73.

Goldwater, Walter, comp. *Radical Periodicals in America, 1890–1950.* Rev. ed. New Haven: Yale University Library, 1966.

Goluboff, Risa L. *The Lost Promise of Civil Rights.* Cambridge, MA: Harvard University Press, 2007.

Gorman, Robert A. *Michael Harrington: Speaking American.* New York: Routledge, 1995.

Gornick, Vivian. *Emma Goldman: Revolution as a Way of Life.* New Haven: Yale University Press, 2011.

Gould, Lewis L. *Four Hats in the Ring: The 1912 Election and the Birth of American Politics.* Lawrence: University Press of Kansas, 2008.

Groening, Matt. *Bart Simpson's Guide to Life, Helped into Print by Matt Groening.* London: HarperCollins, 1993.

Hall, Jacqueline D. "The Long Civil Rights Movement and the Political Uses of the Past." *Journal of American History* 91 (March 2005): 1233–63.

Hall, Mitchell K. *Because of Their Faith: CALCAV and Religious Opposition to the Vietnam War.* New York: Columbia University Press, 1990.

——, ed. *Vietnam War Era: People and Perspectives.* Santa Barbara, CA: ABC CLIO, 2009.

Hamby, Alonzo L. "The New Deal: Avenues for Reconsideration." *Polity* 31 (Summer 1999): 665–81.

Harrington, Michael. *The Accidental Journey.* London: Weidenfeld & Nicolson, 1966.

——. *The Other America: Poverty in the United States.* Baltimore, MD: Penguin, 1969 [1962].

Harris, Howell. "Between Convergence and Exceptionalism: Americans and the British Model of Labor Relations, c. 1867–1920." *Labor History* 48 (May 2007): 141–73.

Harrison, J. F. C. *Robert Owen and the Owenites in Britain and America: The Quest for a New Moral World.* London: Routledge & Kegan Paul, 1969.

Hartz, Louis. *The Liberal Tradition in America.* New York: Harcourt, Brace, 1955.

Hayden, Tom. *Reunion: A Memoir.* New York: Random House, 1988.

Heale, Michael J. *American Anticommunism: Combating the Enemy Within, 1830–1970.* Baltimore: Johns Hopkins University Press, 1990.

——. *McCarthy's Americans: Red Scare Politics in State and Nation, 1935–1965.* Athens: University of Georgia Press, 1998.

——. *Twentieth-Century America: Politics and Power in the United States, 1900–2000.* London: Arnold, 2004.

Hedges, Chris. *Death of the Liberal Class.* New York: Nation Books, 2010.

Hefferle, Caroline. "Students and Political Activism." In *Vietnam War Era: People and Perspectives.* Edited by Mitchell K. Hall. Santa Barbara, CA: ABC CLIO, 2009. Pp. 185–201.

Hillquit, Morris. *Socialism in Theory and Practice.* New York: Macmillan, 1910.

Himmelfarb, Gertrude. *One Nation, Two Cultures.* New York: Knopf, 1999.

Hirshman, Linda R. *Victory: The Triumphant Gay Revolution.* New York: Harper, 2012.

Hodge, Roger D. *The Mendacity of Hope: Barack Obama and the Betrayal of American Liberalism.* New York: Harper, 2010.

Hoff, Joan. *Nixon Reconsidered.* New York: Basic, 1994.

Hofstadter, Richard, ed. *The Progressive Movement, 1900–1915.* Englewood Cliffs, NJ: Prentice-Hall, 1963.

——. *The Age of Reform: From Bryan to FDR.* New York: Bantam, 1955.

Holzman, Michael. *James Jesus Angleton, the CIA, and the Craft of Counterintelligence.* Amherst: University of Massachusetts Press, 2008.

Horowitz, Daniel. *Betty Friedan and the Making of the Feminine Mystique.* Amherst: University of Massachusetts Press, 1998.

Horowitz, David. *Unholy Alliance: Radical Islam and the American Left.* Washington, DC: Regnery, 2004.

"How Can the Health Care of United States Citizens Best be Improved? A Collection of Excerpts and Bibliography Relating to the High School Debate Topic, 1977–1978." Compiled by the Congressional Research Service. *Senate Document* 95–39, 95 Cong., 1 sess., 1977.

Hughes, Geoffrey. *Political Correctness: A History of Semantics and Culture.* Malden, MA: Wiley-Blackwell, 2010.

Hughes, Langston. *I Wonder as I Wander.* New York: Hill and Wang, 1964 [1956].

Hungerford, Thomas L. *Changes in the Distribution of Income among Tax Filers between 1996 and 2006: The Role of Labor Income, Capital Income, and Tax Policy.* Washington, DC: Congressional Research Service, 2011.

Hunter, James J. *Culture Wars: The Struggle to Define America.* New York: Basic Books, 1991.

Hunter, Robert. *Poverty.* New York: Harper Torchbooks, 1965 [1904].

——. *Violence and the Labor Movement.* New York: Macmillan, 1914.

Ingleby, David. "How the NHS Measures Up to other Health Systems." *British Medical Journal* (3 March 2012): 24–27.

Isserman, Maurice. *If I Had a Hammer: The Death of the Old Left and the Birth of the New Left.* Urbana: University of Illinois Press, 1987.

——. *The Other American: The Life of Michael Harrington.* New York: Public Affairs, 2000.

Jacobs, Lawrence R. "Barack Obama and the Angry Left: The Fight for Progressive Realism." In *Obama at the Crossroads: Politics, Markets, and the Battle for America's Future.* Edited by Lawrence R. Jacobs and Desmond King. Oxford: Oxford University Press, 2012. Pp. 181–94.

Jacobs, Paul. "The Anti-Zionist Left and the Jews." In "Jews and the Left," *Journal of Palestine Studies* 4 (Spring 1975): 155–60.

James, Winston. *Holding Aloft the Banner of Ethiopia: Caribbean Radicalism in Early Twentieth-Century America.* London: Verso, 1998.

Jeffreys-Jones, Rhodri. "Soziale Folgen der Industrialisierung, Imperialismus und der Weltkrieg 1890–1920." In *Die Vereinigten Staaten.* Edited by W. P. Adams. Frankfurt am Main: Fischer Verlag, 1977. Pp. 235–82.

——. "Changes in the Nomenclature of the American Left." *Journal of American Studies* 44 (February 2010): 83–100.

——. *Changing Differences: Women and the Shaping of American Foreign Policy, 1917–1994.* New Brunswick, NJ: Rutgers University Press, 1995.

——. *In Spies We Trust: The Story of Western Intelligence.* Oxford: Oxford University Press, 2013.

——. *Peace Now! American Society and the Ending of the Vietnam War.* New Haven: Yale University Press, 1999.

——. *The CIA and American Democracy.* New Haven: Yale University Press, 1989.

——. *The FBI: A History.* New Haven: Yale University Press, 2007.

——. *Violence and Reform in American History.* New York: New Viewpoints, 1978.

Jensen, Joan M. "All Pink Sisters: The War Department and the Feminist Movement of the 1920s." In *Decades of Discontent: The Women's Movement, 1920–1940.* Edited by Lois Scharf and Joan M. Jensen. Westport, CT: Greenwood, 1983. Pp. 200–22.

Johanningsmeier, Edward P. *Forging American Communism: The Life of William Z. Foster.* Princeton, NJ: Princeton University Press, 1994.

Johnson, David K. *The Lavender Scare: The Cold War Persecution of Gays and Lesbians in the Federal Government.* Chicago: University of Chicago Press, 2004.

Johnson, James W. *Along this Way: The Autobiography of James Weldon Johnson.* New York: Penguin, 1990 [1955].

Johnstone, Andrew and Helen Laville, eds. *The U.S. Public and American Foreign Policy.* London: Routledge, 2010.

Judd, Richard W. *Socialist Cities: Municipal Politics and the Grass Roots of American Socialism.* Albany: State University of New York Press, 1989.

Kaner, Norman J. "Towards a Minority of One: Vito Marcantonio and American Foreign Policy." Rutgers University PhD, 1968.

Karlinsky, Simon. "Russia's Gay Literature and Culture: The Impact of the October Revolution." In *Hidden From History: Reclaiming the Gay and Lesbian Past.* Edited by Martin B. Duberman, Martha Vicinus and George Chauncey. New York: New American Library, 1989.

Karson, Marc. *American Labor Unions and Politics, 1900–1918.* Boston: Beacon Press, 1965.

Kaufman, Will. *Woody Guthrie, American Radical.* Urbana: University of Illinois Press, 2011.

Kazin, Alfred. *New York Jew.* New York: Knopf, 1978.

Kazin, Michael. *American Dreamers: How the Left Changed a Nation.* New York: Knopf, 2011.

——. *The Populist Persuasion: An American History.* New York: Basic, 1995.

Kelly-Woessner, April and Matthew C. Woessner. "My Professor is a Partisan Hack: How Perceptions of a Professor's Political Views Affect Student

Course Evaluations." *PS: Political Science and Politics* 39 (July 2006): 495–501.

Kenny, Kevin. *The American Irish: A History.* Harlow: Longman, 2000.

Kessner, Thomas. *Fiorello H. La Guardia and the Making of Modern New York.* New York: McGraw-Hill, 1989.

Kipnis, Ira. *The American Socialist Movement, 1897–1912.* New York: Columbia University Press, 1952.

Klehr, Harvey, John E. Haynes and Fridrikh I. Firsov. *The Secret World of American Communism.* New Haven: Yale University Press, 1995.

Klein, Jennifer. *For All These Rights: Business, Labor, and the Shaping of America's Public-Private Welfare State.* Princeton, NJ: Princeton University Press, 2006.

Klein, Naomi. *No Logo: No Space, No Choice, No Jobs.* London: Flamingo, 2000.

Kolchin, Peter. *American Slavery.* London: Penguin, 1995.

Kolin, Andrew. *State Power and Democracy: Before and During the Presidency of George W. Bush.* New York: Palgrave Macmillan, 2011.

Kornbluh, Joyce L., ed. *Rebel Voices: An IWW Anthology.* Ann Arbor: University of Michigan Press, 1964.

Krug, Edward A. *The Shaping of the American High School.* Madison: University of Wisconsin Press, 1972.

Kuper, Adam and Jessica Kuper, eds. *The Social Science Encyclopedia.* 2nd ed. London: Routledge, 1996.

Kutulas, Judy. *The American Civil Liberties Union and the Making of Modern Liberalism.* Chapel Hill: University of North Carolina Press, 2006.

Laski, Harold J. *The American Democracy: A Commentary and an Interpretation.* London: George Allen & Unwin, 1949.

Lee, A. Robert. *Black American Fiction since Richard Wright.* London: British Association for American Studies, 1983.

Leiby, James. *Carroll Wright and Labor Reform: The Origin of Labor Statistics.* Cambridge, MA: Harvard University Press, 1960.

Lens, Sidney. *The Military-Industrial Complex.* London: Stanmore Press, 1971.

Leuchtenburg, William E. *Franklin D. Roosevelt and the New Deal, 1932–1940.* New York: Harper & Row, 1963.

Levine, Daniel. *Poverty and Society: The Growth of the American Welfare State in International Comparison.* New Brunswick, NJ: Rutgers University Press, 1988.

Levine, Linda. *The U.S. Income Distribution and Mobility: Trends and International Comparisons.* Congressional Research Service, 2012.

Levy, Peter B. *The New Left and Labor in the 1960s.* Urbana: University of Illinois Press, 1994.

Lewis, David L. "The Intellectual Luminaries of the Harlem Renaissance." *Journal of Blacks in Higher Education* 7 (Spring 1995): 68–69.

——. *W. E. B. Du Bois: The Fight for Equality and the American Century, 1919–1963.* New York: Henry Holt, 2000.

Lewy, Guenter. *America in Vietnam.* Oxford: Oxford University Press, 1978.

Lilienthal, David E. *TVA: Democracy on the March.* Chicago: Quadrangle, 1966 [1944].

Lipset, Seymour M. and Gary Marks. *It Didn't Happen Here: Why Socialism Failed in the United States.* New York: Norton, 2000.

Locke, Alain, ed. *The New Negro.* New York: Atheneum, 1975 [1925].

Lockman, Zachary. *Contending Visions of the Middle East: The History and Politics of Orientalism.* 2nd ed. Cambridge: Cambridge University Press, 2010.

London, Jack. "The Shrinking of the Planet." In *Revolution and Other Essays.* New York: Macmillan, 1910. Pp. 141–57.

——. *War of the Classes.* New York: Grosset & Dunlop, 1908 [1905].

Lorence, James J. *Gerald J. Boileau and the Progressive-Farmer-Labor Alliance: Politics of the New Deal.* Columbia: University of Minnesota Press, 1994.

——. *The Unemployed People's Movement: Leftists, Liberals and Labor in Georgia, 1929–1941.* Athens: University of Georgia Press, 2009.

Lovin, Hugh T. "Agrarian Radicalism at Ebb Tide: The Michigan Farmer-Labor Party, 1933–1937." *Old Northwest* 5/2 (1979): 149–66.

——. "Thomas R. Amlie's Crusade and the Dissonant Farmers – A New Deal Windfall." *North Dakota Quarterly* 49 (Winter 1981): 91–105.

Lukas, J. Anthony. *Big Trouble.* New York: Simon & Schuster, 1997.

Lynch, Timothy J. and Robert S. Singh. *After Bush: The Case for Continuity in American Foreign Policy.* Cambridge: Cambridge University Press, 2008.

Mailer, Norman. *The Armies of the Night: History as a Novel, the Novel as History.* New York: Plume/Penguin, 1994 [1968].

Malcolm X. *The Autobiography of Malcolm X.* With the assistance of Alex Haley. Harmondsworth: Penguin, 1976 [1965].

Marcuse, Herbert. *One Dimensional Man: Studies in the Ideology of Advanced Industrial Society.* London: Routledge & Kegan Paul, 1964.

Mason, Robert. *Richard Nixon and the Quest for a New Majority.* Chapel Hill: University of North Carolina Press, 2004.

——. *The Republican Party and American Politics from Hoover to Reagan.* Cambridge: Cambridge University Press, 2012.

Matthiessen, Francis O. *American Renaissance: Art and Expression in the Age of Emerson and Whitman.* London: Oxford University Press, 1968 [1941].

Maxwell, William J. *New Negro, Old Left: African-American Writing and Communism Between the Wars.* New York: Columbia University Press, 1999.

McDuffie, Erik S. *Sojourning for Freedom: Black Women, American Communism, and the Making of Black Left Feminism.* Durham: Duke University Press, 2011.

Mead, Margaret. *The American Character.* Harmondsworth: Penguin, 1944.

Meister, Dick. "*La Huelga* Becomes *La Causa.*" In *American Labor Since the New Deal.* Edited by Melvyn Dubofsky. New York: New York Times, 1971.

Message from the President of the United States, transmitting a report of the examination which has been made by the Board of Engineers, with a view to Internal Improvement. Printed by order of the Senate, 18 Cong., 2 sess., 1825.

Meyer, Gerald. "Gay/Lesbian Liberation Movement." In *Encyclopedia of the American Left.* Edited by Mari Jo Buhle, Paul Buhle, and Dan Georgakas. Urbana: University of Illinois Press, 1992. Pp. 257–64.

——. *Vito Marcantonio: Radical Politician, 1902–1954.* Albany: State University of New York Press, 1989.

Miller, Sally M. "Socialism." In *The Encyclopedia of the United States Congress.* 4 vols. Edited by Donald C. Bacon and others. New York: Simon & Schuster, 1995. Pp. 1838–40.

——. *Victor Berger and the Promise of Constructive Socialism, 1910–1920.* Westport, CT: Greenwood, 1973.

Mills, C. Wright. *The Marxists.* Harmondsworth: Penguin, 1967 [1962].

Millward, Robert and John Singleton, eds. *The Political Economy of Nationalisation in Britain 1920–1950.* Cambridge: Cambridge University Press, 1995.

Mitchell, Broadus. *Alexander Hamilton.* 2 vols. New York: Macmillan, 1957, 1962.

——. *Heritage from Hamilton.* New York: Columbia University Press, 1957.

Moley, Raymond. *How to Keep our Liberty: A Program for Political Action.* New York: Knopf, 1952.

Moore, Michael. *Here Comes Trouble: Stories from My Life.* London: Allen Lane, 2011.

Morgan, Arthur E. *The Making of the TVA.* Buffalo, NY: Prometheus, 1974.

——. *The Philosophy of Edward Bellamy.* New York: King's Crown Press, 1945.

Morgan, H. Wayne, ed. *American Socialism 1900–1960.* Englewood Cliffs, NJ: Prentice-Hall, 1964.

Morgan, Ted. *A Covert Life: Jay Lovestone: Communist, Anti-Communist, and Spymaster.* New York: Random House, 1999.

Morris, Kenneth E. *Jimmy Carter: American Moralist.* Athens: University of Georgia Press, 1996.

Moser, John E. *Right Turn: John T. Flynn and the Transformation of American Liberalism.* New York: New York University Press, 2005.

Mowry, George E. *The Era of Theodore Roosevelt and the Birth of Modern America, 1900–1912.* New York: Harper Torchbook, 1958.

Moynihan, Daniel P. *Secrecy: The American Experience.* New Haven: Yale University Press, 1998.

Mundy, Liza. *Michelle: A Biography.* New York: Simon & Schuster, 2008.

Murray, Hugh T. "Changing America and the Changing Image of Scottsboro." *Phylon* 38 (1st Qtr., 1977): 82–92.

——. "The NAACP Versus the Communist Party: The Scottsboro Rape Cases, 1931–1932." *Phylon* 28 (3rd Qtr., 1967): 276–87.

Murrin, John M. and others. *Liberty, Equality, Power: A History of the American People.* 2nd ed. Fort Worth, TX: Harcourt Brace, 1999.

Musolf, Lloyd D. *Uncle Sam's Private, Profit Seeking Corporations Comsat, Fannie Mae, Amtrak and Conrail.* (Lexington, MA: Lexington Books, 1983).

Muzik, Edward J. "Victor L. Berger, a Biography." Northwestern University PhD, 1960.

Myers, Robert J. "Long-Range Trends in Old-Age Assistance." *Social Security Bulletin* 16 (February 1953): 13–14, 27.

Nash, Michael. "Communist History at the Tamiment Library." *American Communist History* 3/2 (2004): 267–85.

"National Health Program: Message from the President of the United States." *House Document* 380, 79 Cong., 1 sess., November 19, 1945.

Nelson, Daniel. *Unemployment Insurance: The American Experience, 1915–1935.* Madison: University of Wisconsin Press, 1969.

Nichols, Christopher M. *Promise and Peril: America at the Dawn of a Global Age.* Cambridge, MA: Harvard University Press, 2011.

Nichols, John. "How Sarah Palin Renewed American Socialism." In *Going Rouge: Sarah Palin, An American Nightmare.* Edited by Richard Kim and Betsy Reed. London: O/R Books, 2009. Pp. 310–15.

Niven, Steven J. *Barack Obama: A Pocket Biography of our 44th President.* New York: Oxford University Press, 2009.

Noah, Timothy. *The Great Divergence: America's Growing Inequality Crisis and What We Can Do About It.* New York: Bloomsbury, 2012.

Norton, Anne. *Leo Strauss and the Politics of American Empire.* New Haven: Yale University Press, 2004.

Nuschler, Dawn. *Social Security Reform.* CRS Issue Brief for Congress. Washington, DC: Congressional Research Service, update of March 23, 2005.

O'Brien, Gail W. "A Historical Essay." In *A Red Family: Junius, Gladys and Barbara Scales.* Edited by Mickey Friedman. Champaign: University of Illinois Press, 2010.

——. *The Color of the Law: Race, Violence, and Justice in the Post-World War II South.* Chapel Hill: University of North Carolina Press, 1999.

O'Neill, William L. *The New Left: A History.* Wheeling, IL: Harlan Davidson, 2001.

——, ed. *The Woman Movement: Feminism in the United States and England.* London: George Allen & Unwin, 1969.

O'Reilly, Kenneth. *"Racial Matters": The FBI's Secret File on Black America, 1960–1972.* New York: Free Press, 1989.

Obama, Barack. *Dreams from my Father: A Story of Race and Inheritance.* Edinburgh: Canongate, 2007 [1995].

——. *The Audacity of Hope: Thoughts on Reclaiming the American Dream.* New York: Three Rivers Press, 2006.

Officer, Lawrence H. *Two Centuries of Compensation for U.S. Production Workers in Manufacturing.* New York: Palgrave Macmillan, 2009.

Oliver, Susan. *Betty Friedan: The Personal is Political.* New York: Pearson, 2008.

Olmsted, Kathryn S. "Linus Pauling: A Case Study in Counterintelligence Run Amok." In *Handbook of Intelligence Studies.* Edited by Loch K. Johnson. London: Routledge, 2007. Pp. 269–78.

Osofsky, Gilbert. *Harlem: The Making of a Ghetto; Negro New York, 1890–1930.* 2nd ed. New York: Harper & Row, 1971.

Painter, Nell Irvin. *The Narrative of Hosea Hudson and His Life as a Negro Communist in the South.* Cambridge, MA: Harvard University Press, 1979.

Patterson, James T. *The Welfare State in America, 1930–1980.* Durham: British Association for American Studies, 1981.

Patterson, William L., ed. *We Charge Genocide: The Historic Petition to the United Nations for Relief from a Crime of the United States Government against the Negro People.* 2nd ed. New York: International Publishers, 1970 [1951].

Payne, Charles. "Debating the Civil Rights Movement: The View from the Trenches." In *Debating the Civil Rights Movement, 1945–1968.* Edited by Steven F. Lawson and Charles Payne. Lanham, MD: Rowman and Littlefield, 2006.

Pedersen, Carl. *Obama's America.* Edinburgh: Edinburgh University Press, 2009.

Pelling, Henry. *America and the British Left from Bright to Bevan.* London: A. & C. Black, 1956.

——. "The American Labour Movement: A British View." *Political Studies* 2 (October 1954): 227–41.

——. *The Rise and Decline of Socialism in Milwaukee.* Reprint from the *Bulletin of the International Institute of Social History*, Amsterdam No. 2. (1955). Leiden: E. J. Brill, (1955).

Penkower, Monty N. *The Federal Writers' Project: A Study in Government Patronage of the Arts.* Urbana: University of Illinois Press, 1977.

Perkins, Frances. *The Roosevelt I Knew.* New York: Viking, 1946.

Perlman, Mark. "A Memoir of Selig Perlman and his Life at the University of Wisconsin." ed. Leon Fink, *Labor History* 32 (Fall 1991): 503–25.

Perlman, Selig. *A Theory of the Labor Movement.* New York: Augustus M. Kelley, 1949 [1928].

Perry, Jeffrey B. *Hubert Harrison: The Voice of Harlem Radicalism, 1883–1918.* New York: Columbia University Press, 2009.

Phelps, Christopher. "Herbert Hill and the Federal Bureau of Investigation." *Labor History* 53 (November 2012): 561–70.

Pierson, Christopher. *Socialism after Communism: The New Market Socialism.* University Park: Pennsylvania State University Press, 1995.

Piven, Frances F. *Challenging Authority: How Ordinary People Change America.* Lanham, MD: Rowman & Littlefield, 2006.

——, ed. *Labor Parties in Postindustrial Societies.* Oxford: Polity Press, 1991.

Plummer, Brenda G. "The Afro-American Response to the Occupation of Haiti, 1915–1934." *Phylon* 43/2 (1982): 125–43.

——. *Rising Wind: Black Americans and U.S. Foreign Affairs, 1935–1960.* Chapel Hill: University of North Carolina Press, 1996.

Powell, Bollin R., Jr. *Compilation and Analysis of Congressional Debates on the Right of the Federal Government to Operate Electric Power Projects.* St. Louis, MO: St. Louis Law Printing Company, 1935.

Powell, Jim. *FDR's Folly: How Roosevelt and his New Deal prolonged the Great Depression.* New York: Crown Forum, 2003.

Prados, John. *Lost Crusader: The Secret Wars of CIA Director William Colby.* Oxford: Oxford University Press, 2003.

Preston, Andrew. "Religion and World Order at the Dawn of the American Century." In *The U.S. Public and American Foreign Policy.* Edited by Andrew Johnstone and Helen Laville. London: Routledge, 2010. Pp. 73–86.

Priest, Andrew. "Power to the People? American Public Opinion and the Vietnam War." In *The U.S. Public and American Foreign Policy.* Edited by Andrew Johnstone and Helen Laville. London: Routledge, 2010. Pp. 41–55.

Pritchett, C. Herman. "The Government Corporation Control Act of 1945." *American Political Science Review* 40 (June 1946): 495–509.

Putnam, Robert D. *Bowling Alone: The Collapse and Revival of American Community.* New York: Simon & Schuster, 2000.

Quint, Howard. *The Forging of American Socialism: Origins of the Modern Movement.* Columbia, SC: University of South Carolina Press, 1953.

Rasmussen, Scott and Douglas Schoen. *Mad as Hell: How the Tea Party Movement is Fundamentally Remaking Our Two-party System.* New York: Harper, 2010.

Reagan, Ronald. *An American Life.* London: Hutchinson, 1990.

Record, Wilson. *The Negro and the Communist Party.* New York: Atheneum, 1971.

Reed, Adolph L. *W. E. B. Du Bois and American Political Thought: Fabianism and the Color Line.* New York: Oxford University Press.

Reeves, Thomas C. *The Life and Times of Joe McCarthy: A Biography.* New York: Stein & Day, 1982.

Remnick, David. *The Bridge: The Life and Rise of Barack Obama.* London: Picador, 2010.

Renshaw, Patrick. *The Wobblies: The Story of Syndicalism in the United States.* Garden City, NY: Doubleday, 1967.

Richardson, Peter. *A Bomb in Every Issue: How the Short, Unruly Life of Ramparts Magazine Changed America.* New York: The New Press, 2009.

Rideout, Walter B. *The Radical Novel in the United States, 1900–1954: Some*

Interrelations of Literature and Society. Cambridge, MA: Harvard University Press, 1956.

Rogoff, Harry. *An East Side Epic: The Life and Work of Meyer London.* New York: Vanguard Press, 1930.

Roof, Tracy. *American Labor, Congress, and the Welfare State, 1935–2010.* Baltimore: Johns Hopkins University Press, 2011.

Roosevelt, Theodore. "The New Nationalism." In *The New Nationalism*, by Theodore Roosevelt, edited by William E. Leuchtenburg. Englewood Cliffs, NJ: Prentice-Hall, 1961 [1910]. Pp. 21–39.

Rorabaugh, W. J. *Berkeley at War: The 1960s.* New York: Oxford University Press, 1989.

Rosemont, Franklin. *Joe Hill: The IWW and the Making of Revolutionary Workingclass Counterculture.* Chicago: Charles H. Kerr, 2003.

Rosen, Elliot A. *Hoover, Roosevelt, and the Brains Trust: From Depression to the New Deal.* New York: Columbia University Press, 1977.

Rosen, Ruth. *The World Split Open: How the Modern Women's Movement Changed America.* New York: Viking, 2000.

Rossinow, Doug. *The Politics of Authenticity: Liberalism, Christianity, and the New Left in America.* New York: Columbia University Press, 1998.

Rovere, Richard H. *Senator Joe McCarthy.* Cleveland, Ohio: World Publishing Company, 1959.

Rutherford, Malcolm. "Wisconsin Institutionalism: John R. Commons and his Students." *Labor History* 47 (May 2006): 161–88.

Said, Edward. *Orientalism.* London: Penguin, 1995 [1978].

"Sale of Hoboken Manufacturers' Railroad." *House Report* 767, 68 Cong., 1 sess., May 1924.

Salmond, John A. "The Civilian Conservation Corps and the Negro." In *Understanding Negro History.* Edited by Dwight D. Hoover. Chicago: Quadrangle, 1868. Pp. 383–400.

Salvatore, Nick. *Eugene V. Debs: Citizen and Socialist.* Urbana: University of Illinois Press, 1982.

Sargent, Lyman T. *New Left Thought: An Introduction.* Homewood, IL: Dorsey Press, 1972.

Saunders, Frances S. *Who Paid the Piper? The CIA and the Cultural Cold War.* London: Granta, 1999.

"Savannah River." *House Document.* 106, 21 Cong., 1 sess., May 1830.

Schaffer, Alan. "Caucus in a Phone Booth: The Congressional Career of Vito Marcantonio, 1934–1950." University of Virginia PhD, 1962.

Scheiber, Noam. *The Escape Artists: How Obama's Team Fumbled the Recovery.* New York: Simon & Schuster, 2012.

Schipper, Martin, comp. *A Guide to U.S. Commission on Industrial Relations, 1912–1915: Unpublished Records of the Division of Research and Investigation:*

Reports, Staff Studies, and Background Research Materials. Frederick, MD: University Publications of America, 1985.

Schlesinger, Arthur M., Jr. *The Coming of the New Deal.* Boston: Houghton Mifflin, 1959.

———. *The Vital Center: The Politics of Freedom.* Boston: Houghton Mifflin, 1949.

Schrecker, Ellen. *Many are the Crimes: McCarthyism in America.* Boston: Little, Brown, 1998.

———. *The Lost Soul of Higher Education: Corporatization, the Assault on Academic Freedom, and the End of the American University.* New York: New Press, 2010.

Schwantes, Carlos A. *Radical Heritage: Labor, Socialism, and Reform in Washington and British Columbia, 1885–1917.* Seattle: University of Washington Press, 1979.

Schwarz, Jordan A. *The New Dealers: Power Politics in the Age of Roosevelt.* New York: Vintage, 1994.

Scipes, Kim. *AFL-CIO's Secret War against Developing Country Workers: Solidarity or Sabotage?* Lanham, MD: Lexington Books, 2010.

Sears, John B. "Peace Work: The Antiwar Tradition in American Labor from the Cold War to the Iraq War." *Diplomatic History* 34 (September 2010): 699–720.

Shannon, David A. *The Socialist Party of America: A History.* Chicago: Quadrangle, 1967.

Shaw, G. Bernard. *The Political Madhouse in America and Nearer Home.* London: Constable, 1933.

Shaw, Randy. *Beyond the Fields: César Chávez, the UFW, and the Struggle for Justice in the 21st Century.* Berkeley: University of California Press, 2008.

Shelton, Michael W. *Talk of Power, Power of Talk: The 1994 Health Care Reform Debate and Beyond.* Westport, CT: Praeger, 2000.

Sherry, Michael S. *Gay Artists in Modern American Culture.* Chapel Hill: University of North Carolina Press, 2007.

Shlaes, Amity. *The Forgotten Man: A New History of the Great Depression.* New York: HarperCollins, 2007.

———. *Toward Tax Reform: Recommendations for President Obama's Task Force.* Falls Church, VA: Tax Analysis, 2009.

Sills, David L., ed. *International Encyclopedia of the Social Sciences.* New York: Macmillan, 1968.

Sinclair, Andrew. *Jack: A Biography of Jack London.* London: Weidenfeld & Nicolson, 1978.

Sinclair, Upton. *The Autobiography of Upton Sinclair.* London: Allen, 1963.

Singh, Robert. *Barack Obama's Post-American Foreign Policy: The Limits of Engagement.* London: Bloomsbury Academic, 2012.

Sklar, Kathryn K. *Florence Kelley and the Nation's Work: The Rise of Women's Political Culture, 1830–1900.* New Haven: Yale University Press, 1995.

Sklar, Martin J. "Capitalism and Socialism in the Emergence of Modern America: The Formative Era, 1890–1916." In *Reconstructing History: The Emergence of a New Historical Society.* Edited by Elizabeth Fox-Genovese and Elisabeth Lasch-Quinn. New York: Routledge, 1999.

Small, Melvin. "Bring the Boys Home Now! Antiwar Activism and Withdrawal from Vietnam – and Iraq." *Diplomatic History* 34 (June 2010): 543–53.

——.*Johnson, Nixon, and the Doves.* New Brunswick, NJ: Rutgers University Press, 1988.

Smith, Bradley F. *The Shadow Warriors: OSS and the Origins of the CIA.* New York: Basic, 1983.

Smith, Gibbs M. *Joe Hill.* Salt Lake City: University of Utah Press, 1969.

Sombart, Werner. *Why is there no Socialism in the United States?* Trans. from 1906 German-language edition by Patricia M. Hocking and C. T. Husbands. London: Macmillan, 1976.

Sorel, Georges. *Reflections on Violence.* Trans. T. E. Hulme. New York: Collier, 1961 [1914]. Originally in French, 1908.

Spargo, John. *Socialism: A Summary and Interpretation of Socialist Principles.* New York: Macmillan, 1906.

——.*The Bitter Cry of the Children.* Chicago: Quadrangle, 1968 [1906].

Starr, Paul. *Remedy and Reaction: The Peculiar American Struggle over Health Care Reform.* New Haven: Yale University Press, 2011.

——.*The Social Transformation of American Medicine.* New York: Basic, 1982.

Stears, Marc. *Progressives, Pluralists, and the Problems of the State: Ideologies of Reform in the United States and Britain, 1909–1926.* Oxford: Oxford University Press, 2006.

Steinfels, Peter. *The Neoconservatives: The Men Who are Changing America's Politics.* New York: Simon & Schuster, 1979.

Stevens, Richard P. *American Zionism and U.S. Foreign Policy.* Beirut, Lebanon: Institute for Palestine Studies, 1970.

Stille, Alexander. "The Betrayal of History." *New York Review of Books* (June 11, 1998): 15–16, 18–20.

Stricker, Frank. *Why America Lost the War on Poverty – And How to Win It.* Chapel Hill: University of North Carolina Press, 2007.

"Survey of the Great Lakes-St. Lawrence Seaway and Power Project: Message from the President of the United States transmitting Reports on the Proposed Great Lakes-St. Lawrence Project." 2 vols. *Senate Document* 116, 73 Cong., 2 sess., January 1934.

Swartz, David R. *Moral Minority: The Evangelical Left in an Age of Conservatism.* Philadelphia: University of Pennsylvania Press, 2012.

Tawney, Richard H. *The American Labour Movement and Other Essays*. Edited by J. M. Winter. Brighton: Harvester Press, 1979.

Temkin, Moshik. *The Sacco-Vanzetti Affair: America on Trial*. New Haven, CT: Yale University Press, 2009.

"Tennessee Valley Authority," *Hearings before the Committee on Military Affairs*. House, 74 Cong., 1 sess, March 28, 29, 30, April 2, 3, 9, 10, 1935.

Thomas, William H., Jr. *Unsafe for Democracy: World War I and the U.S. Justice Department's Covert Campaign to Suppress Dissent*. Madison: University of Wisconsin Press, 2008.

Thorpe, Andrew. *A History of the British Labour Party*. 2nd ed. Basingstoke: Palgrave, 2001.

Tyler, Robert. *Rebels of the Woods: The IWW in the Pacific Northwest*. Eugene: University of Oregon Press, 1967.

Van Vechten, Carl. *Peter Whiffle*. New York: Knopf, 1927.

Walker, Forrest A. "Compulsory Health Insurance: 'The Next Step in Social Legislation'." *Journal of American History* 56 (September 1969): 290–304.

Wallace, Henry A. *Democracy Reborn*. London: Hammond, Hammond, 1945.

——. *Sixty Million Jobs*. London: William Heinemann, 1946.

Warner, Sam B. *Street Car Suburbs: The Process of Growth in Boston, 1870–1900*. Cambridge, MA: Harvard University Press, 1962.

Washburn, Jennifer. *University, Inc.: The Corporate Corruption of American Higher Education*. New York: Basic Books, 2005.

Wayne, Stephen J. *Personality and Politics: Obama For and Against Himself*. Washington, DC: CQ Press, 2012.

Webel, Baird and Marc Labonte. *Government Interventions in Response to Financial Turmoil*. Washington, DC: Congressional Research Service, February 1, 2010.

Weinstein, James. *The Decline of Socialism in America, 1912–1925*. New York: Monthly Review Press, 1967.

——. *The Long Detour: The History and Future of the American Left*. Boulder, CO: Westview Press, 2003.

Weisbord, Robert G. "Black America and the Italian-Ethiopian Crisis: An Episode in Pan-Negroism." *Historian* 34 (February 1972): 230–41.

Wells, Wyatt. "Public Power in the Eisenhower Administration." *Journal of Policy History* 20/2 (2008): 227–62.

Whalen, Jack and Richard Flacks. *Beyond the Barricades: The Sixties Generation Grows Up*. Philadelphia: Temple University Press, 1989.

Whiting, Richard C. *The Labour Party and Taxation: Party Identity and Political Purpose in Twentieth-Century Britain*. Cambridge: Cambridge University Press, 2000.

Whitman, Alden. *Labor Parties 1827–1834*. New York: International Publishers, 1943.

Wilentz, Sean. "Socialism." In *A Companion to American Thought*. Edited by Richard Wightman Fox and James T. Kloppenberg. Oxford: Blackwell, 1995. Pp. 637–41.

Wilford, Hugh. "The Communist International and the American Communist Party." In *International Communism and the Communist International*. Edited by Tim Rees and Andrew Thorpe. Manchester: Manchester University Press, 1998. Pp. 225–33.

——. *The CIA, the British Left and the Cold War*. London: Frank Cass, 2003.

——. *The Mighty Wurlitzer: How the CIA Played America*. Cambridge, MA: Harvard University Press, 2008.

Wilkinson, Patrick. "The Selfless and the Helpless: Maternalist Origins of the Welfare State." *Feminist Studies* 25 (Autumn 1999): 571–97.

Williams, William A. *The Tragedy of American Diplomacy*. Cleveland, OH: World Publishing Company, 1959.

Wills, Garry. *Reagan's America*. New York: Penguin, 1988.

Wish, Harvey, ed. *The Negro Since Emancipation*. Englewood Cliffs, NJ: Prentice-Hall, 1964.

Wolf, Sherry. *Sexuality and Socialism: History, Politics and Theory of LBGT Liberation*. Chicago: Haymarket Books, 2009.

Wolff, Edward N. *Top Heavy: A Study of the Increasing Inequality of Wealth in America*. New York: Twentieth Century Fund Press, 1995.

Wolfskill, George. *The Revolt of the Conservatives: A History of the American Liberty League, 1934–1940*. Boston: Houghton Mifflin, 1962.

Wynn, Neil A. *From Progressivism to Prosperity: World War I and American Society*. New York: Holmes and Meier, 1986.

Yellowitz, Irwin. "The Origins of Unemployment Reform in the United States." *Labor History* 9 (September 1968): 338–60.

Young, Marilyn. "Reflections on the Anti-War Movement, Then and Now." *Historein* 9 (annual, Greece, 2009): 67–75.

Zaretsky, Eli. *Why America Needs a Left: A Historical Argument*. Cambridge: Polity, 2012.

Zarnow, Leandra. "Braving Jim Crow to Save Willie McGee: Bella Abzug, the Legal Left, and Civil Rights Innovation, 1948–1951." *Law and Social Inquiry* 33 (Fall 2008): 1003–41.

Zinn, Howard, ed. *New Deal Thought*. Indianapolis, IN: Hackett, 2003 [1966].

——. *A People's History of the United States, 1492 – Present*. New York: HarperPerennial, 2005 [1980].

INDEX

Comprehensive Health Insurance Plan, 139–40
COMSAT Corporation, 138
Comstock Act (1873), 33
The Condition of the Working Class in England in 1844 (Engels), 29
Congress, socialist members, 40–2, *43*, 44–6
Congress of Industrial Organizations *see* CIO
Congress of Racial Equality (CORE), 114, 133
Congressional Record, 93
Conrail, 150
conservatism, 5, 7, 78, 97, 101; *see also* Republican Party
constructionists, 38, 45–6
consumer rights, 30, 197
consumerism, 158
Continental Army, 84
contraception, 33–4, 70, 135–6, 197
convergence theory, 158
Coolidge, Calvin, 85
cooperativism, 50, 51, 87
Copland, Aaron, 11, 57, 82, 145
Coppola, Francis Ford, 148
CORE (Congress of Racial Equality), 114, 133
counterculture, 147–8
CRC (Civil Rights Congress), 110–13
Crisis, 67, 71, 145
Cruse, Harold, 54
Cuba, 150; *see also* Castro, Fidel
Cullen, Countee, 54, 62, 145
culture wars, 56, 148, 159, 171–2
The Culture Wars (Hunter), 159, 196

The Daily Show, 171
Daily Worker, 45, 77, 94
Daily World, 148–9
Darcy, Sam, 59, 60
Darrow, Clarence, 28, 65
Debs, Eugene, 2, 16, 34–6, 42, 44, 50
debt peonage, 66–7
Dellums, Ronald V.
  in Congress, *43*, 45, 61, 128–9, 151, 155
  conservatives against, 150
  DSA, 41
  and Sanders, 161
Democratic Party
  corruption, 47
  fusion candidate, 51
  gay rights, 144
  members of Congress, *43*
  New Deal, 76
  Olson, 61
  presidential elections, 16
  public investment, 14

social reform, 12
and socialism, 38, 51
democratic socialism
  conservatives on, 6
  and Italian communists, 115
  King, 133
  Perlman, 19
  Reagan opposing, 152
  Spain, 72
  support for, 44–5
Democratic Socialists of America (DSA)
  Dellums, 41
  friends of Obama, 178
  Harrington, 152, 153
  on homosexuality, 146
  Meyerson, 177
  and Sanders, 161
  and Socialist Party USA, 171
  supporters in Congress, 45
Denmark, 96
Department of Health, Education and Welfare, 107
Department of Justice, 25, 67, 110
Department of Labor, 19
dependency, 128
depression *see* Great Depression
Devine, Edward T., 16, 22
Dewey, John, 3, 25, 28, 50, 56, 80
Dewey, Thomas E., 101–2, 104
Dies Jr., Martin, 91
Diggs, Anna L., 42–3
direct action, 130, 133, 144
disinformation campaign, 20
Douglas, Helen, 102, 103
Douglas, Paul, 42, *43*, 80
Douglass, Frederick, 62–3
Dreams From My Father (Obama), 6
Dreiser, Theodore, 11, 32
Dreler, Peter, 10
drone warfare, 188
Drucker, Peter, 158
DSA *see* Democratic Socialists of America
Du Bois, W. E. B., 31, 67
  on Ethiopia, 70
  in Ghana, 131
  Harlem Renaissance, 54, 55
  on homosexuality, 145
  NAACP, 30–1
  public ownership, 113
  Russian visit, 64
  socialism, 12, 113
Du Bois Clubs of America, 131–2, 134
Dubinsky, David, 96
Dylan, Bob, 11, 31, 129